STAMFORD SPORTS

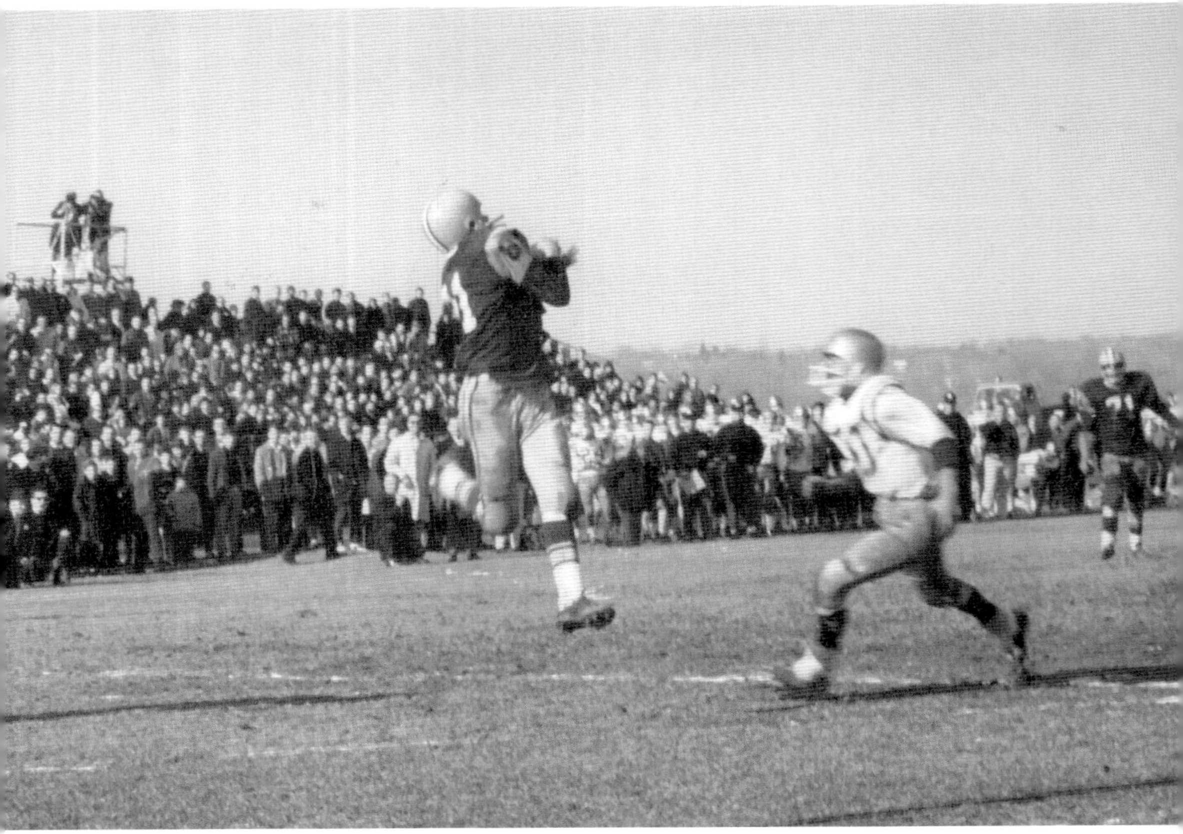

Dan Burke's Touchdown Catch, 1965. Dan Burke is a longtime volunteer for the Stamford Historical Society and a major contributor to this book. He attended Stamford Catholic High School and played varsity football there—he still has his letter jacket. Burke is seen here going up for a touchdown pass on Thanksgiving Day, 1965.

Front Cover: These unidentified Stamford players are on an outing at the Stamford Rifle Club in Long Ridge.

Cover Background: Private girls' schools in Stamford generally had larger and more consistent sports programs than their public counterparts, especially between 1930 and 1949, when finances were an issue. Here, the 1936 Willard School girls' hockey team poses on the grounds of the school.

Back Cover: This formal photograph was taken of a duckpin bowling team in the early 1900s.

STAMFORD SPORTS

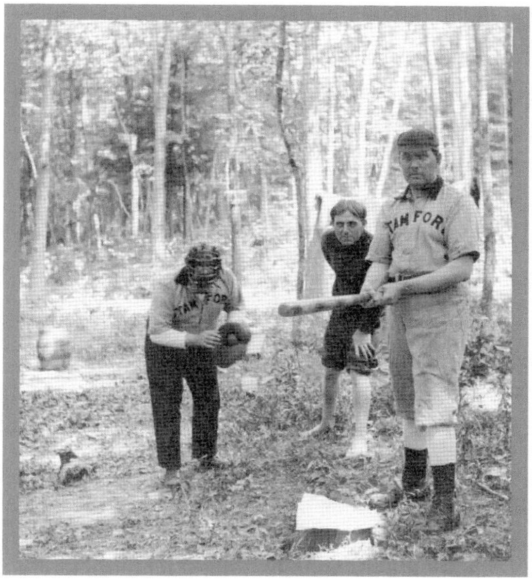

Stamford Historical Society

ARCADIA PUBLISHING

ISBN 978-0-7385-9808-6

Published by Arcadia Publishing
Charleston, South Carolina

Printed in the United States of America

Library of Congress Control Number: 2012945150

For all general information, please contact Arcadia Publishing:
Telephone 843-853-2070
Fax 843-853-0044
E-mail sales@arcadiapublishing.com
For customer service and orders:
Toll-Free 1-888-313-2665

Visit us on the Internet at www.arcadiapublishing.com

Dedicated to every fan who cannot speak the next day,
to every player who cannot stop the tears of joy,
to every sportswriter who cannot find the words

CONTENTS

ACKNOWLEDGMENTS

This book was created for the Stamford Historical Society through the primary efforts of Kathy Ciuci, our photograph archivist; Dan Burke, library volunteer and curator of several exhibits; and Thomas Zoubek, our executive director and fan-in-chief. Throwing all caution to the wind, Kathy agreed to take the lead and has project-managed, compiled, and selected the photographs; laid out the book; and authored a goodly part of the copy. Dan and Tom have provided a wealth of copy, insights, anecdotes, research, and copy editing to the project.

The following people have helped tremendously to collect, research, and tell wonderful stories about the photographs presented here. We wish to acknowledge the generosity of time and spirit first and foremost of our librarians, Grace Bounty and Ronald Marcus. Grace and Ron have a vast knowledge of Stamford history, geography, and culture and have provided this knowledge as well as their time and skills in researching and proofreading this volume. Patricia Markiewicz, our newest photograph-room volunteer, has helped tremendously as well, with research, layout, and proofreading. We especially would like to acknowledge the athletes and organizations who have provided pictures, reminiscences, and enthusiasm for the project. They are as follows: Joseph Deleo, Andrew Dzamba, Nick Scutti, Jack Hagan, John Kuczo, Dr. Donna Lopiano, Gerry Lione, Pat Markiewicz, the Allyson Rioux Memorial Foundation, and the Brakettes softball organization.

Unless otherwise noted, all photographs on the cover and in this book are property of the Stamford Historical Society. You may request copies of photographs by visiting our website, www.stamfordhistory.org.

INTRODUCTION

Until the 1840s, Stamford was a moderately sized coastal village in southwestern Connecticut. Founded in 1641, it remained an insular, parochial community of mostly farmers. By the early 1800s, commerce grew and developed along the coastline, spurred on by the opening of a ship canal constructed by Alfred Bishop in 1833. It may seem an odd leap, but this canal, along with the construction of the New Haven Railroad line in 1848, was perhaps the largest driving force behind Stamford's development as a huge sports town. With these two advances came a boom in manufacturing and an influx of European immigrants that transformed Stamford from a small, homogenous New England town to a large, multiethnic city. Stamford also became more cosmopolitan, as businessmen commuted to New York City on the railroad and New Yorkers began sending their sons and daughters to a number of private schools that opened in Stamford in the 1830s and 1840s. By the 1860s, these two institutions—manufacturing enterprises and private schools—began organizing the first baseball and football teams, and a sporting town was born.

Today, Stamford remains enamored with sport. At the Stamford Historical Society, the interests of Stamford in general are reflected in our staff of volunteers, and sports and sporting events—and, of course, sports history—are often the topic of animated and passionate conversation. This book brings together our passion for sports, the photographs and reminiscences of Stamford's athletes and fans, and our own growing collection of sports photographs. Through photographs, our hope is to not only to convey the history of sports in Stamford, but to explore how sports have helped create a single Stamford community from its many ethnic and class-centric neighborhoods. With such a rapid influx of peoples and races, Stamford had great potential for ethnic and class strife; yet, as the 20th century progressed, Stamford remained fairly peaceful and relatively free of these types of conflicts. We contend that sports, perhaps more than any other factor, forged understanding, friendship, and community among all of its residents as they played with and against each other on the playing fields of Stamford.

We also attempt to illustrate how this theme has played out throughout the later 20th century. Stamford sports have been consistently ahead of the times in terms of race and gender, and a number of photographs in this collection speak to the expansion of sports as inclusive and available to all Stamford residents. Stamford residents have also played key roles in race and gender equality in sports, and their photographs and stories are included here. Our photographic history covers a full century, from the first sports photographs of the 1880s through the expansion of sports of all types and for all people throughout the 1970s and 1980s.

As a typical East Coast city, Stamford's most popular sports have always been baseball and football. This has been true since the very earliest days of baseball in the 1860s and football in the 1880s. They are the sports most played by schools, industries, religious groups, and community organizations. Thus, understandably perhaps, the bulk of our sports photographs are of baseball and football. Add to this that our own collection has been greatly supplemented by some of

Stamford's leading baseball and football players and coaches—including wonderful loans from the Kuczo, Lione, and Deleo families—and it is perhaps a given fact that this book is heavily weighted with photographs from these two sports. That being said, we have been delighted to find a great number of photographs from nearly all of the sports popular in Stamford, and we have included the greatest breadth possible within the confines of space and our own available photographs.

However, to forewarn the reader, we would like to say a few things to put the photographs and their history into the context of this book. Most importantly, the reader should be aware that as a photographic history, the content of the book is limited by the photographs we have available to us. Our collection, created as it was by the generous donations of our community, is not comprehensive. We may have dozens of photographs of certain teams and athletes, but few or none of others. We have included the broadest and most inclusive collection possible, but we realize that there are gaps of one type or another throughout the book.

As a sports book, we have included a number of team photographs and have provided the names of the players if available. The standard we have followed in listing the names is to move from front to back, or nearest to farthest. Thus, the nearest or front row is first and the farthest or back row is last. Also, the reader should be aware that although there are a great number of wonderful images available in our collection of newspapers, yearbooks, company newsletters, and various Stamford-related books, these are not included here, no matter how much we love them. The images in the book are limited to actual photographs, postcards, drawings, and other original media in our collection or in the collections loaned to us for our use. As a formal book of photographs, copies of photographs printed in other media fall outside its scope.

A note on sources: as a sports history, we have used the wealth of information available to us in yearbooks, newsletters, newspapers, and city directories. As multivolume works spanning over a century, we have not included these sources with bibliographic entries. All materials, however, are available at the Stamford Historical Society, and most are available for research to our visitors.

Our thanks go out especially to our contributors, who have so generously provided so many wonderful photographs and stories. We very much hope that our love and enthusiasm comes through for all readers of this book. The project was born from love of sports and Stamford history, and the greatest compliment we could receive is that this leaps out from the pages of this book.

Now, play ball!

1

The Earliest Sports Photographs

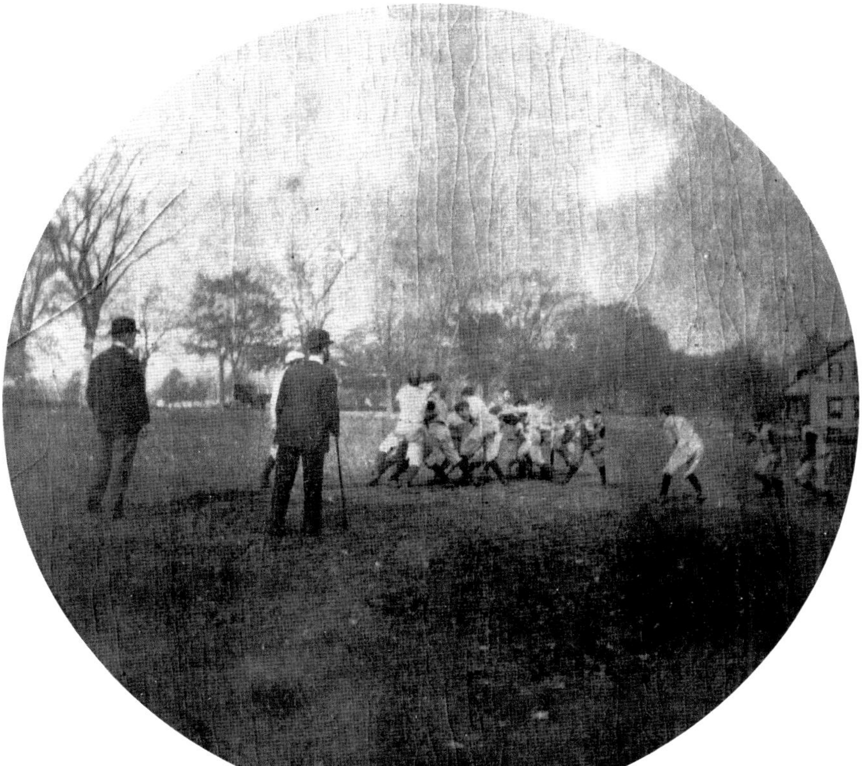

Betts Academy Football Game. The origins of baseball are murky. While some believe the game was invented by a single person, others believe it evolved through a series of children's games. However it may have emerged as an organized sport, Stamfordites were playing it at least as early as 1862, and likely in the 1840s. An 1863 article in the *Starrford Advocate* chronicles a game between Stamford and Norwalk schoolboys, mentioning it as "the third annual game between the nine of Stamford and the nine of Norwalk." In this chapter, we have selected a number of photographs from the early years of organized sports in Stamford.

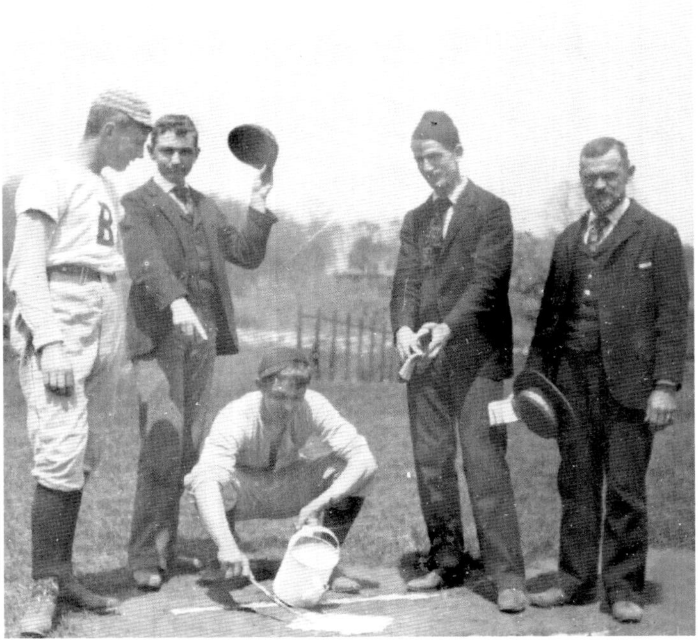

LINING THE BATTER'S BOX, C. 1890. Betts was one of the very first schools in Stamford to field a team in any sport. James Betts established the school in 1838. In the years following, numerous other private boarding and day schools for both boys and girls were established in Stamford. Nearly all incorporated physical education and athletics as part of their academic programs, but Betts promoted their athletics programs and facilities more than any other.

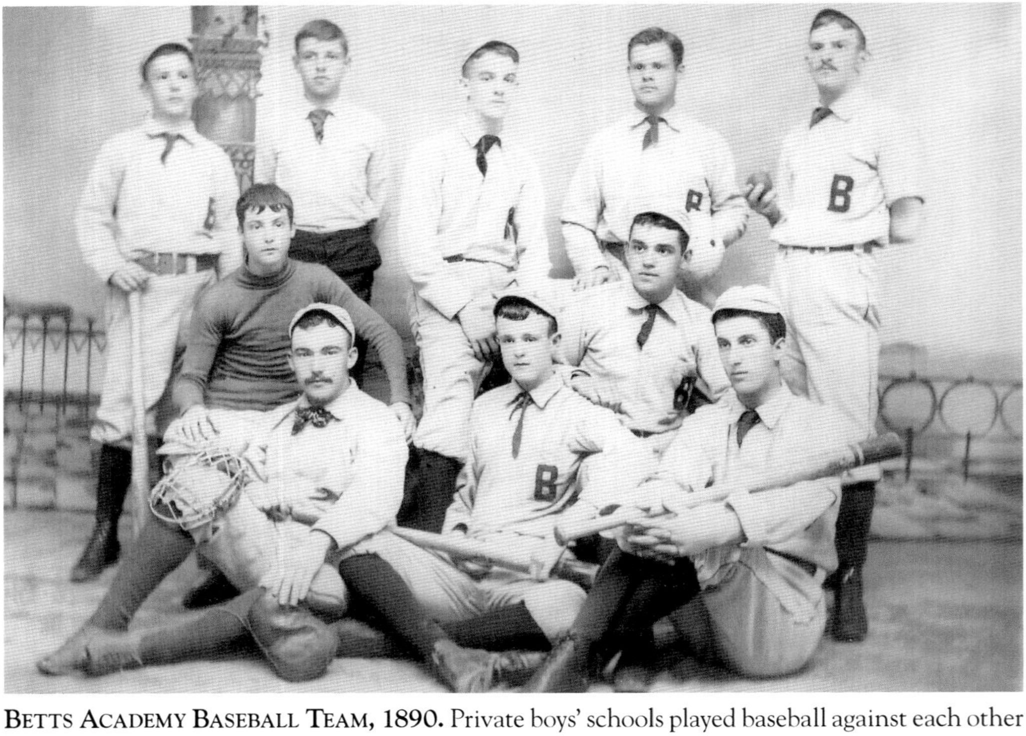

BETTS ACADEMY BASEBALL TEAM, 1890. Private boys' schools played baseball against each other throughout the late 1800s. The 1890 Betts Academy baseball team is seen here. Only four players are identified in this photograph: in the first row, second and third from the left, are Remington and Mead; and in the third row, second and third from the left, are Boden and Grote.

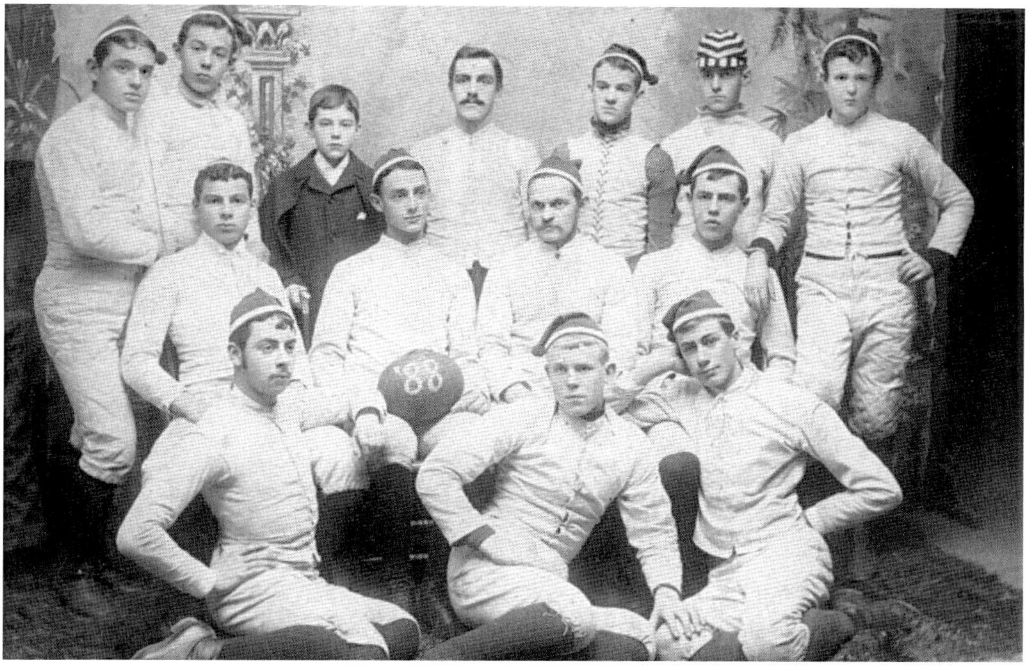

BETTS ACADEMY FOOTBALL TEAM, 1888. Although baseball came first, football was not far behind. Stamford High School records show that they had a football team as early as 1895. As a growing city, Stamford fielded a number of football teams that played against each other and against teams from other towns. Betts Academy was a private boys' school in north-central Stamford on Strawberry Hill Avenue, the current location of Stamford High School. Above, from left to right are (first row) Grote, Morrison, Miller, Mead, and Boden; (second row) Gonzalez, Hillyer, Betts, and unidentified; (third row) DuBois, Boden, and unidentified.

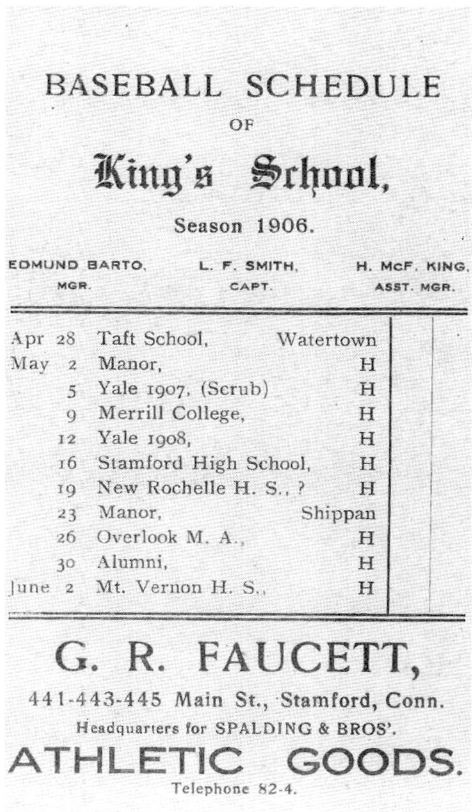

BASEBALL SCHEDULE

OF

King's School,

Season 1906.

EDMUND BARTO, MGR. — L. F. SMITH, CAPT. — H. McF. KING, ASST. MGR.

Date	Opponent	Place
Apr 28	Taft School,	Watertown
May 2	Manor,	H
5	Yale 1907, (Scrub)	H
9	Merrill College,	H
12	Yale 1908,	H
16	Stamford High School,	H
19	New Rochelle H. S., ?	H
23	Manor,	Shippan
26	Overlook M. A.,	H
30	Alumni,	H
June 2	Mt. Vernon H. S.,	H

G. R. FAUCETT,

441-443-445 Main St., Stamford, Conn.

Headquarters for SPALDING & BROS'.

ATHLETIC GOODS.

Telephone 82-4.

KING SCHOOL BASEBALL SCHEDULE, 1906. This schedule from 1906 includes both the out-of-town and local schools—Merrill College, Manor School, King School, Stamford High School—that played each other regularly in both baseball and football at the time. Note here that high schools often played colleges; in fact, the Merrill Business School football team included college graduates.

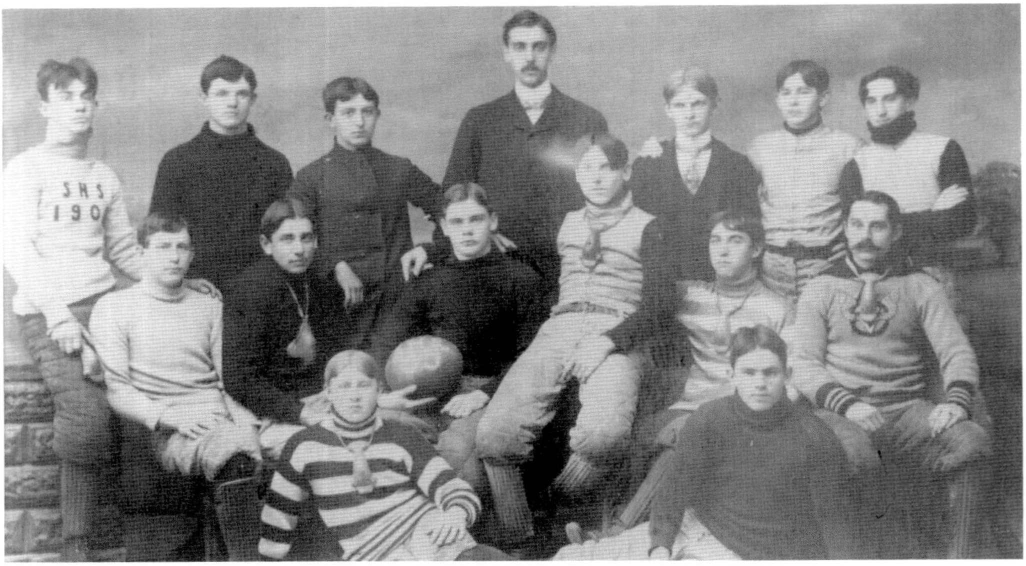

STAMFORD HIGH SCHOOL'S FIRST UNIFORMED TEAM, 1899–1900. Stamford High School's earliest teams were not funded, and players had to supply their own equipment. The team members are identified by their last name. They are, from left to right, (first row) Quinn and Scofield; (second row) Hoyt, Holly, Hart, Faucett, Nolan, and Peckham; (third row) Alexander, Wood, Button, Jenney, Morgan, Ryle, and Downey.

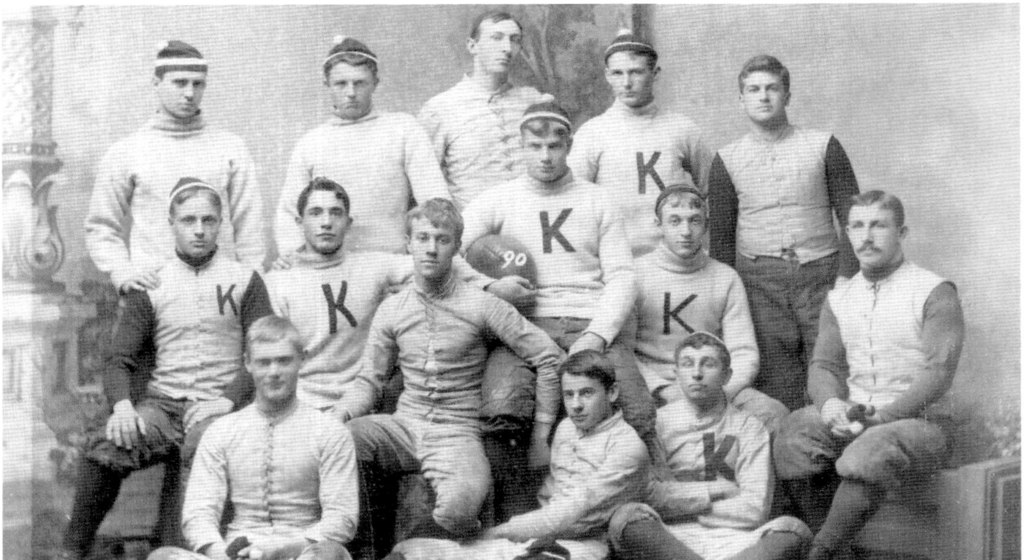

KING SCHOOL FOOTBALL TEAM, 1890. King School, a preparatory school for boys, competed in football, baseball, and basketball from the earliest days of these games. The school's brochure from 1906 says, regarding exercises and sports, "A field of three acres gives an opportunity for out-of-door sports, which are encouraged under the care of an instructor. During the winter months, systematic exercise is taken under a trained teacher in a well-appointed gymnasium."

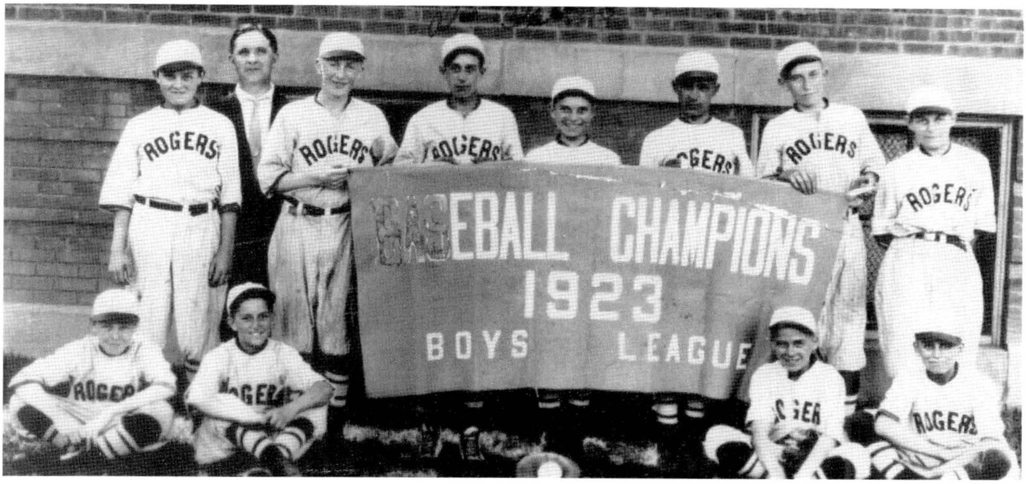

ROGERS SCHOOL BASEBALL TEAM, 1923. The friendly competition between neighborhood teams in Stamford was often how kids got to know one another. As neighborhoods in Stamford in this era corresponded to ethnicities, teams of Irish kids played teams of Italian kids or Polish kids. As the children grew older, they would find themselves on teams of mixed ethnicities playing with people they knew from their youth. In this manner, these teams provided social cement, helping to forge a single community out of the diverse neighborhoods.

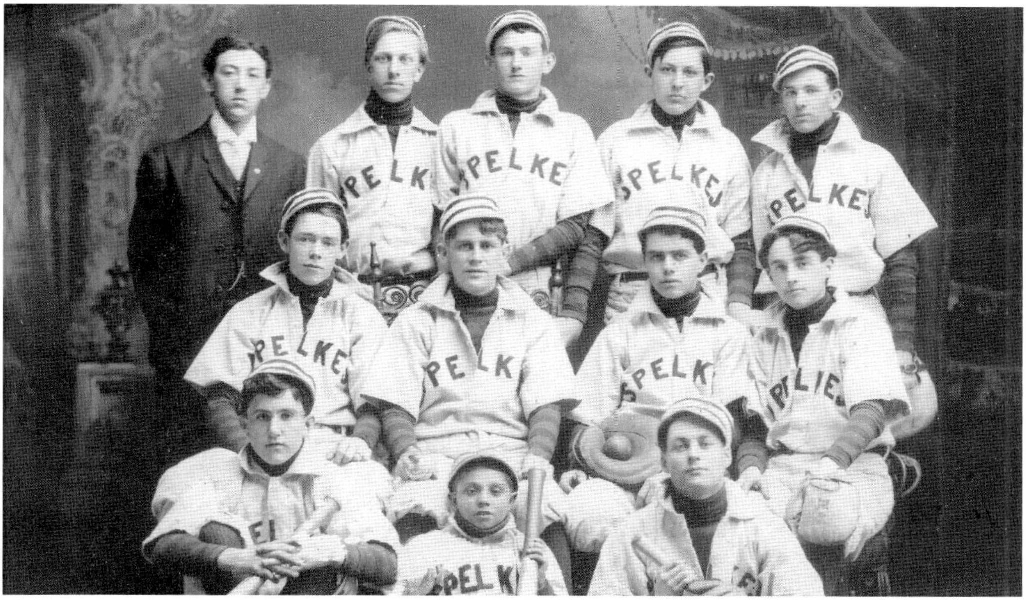

SPELKE BASEBALL TEAM, 1905. This photograph shows an early baseball team privately owned by Abram Spelke (top left, in suit), a real estate developer and prominent Stamford businessman and public servant. Although Spelke, who also managed the team, was Jewish, he successfully brought together a team that crossed religious and ethnic boundaries. From left to right are (first row) O'Keefe, "Spider" Rabinowitz, and Burke; (second row) Donnelly, Sauter, Nichols, and Smith; (third row) Abram Spelke, Hoyt, Cuddy, Smith, and Howard.

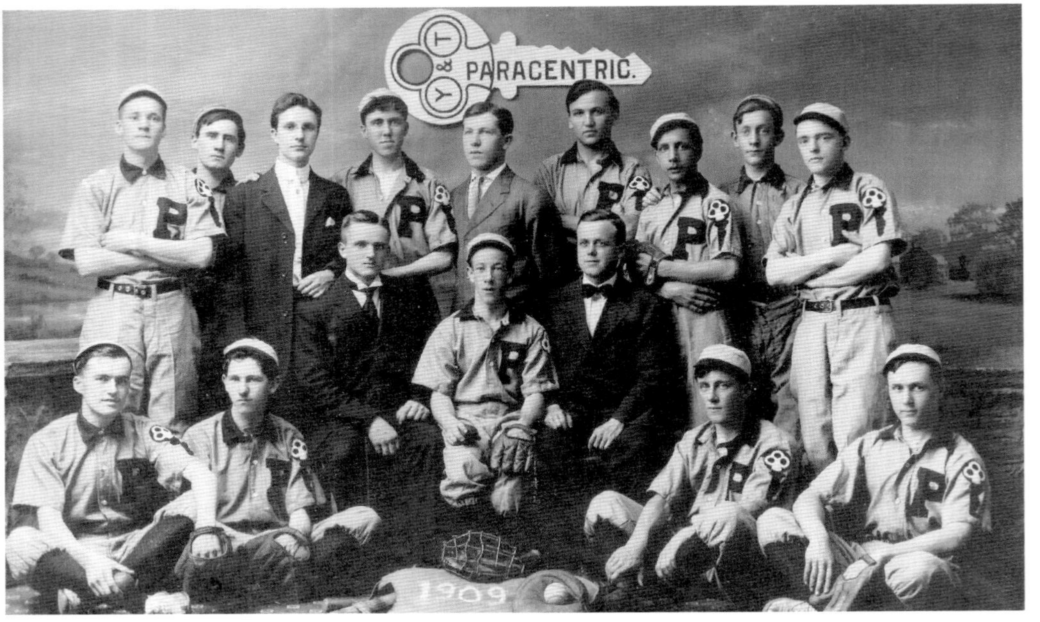

The Yale & Towne Paracentrics, 1909. One of the early Yale & Towne teams is seen here. It was named after the Paracentric Keyway, designed by W.H. Taylor, a Yale & Towne inventor. They are, from left to right, (first row) Charles Wight, Jack Ryan, Terry Murphy, and Billy Williams; (second row) Brace Wynkoop (vice president), Bill Palmer (captain), and Howard Scofield (president); (third row) Charlie Aronson, Bill Hyland, Cliff Wicks (publicity), Walt Brooks, Mike Ryan (manager), John Wasserlein, Leon Kaylor, H. Dalgren, and Patsy O'Keefe.

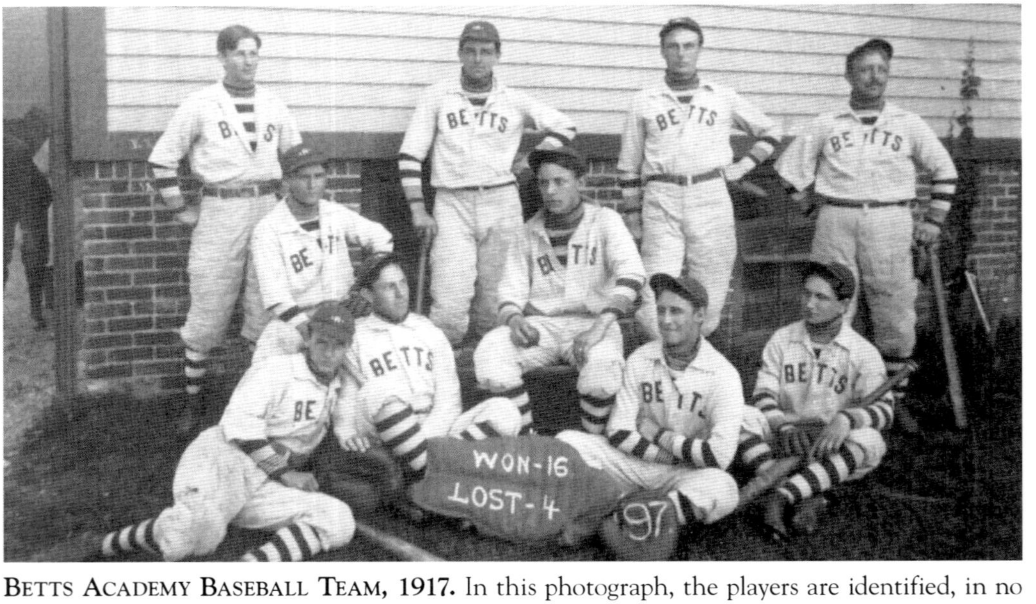

Betts Academy Baseball Team, 1917. In this photograph, the players are identified, in no particular order, as Brainard, Olcott, Smith, Leach, Flake, Ferguson, Walter, and Davies. Note that the players were by then using padded gloves.

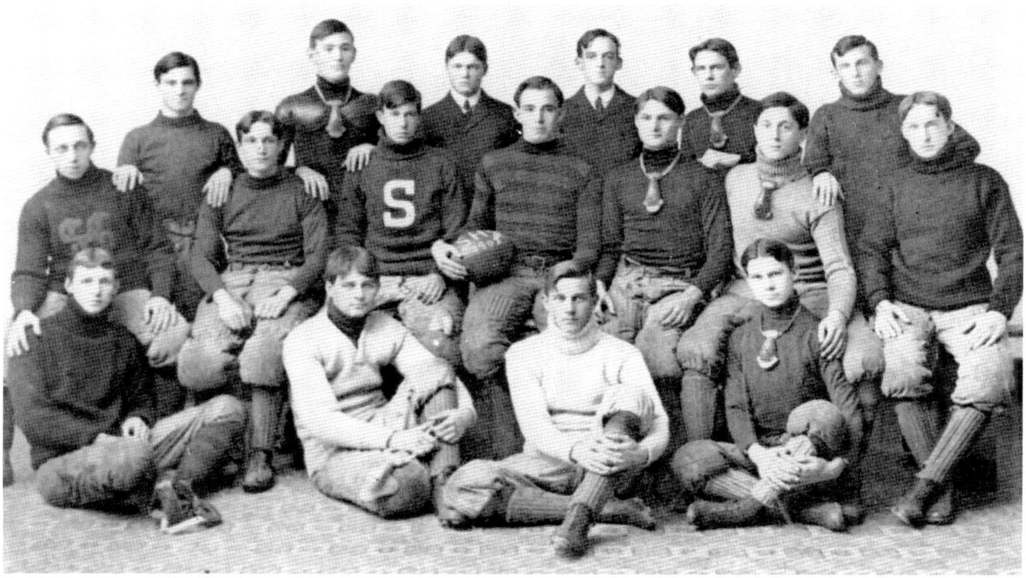

Stamford High School Football Team, 1903. This team went undefeated, with five wins, zero losses, and three cancellations. While the earliest teams used no protective equipment, this photograph shows the introduction of nose guards, shoulder pads, and padded pants.

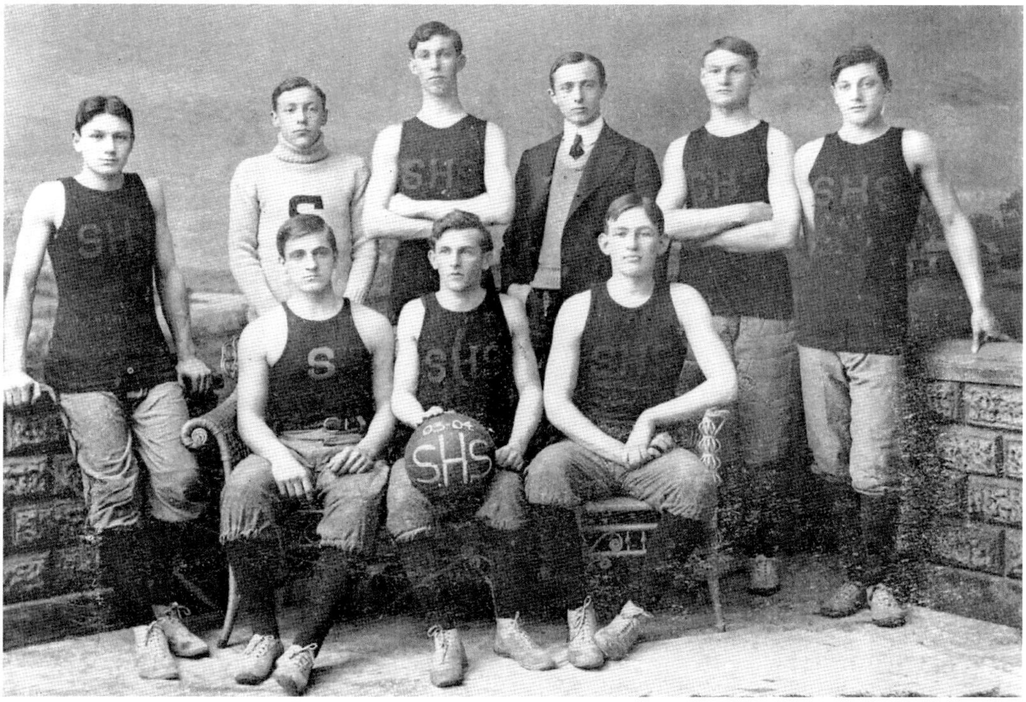

Stamford High School Basketball Team, 1903–1904. The school's magazine, the *Quarterly*, did not list all of the boys' names, but does identify the captain as George Cavanaugh and the manager as Alexander Hans.

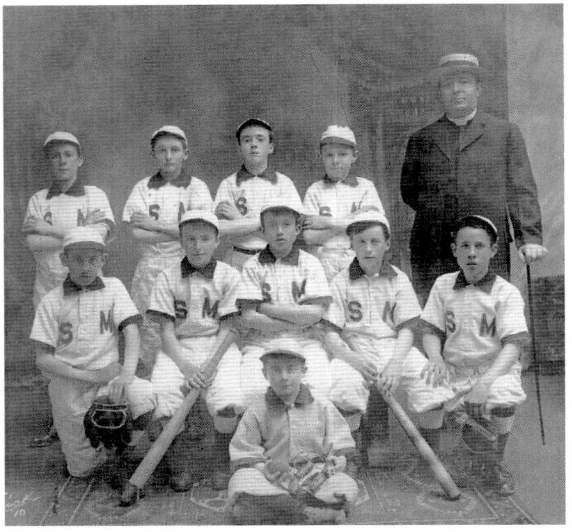

St. Mary's Baseball Team, 1907. Serving Stamford's rapidly expanding Irish community, St. Mary's Roman Catholic Church sponsored one of the few organized boys' teams at the time. Most boys played pickup games or played for school teams when they were older. Organized league play on a large scale would not come to Stamford until the early 1950s. From left to right are (front) unidentified; (first row) Jas. Mulreed, Kerrigan, unidentified, McHugh, and Kinsella; (second row) Kinsello, unidentified, Tom Gill, Dan Graf Jr., and Father Kerrigan.

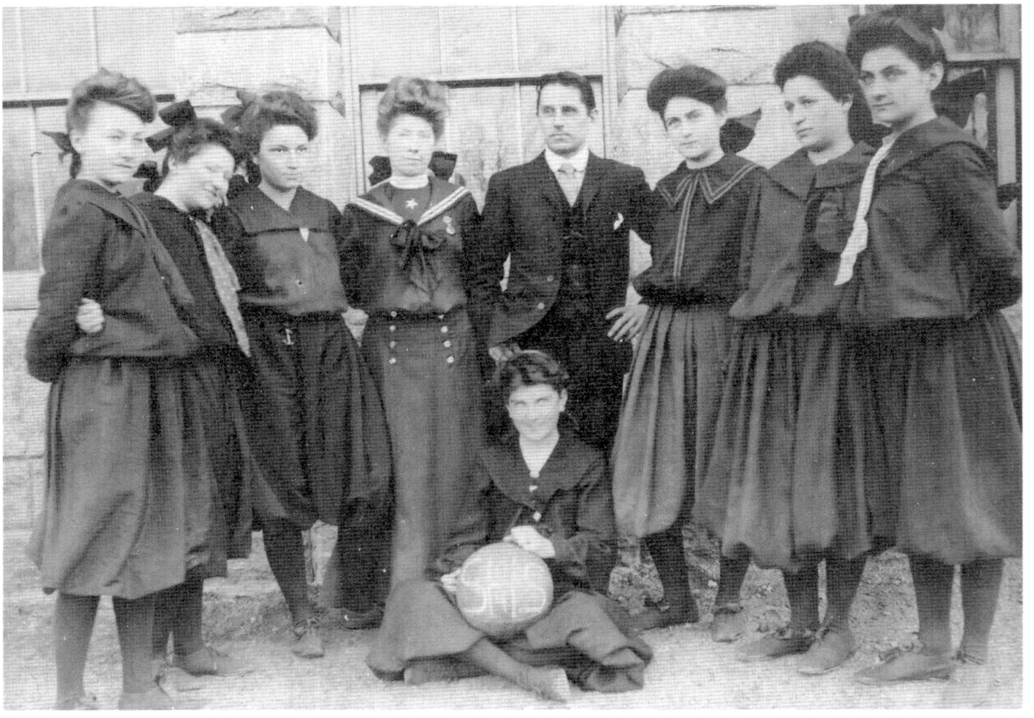

Stamford High School Girls' Basketball Team, 1903–1904. Stamford High School sponsored a girls' team early in the game's history. The women's game was begun at Smith College by Senda Berenson. The court was divided into three areas, and girls were not allowed to move from their assigned areas. According to the *Quarterly*, the class of 1902 offered a silver cup as a tournament prize, "realizing the need of something to awaken the athletic life of school." The 1903–1904 team responded by defeating the Mount Vernon, New Haven, and Bridgeport high schools to become state champions.

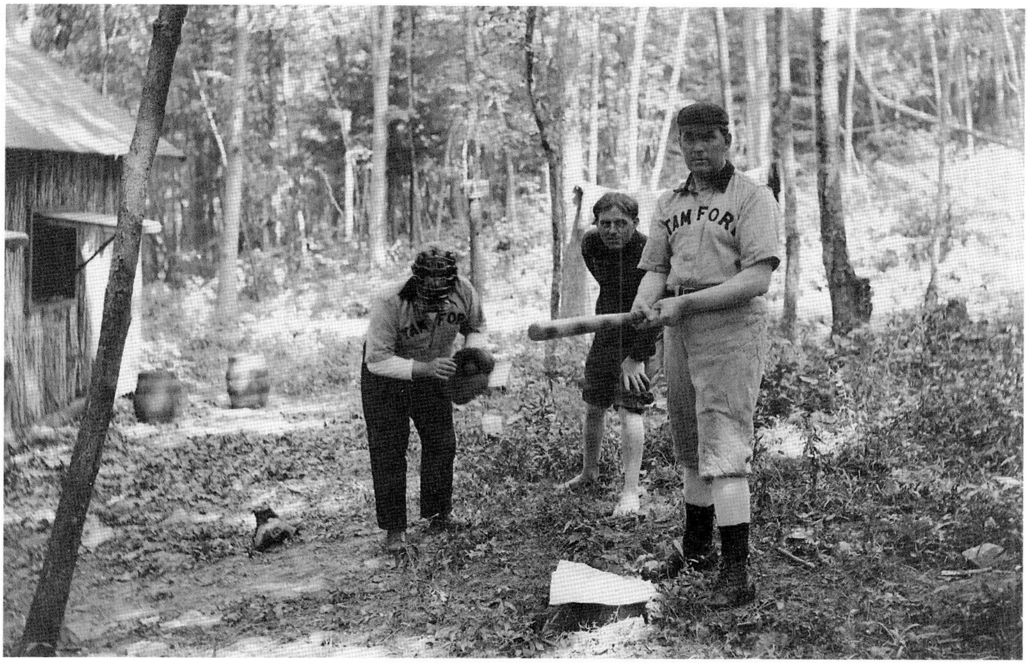

STAMFORD BASEBALL CLUB, C. 1905. Although neither of these photographs included information about the players or the location, the cabin on the left in the photograph above belonged to the Stamford Rifle Club. The cabin was located on Mianus Ridge in the Long Ridge section of north Stamford.

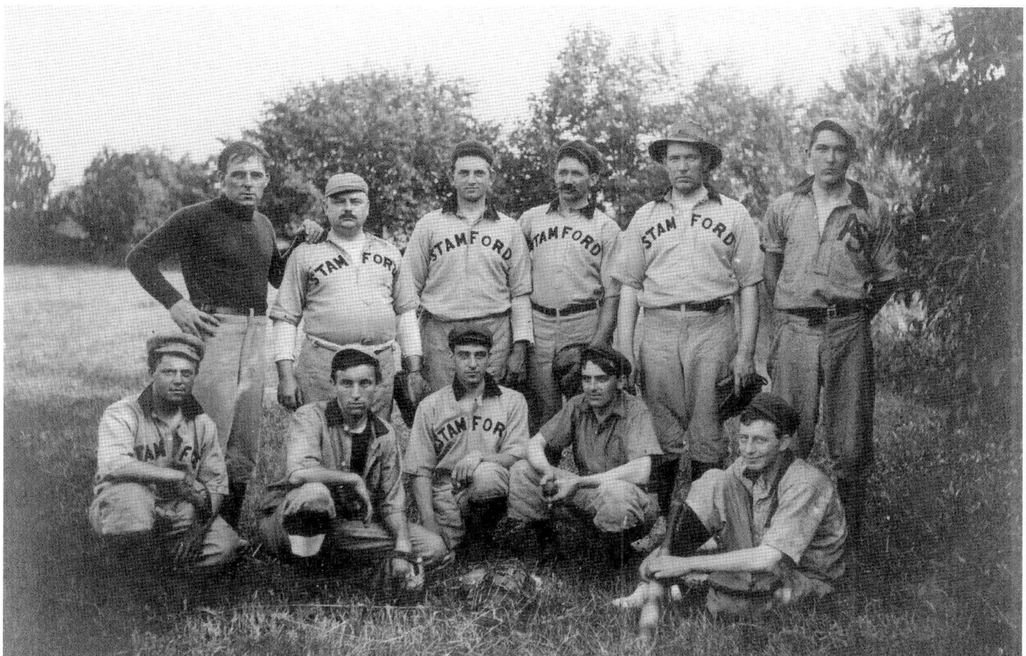

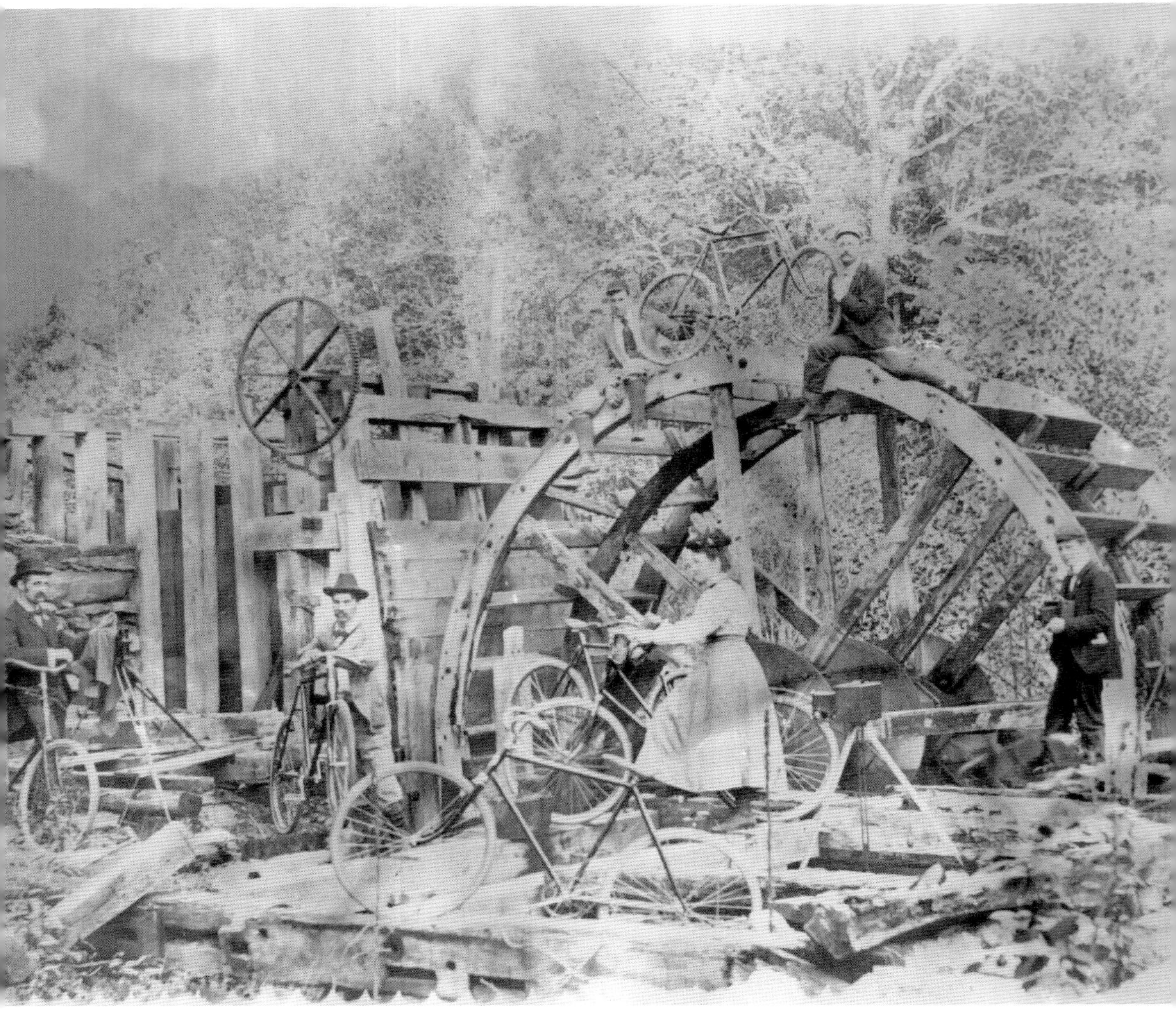

BICYCLE CLUB AT THE WIRE MILL WHEEL, 1892. Bicycling was a very popular pastime in the 1890s in Stamford, and the Bicycle Club was probably the earliest sports organization that admitted both men and women. The woman seen here is Amy Peckham, the wife of Dr. Ellery Peckham. The image is from a glass-plate negative.

2

A DIVERSITY OF SPORT

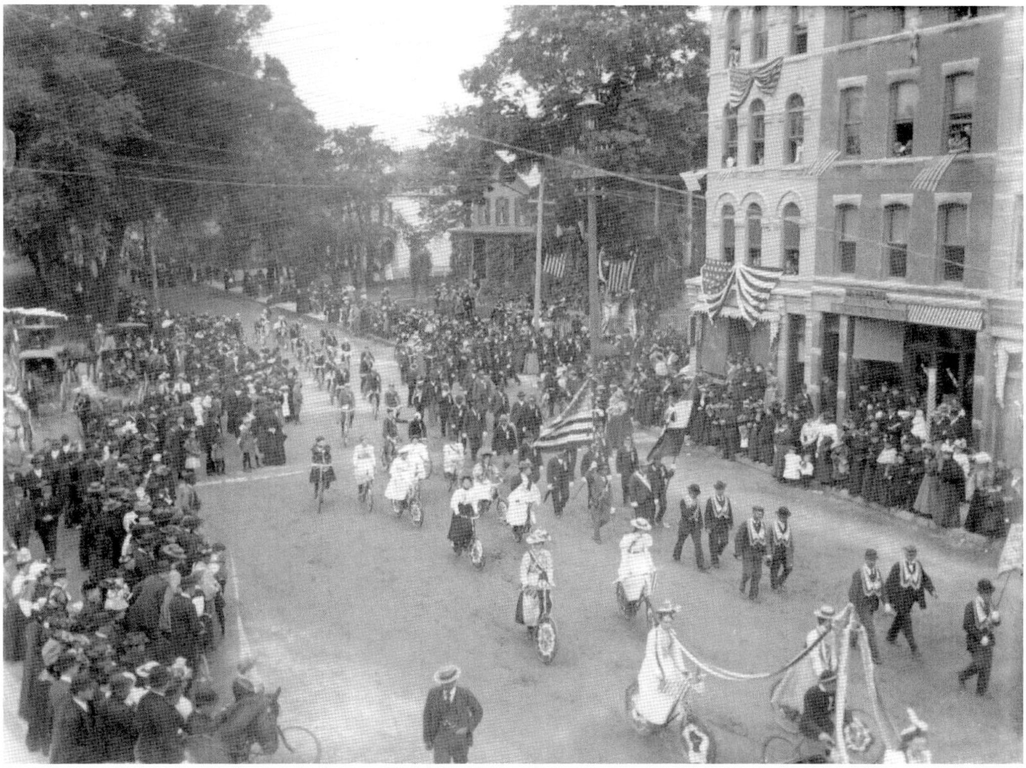

CYCLISTS CLUB, DECORATION DAY PARADE, 1898. In the early 1900s, Stamford's immigrant population was rapidly growing. Industrial leagues brought the diverse working communities together for many sports and activities. Athletic organizations were formed by Stamford's many cultural and religious organizations, and these clubs often branched out beyond the standard baseball and football teams. The burgeoning population, driven by industrial growth, also created a large, affluent population center capable of supporting paid diversions not available in smaller towns. In Stamford, these included big moneymakers such as prizefighting and horse racing.

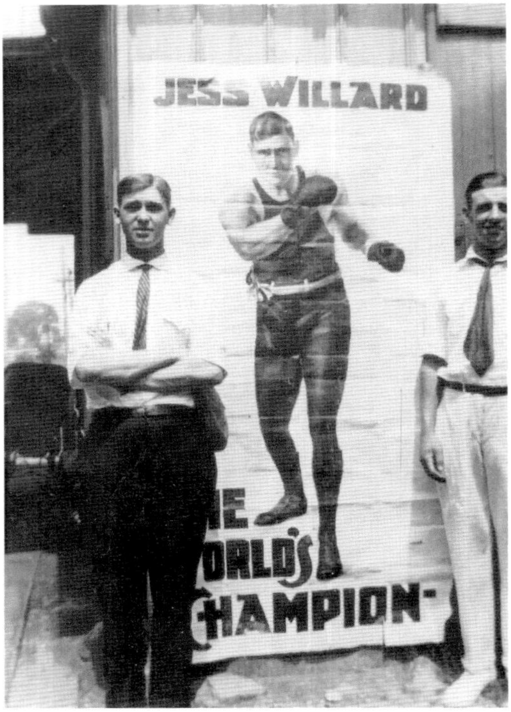

JESS WILLARD POSTER. Billie Weed and Cornie May of Stamford pose in front of a Jess Willard poster. Willard was the long-reigning heavyweight-boxing champion known as "The Great White Hope." Because of its proximity to New York City and its growing size, Stamford was able to bring big names in prizefighting to its venues.

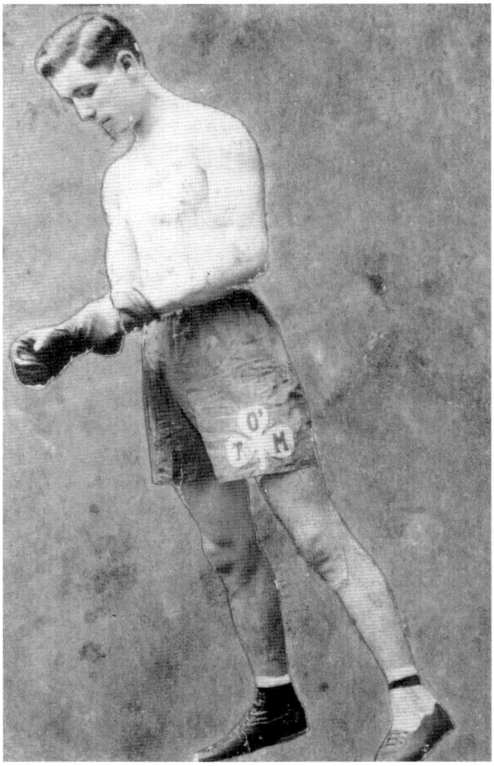

TERRENCE O'MOORE. This advertising photograph shows John Moore, a first-generation Irish boy and Stamford resident who fought as a lightweight under the names "Irish Jackie Moore" and "Terrence O'Moore." Note the initials on his trunks.

ANGELO PACE AND B.H. PEATT. Here, "Young Angelo" Pace (right) of Stamford faces off against B.H. Peatt. Pace fought nationally in the 1920s and often returned to fight in Stamford.

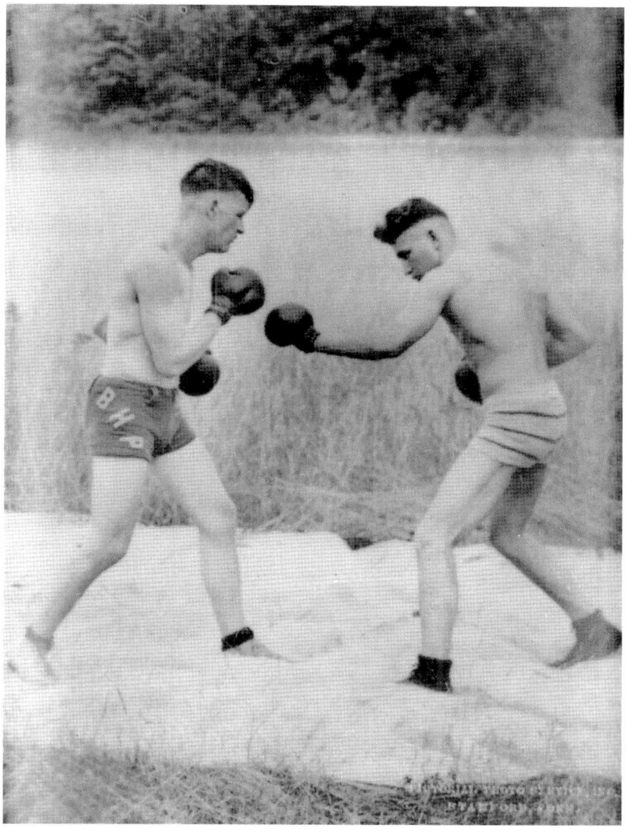

POLICE ATHLETIC LEAGUE BOXERS, 1950S. Boxing continued its popularity in Stamford through the 1950s. The boxers below trained at the Police Athletic League.

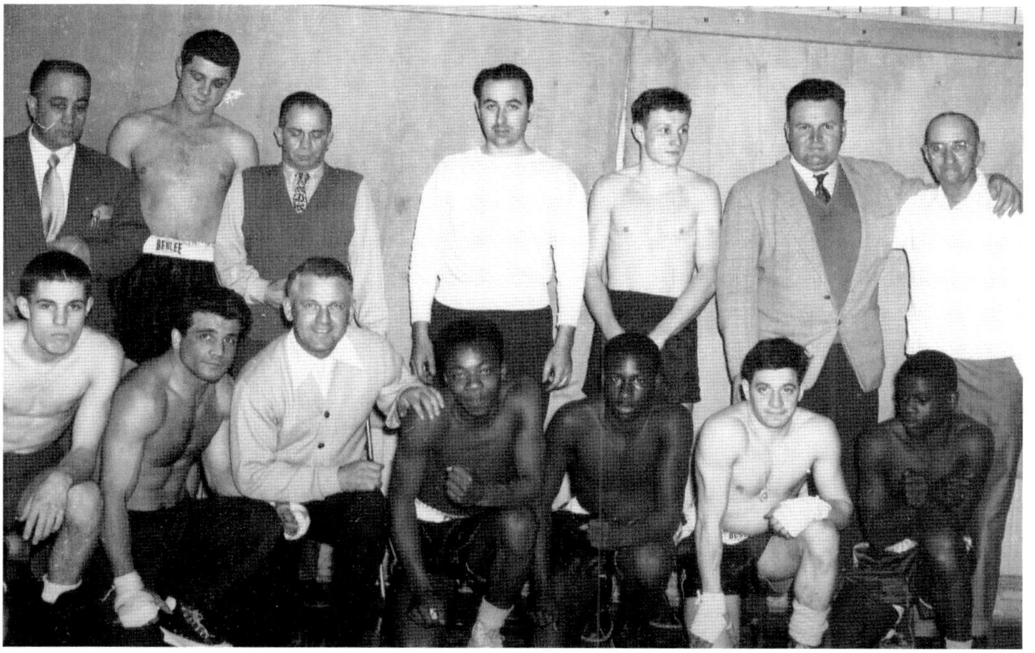

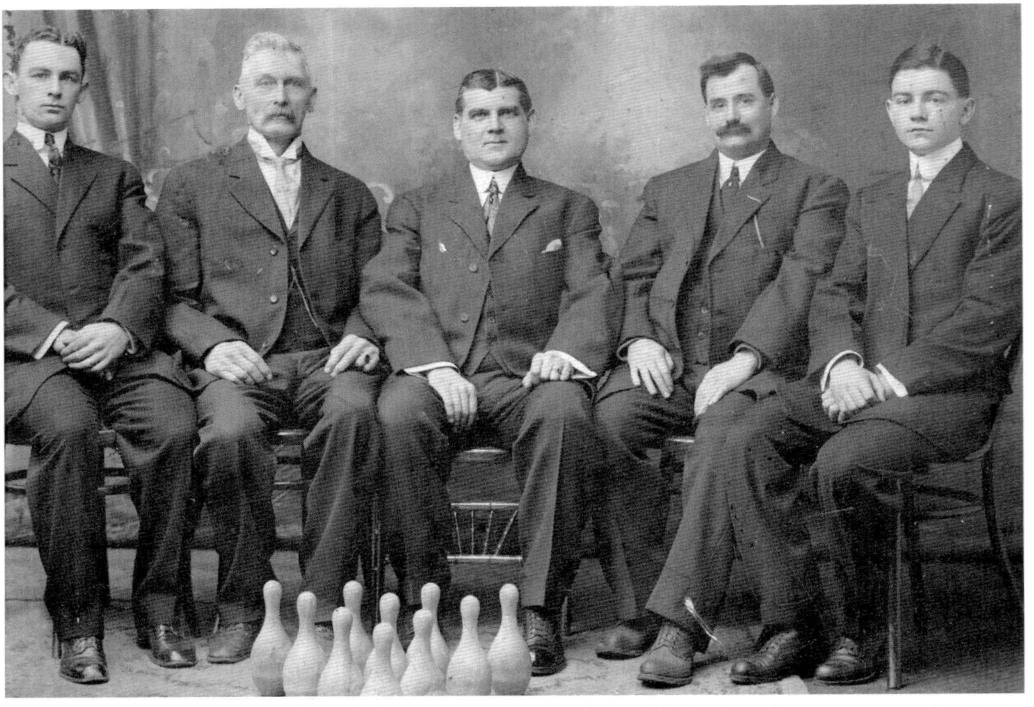

Bowling Team. This is a formal photograph of an early 1900s duckpin bowling team. Duckpin bowling was much more popular in the first half of the century than "Big Pin" bowling, as regular bowling was known then. Both variations sustained popular leagues in Stamford.

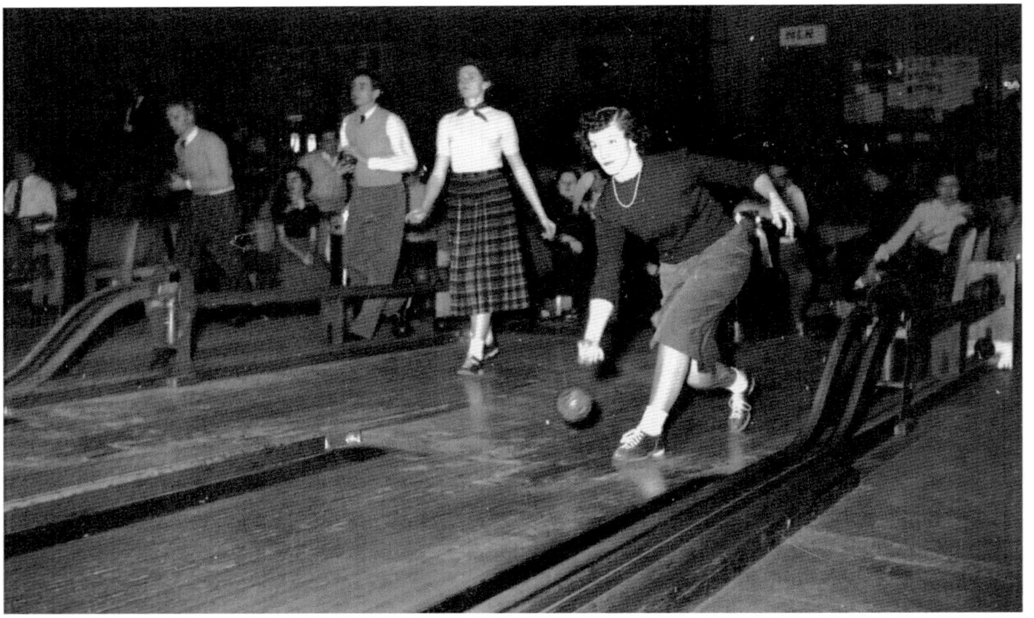

Duckpin Bowling. In 1948, Stamford youths bowl at duckpins, a popular pastime in Stamford.

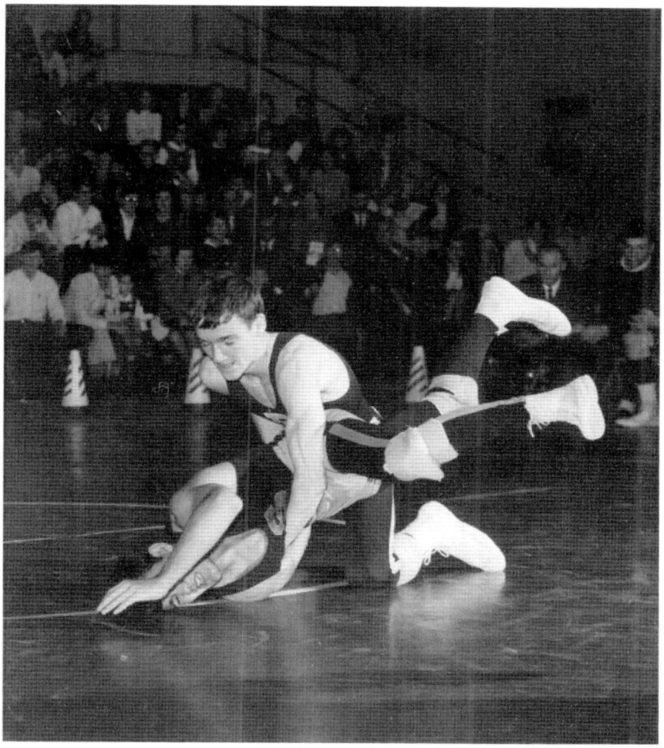

Rippowam Wrestlers, 1967. This action shot shows a wrestling match at Rippowam High School. Rippowam opened as an extra high school when the baby boomer population began straining the limits of Stamford High School. Rippowam had an outstanding sports program, with a wide variety of programs, including swimming and wrestling. The wrestler on top here is captain Bob Franklin. (Courtesy of John Kuczo.)

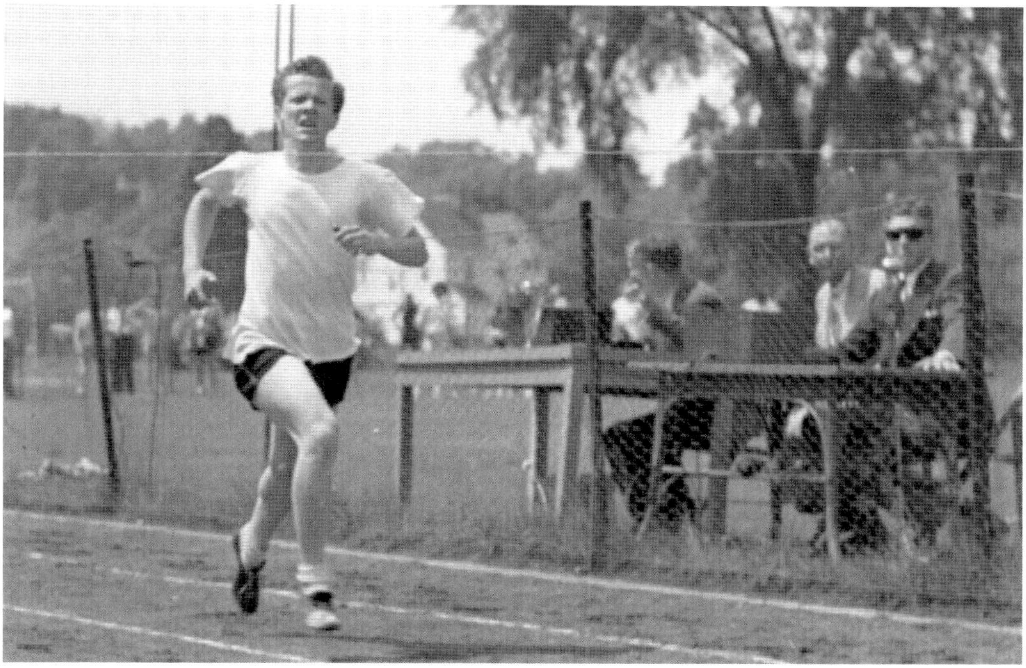

Stamford High School Track Meet, 1948. A runner digs it out for the finish line at a Stamford High track meet.

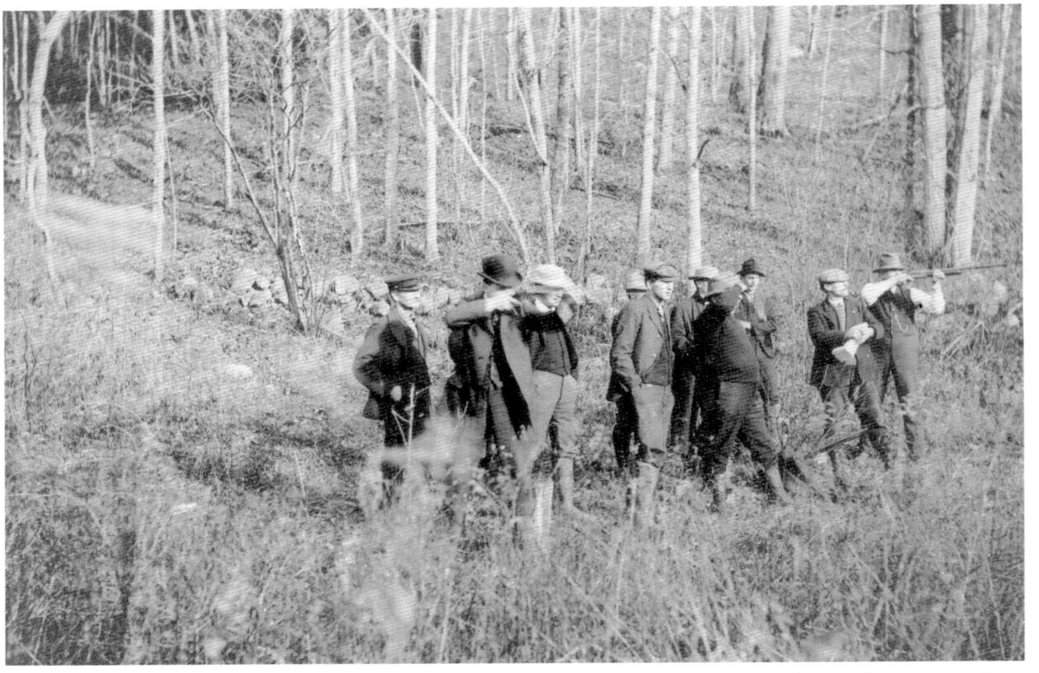

THE STAMFORD RIFLE CLUB, C. 1910. Members of the Stamford Rifle Club trapshoot near their cabin in Long Ridge.

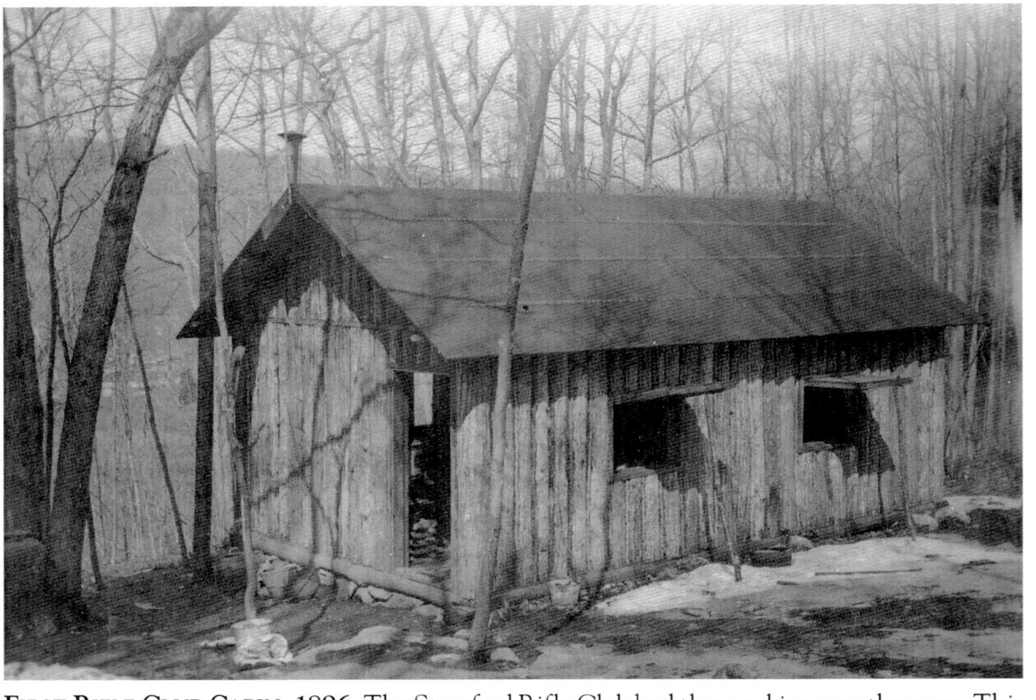

FIRST RIFLE CLUB CABIN, 1896. The Stamford Rifle Club had three cabins over the years. This cabin, on the slopes of Mianus Ridge in northern Stamford, burned down in 1900.

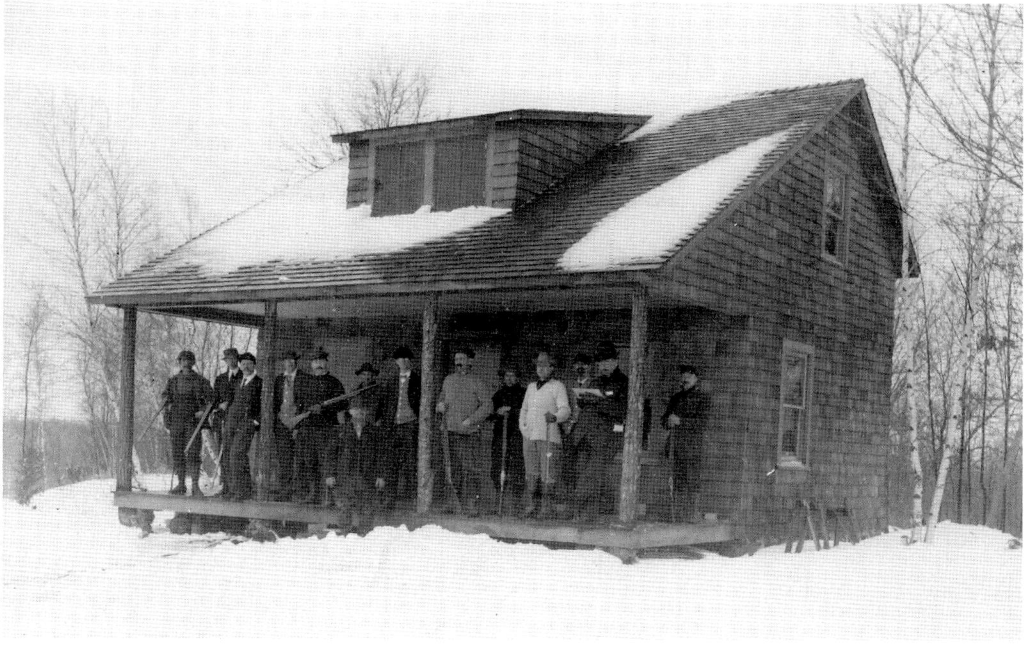

THIRD RIFLE CLUB CABIN, 1906. The back of the photograph above identifies this cabin as being on the second camp of the Stamford Rifle Club. The first two cabins were built at their first camp on Mianus Ridge.

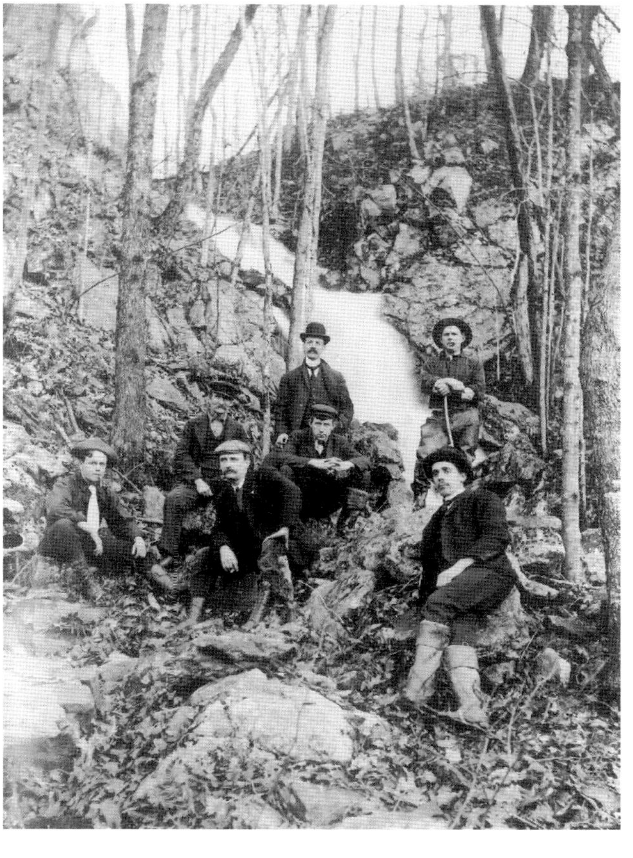

RIFLE CLUB AT BUTTERMILK FALLS, 1909. The Stamford Rifle Club poses near their cabin in Long Ridge.

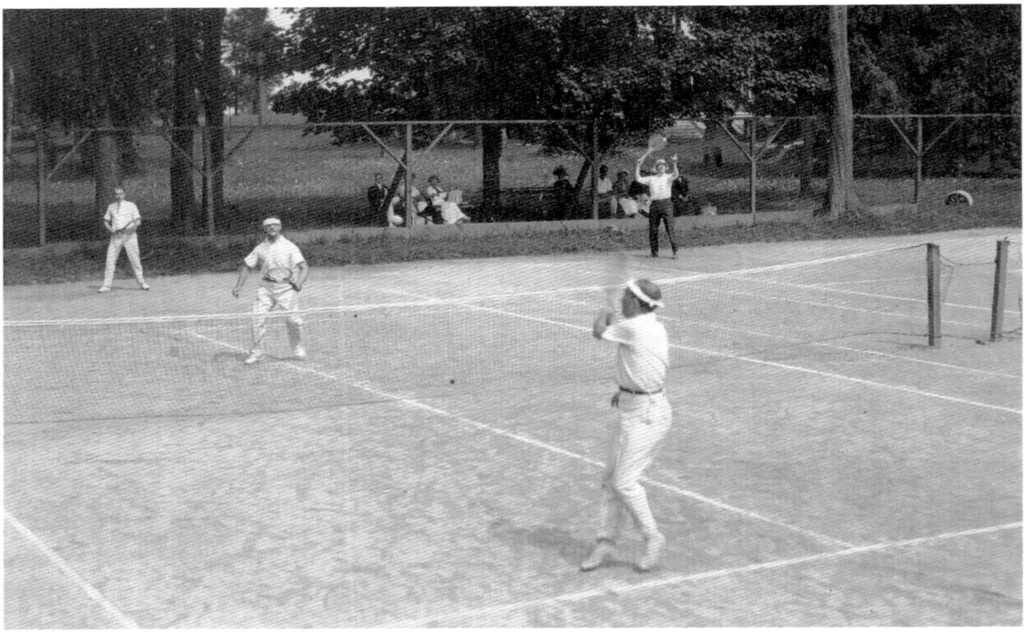

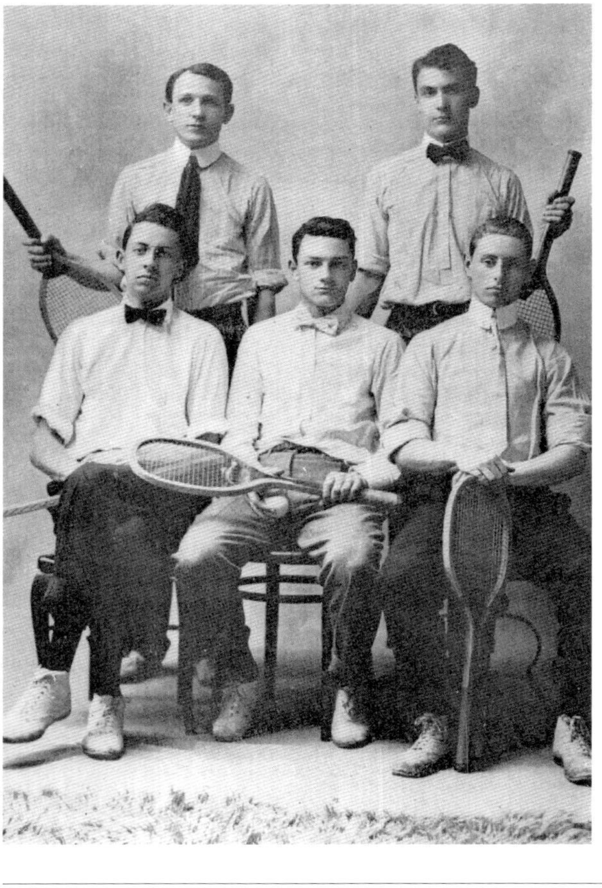

TENNIS COURTS IN SHIPPAN POINT. The photograph above is part of a photograph album compiled by the Shippan Point Land Company. Shippan was developed as a neighborhood for the affluent, and the images of mansions, beaches, and private clubs cater to these potential buyers. The photograph was most likely taken at the Stamford Yacht Club in Shippan.

STAMFORD HIGH SCHOOL TENNIS TEAM, 1906. While tennis was associated with private clubs such as the Stamford Yacht Club, the sport was not restricted to the affluent in Stamford. Stamford High School's 1906 tennis team is seen here. Stamford's public parks, such as Halloween Park (later Cummings Park) included tennis courts by the early 1900s.

CYO-SPONSORED BOXING MATCH, 1949. In these two photographs, two unidentified fighters duke it out at an event sponsored by the Catholic Youth Organization (CYO). This religious organization, like many around Stamford, actively supported and promoted sports and athletic events of all types. Prizefights were well attended and drew large crowds to venues such as Mitchell Field. These images are from original cellulose acetate negatives, which are prone to bubbling when they deteriorate.

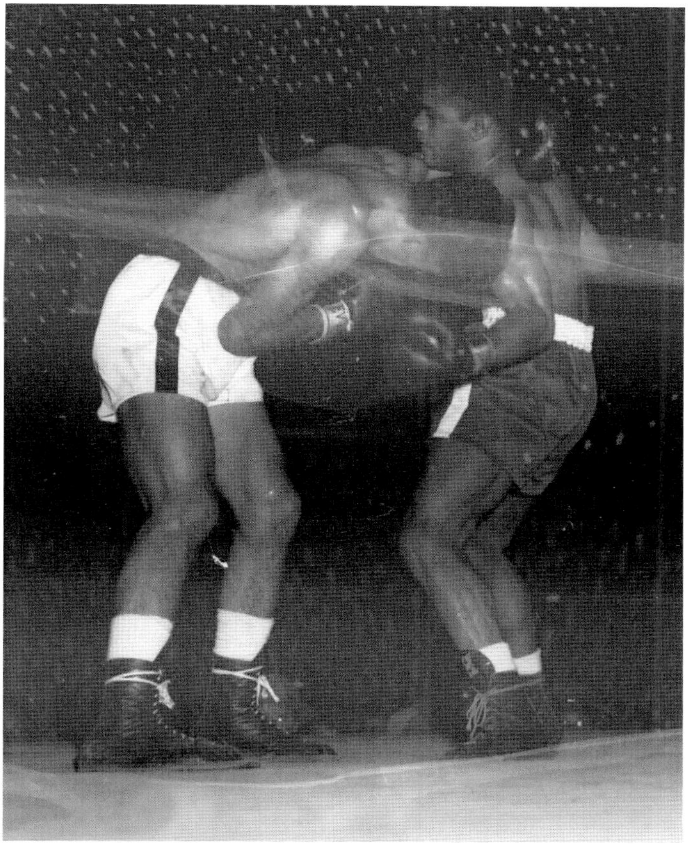

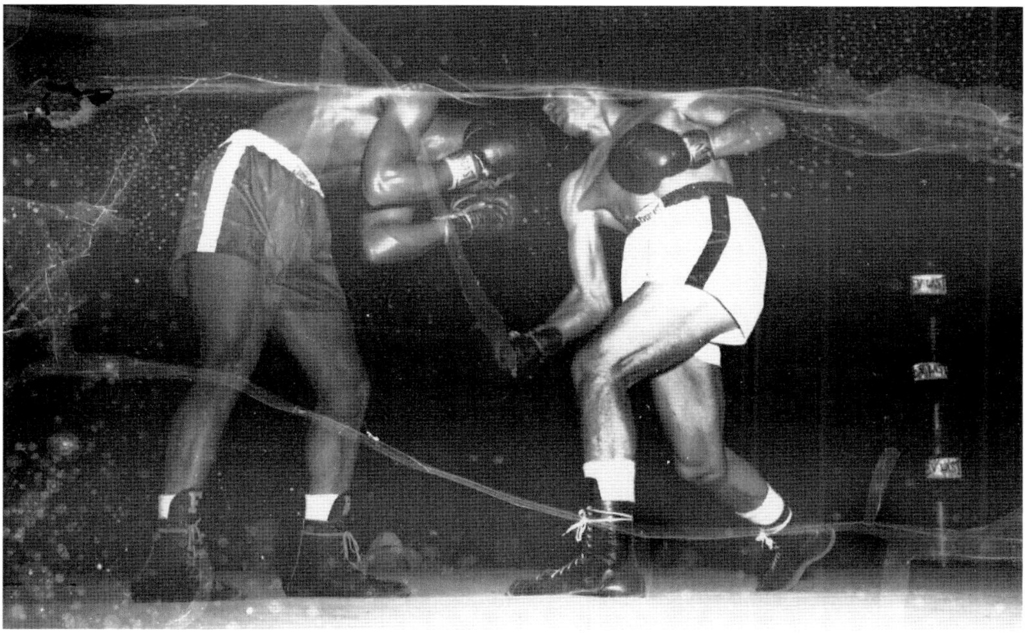

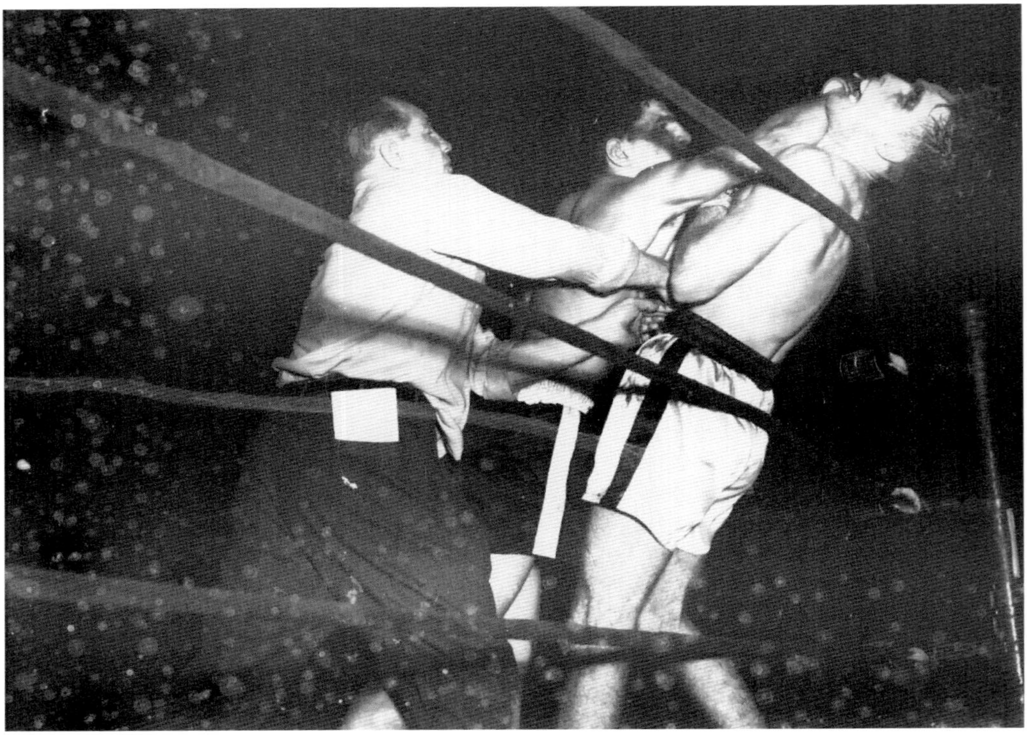

CYO Boxing Match, 1949. Here, a boxer takes a direct hit to the jaw. The damage to the negative barely impairs the intensity of the image.

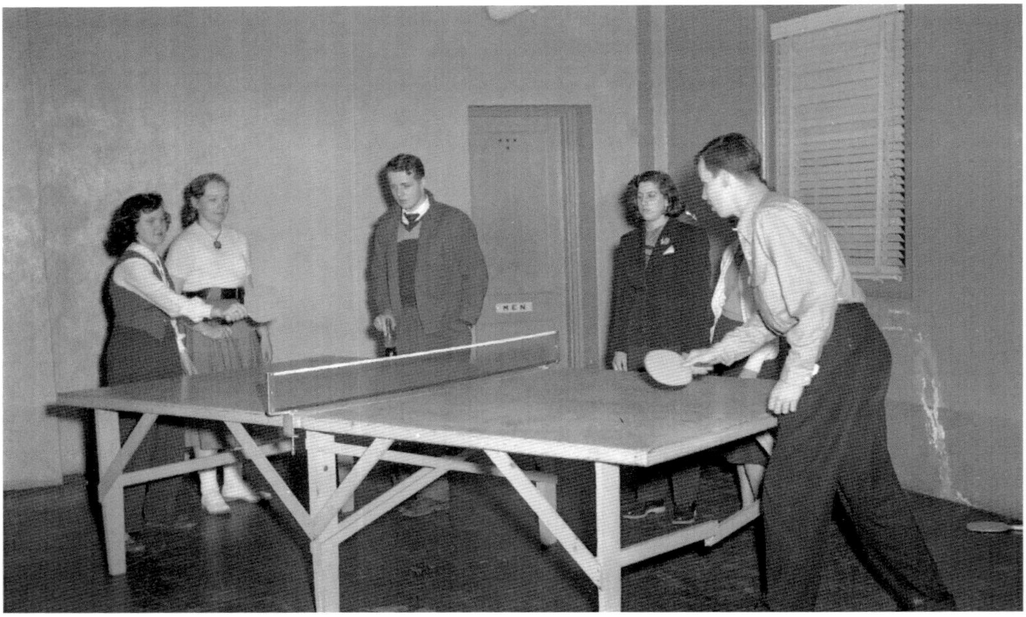

Youths Playing Table Tennis, c. 1950. The CYO sponsored a number of teams and sporting events and also maintained recreational facilities, such as this one complete with table tennis.

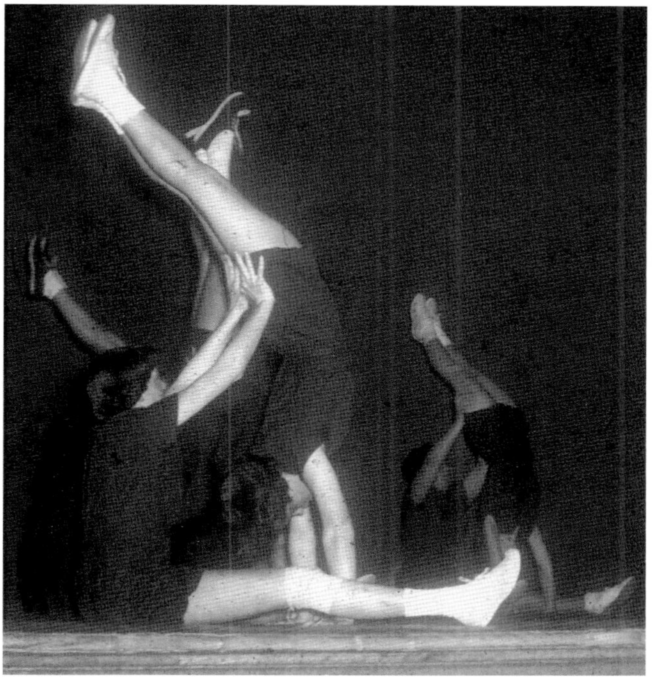

DOLAN JUNIOR HIGH SCHOOL TUMBLING TEAM, 1951. Stamford schools offered a wide variety of sports programs to its young men and women, including badminton, golf, gymnastics, wrestling, and swimming. This image of the Dolan Junior High tumbling team was used as part of a school orientation slide show.

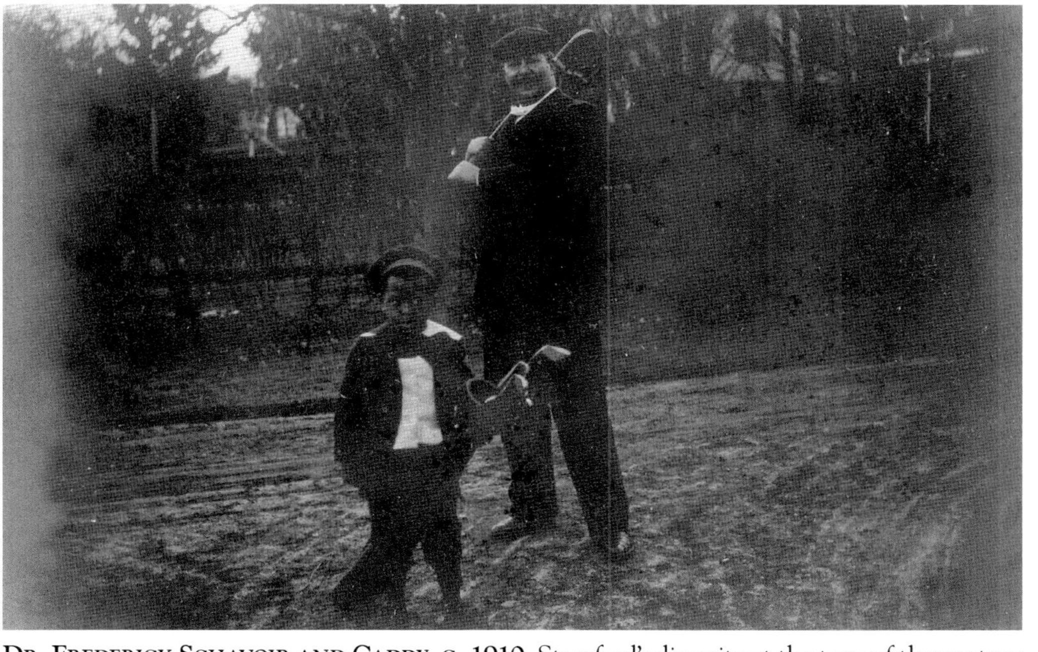

DR. FREDERICK SCHAVOIR AND CADDY, C. 1910. Stamford's diversity at the turn of the century did not extend to race. Here, prominent physician Dr. Fred Schavoir poses with his very young African American caddy at the Hillandale Golf Club. Beginning in the 1920s, Stamford began assimilating a large influx of African American laborers and remained ahead of the American curve in terms of integrating blacks into its athletic teams.

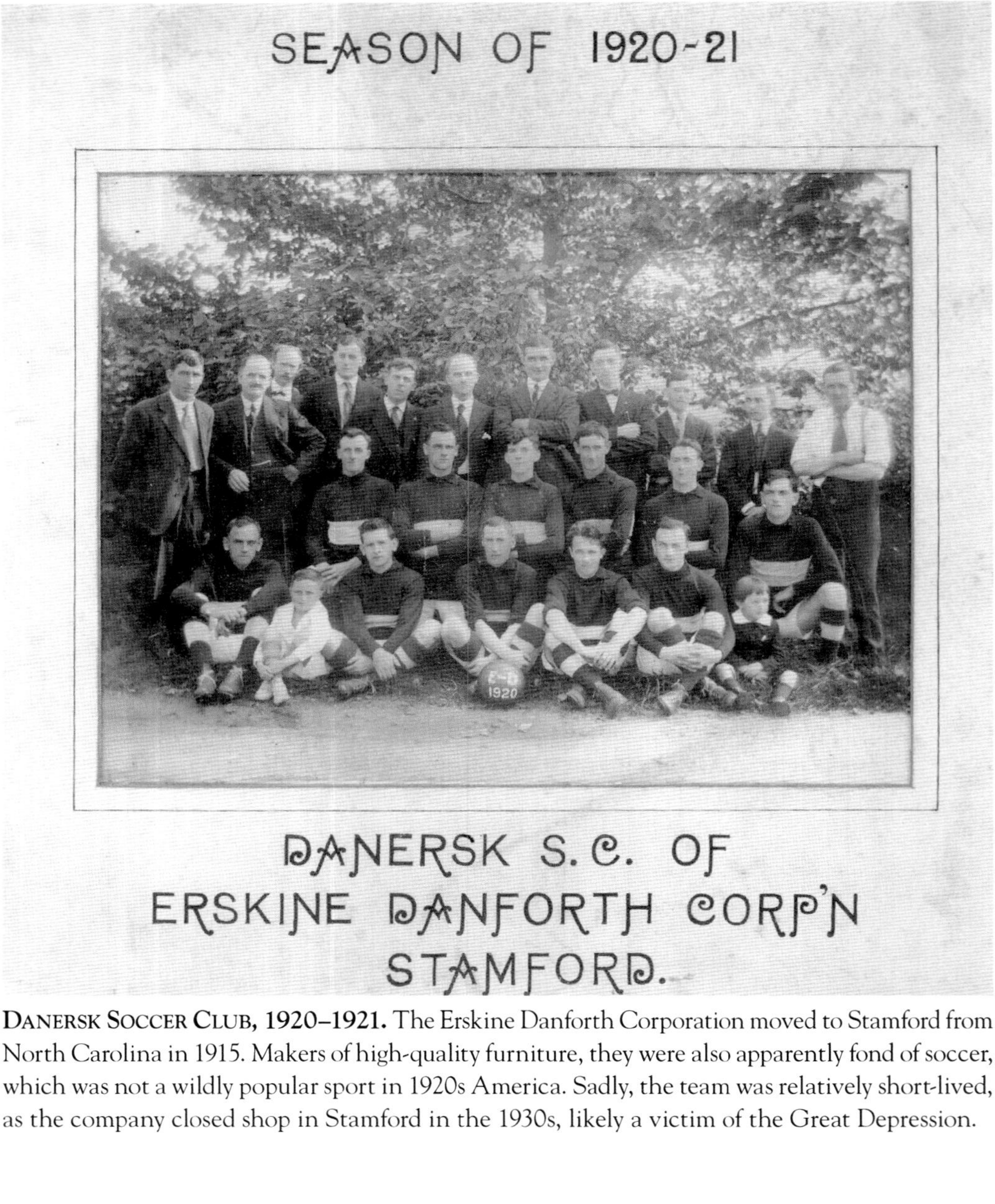

DANERSK SOCCER CLUB, 1920–1921. The Erskine Danforth Corporation moved to Stamford from North Carolina in 1915. Makers of high-quality furniture, they were also apparently fond of soccer, which was not a wildly popular sport in 1920s America. Sadly, the team was relatively short-lived, as the company closed shop in Stamford in the 1930s, likely a victim of the Great Depression.

3

PLAYING FIELDS OF STAMFORD

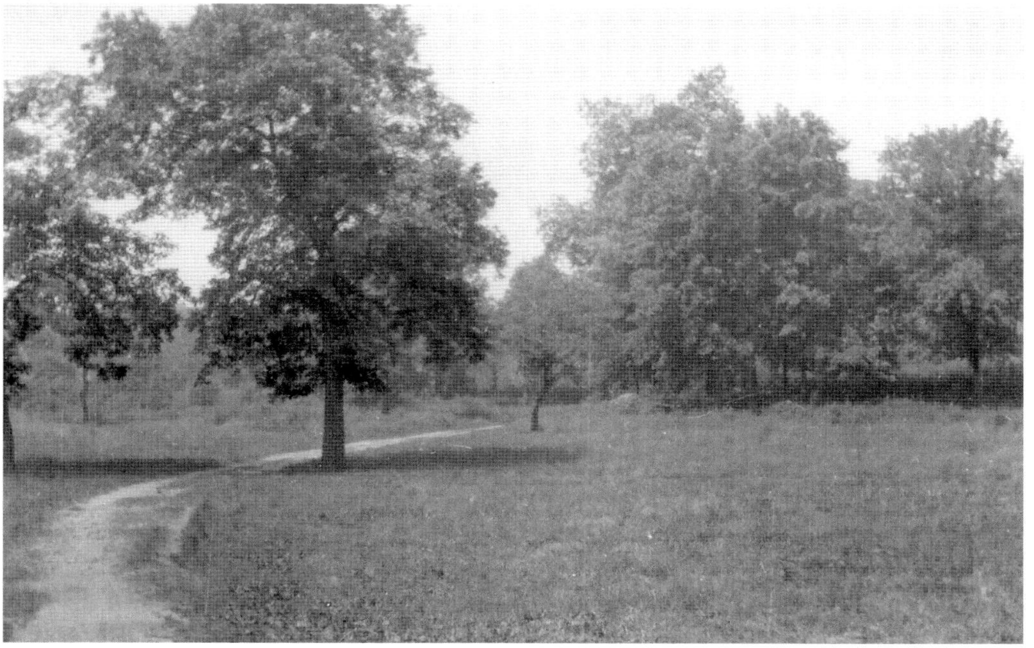

WOODSIDE PARK, 1946. One of the oldest and most used parks in Stamford, Woodside Park was originally on the property of the Ferris brothers, who probably tired of chasing off young baseball players and opened the land to the public in 1868. The area, at what is now Washington Boulevard and Bridge Street, had a horse track, and early baseball games were often marketed in conjunction with horse races, or "trots," as they were called in the advertisements. The path in this photograph is part of a great loop that still exists today and was originally the horse track. The park was later renamed Scalzi Park after Stamford player and coach John Scalzi. Stamford maintained a great many parks and playing fields, with the largest and most popular for sport being Woodside, Cummings, Halloween, the "Dyke," Mitchell Field, Belltown Field, and Cove Island Park.

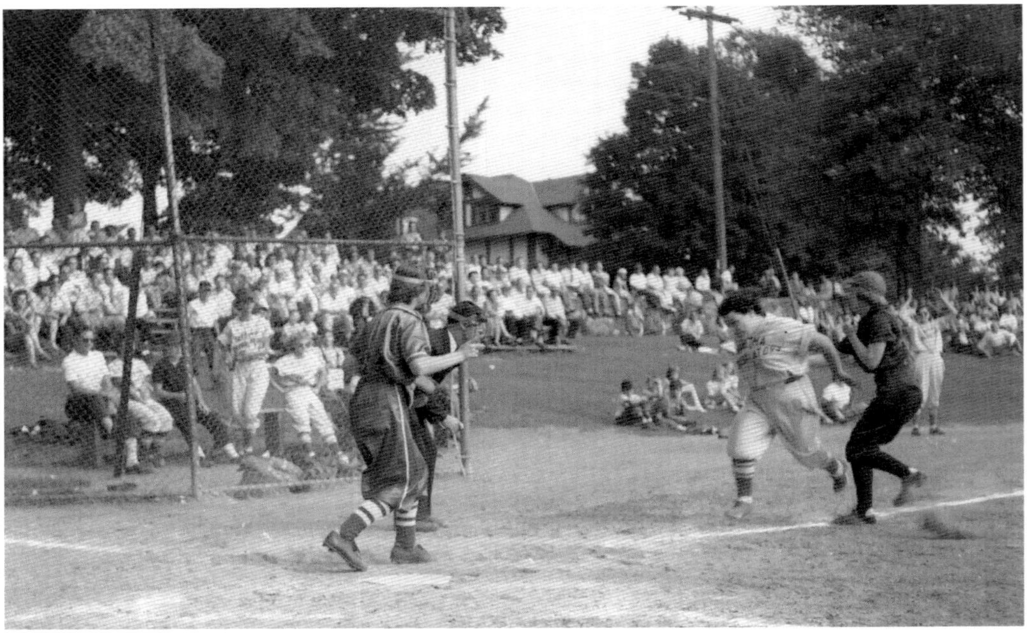

NUTMEGS GAME AT BARRETT FIELD, 1948. Later renamed Barrett Field, Belltown Field saw heavy use by softball and baseball teams on Stamford's east side. Large crowds came out to Belltown in the 1930s and 1940s to watch the Nutmegs play fast-pitch softball.

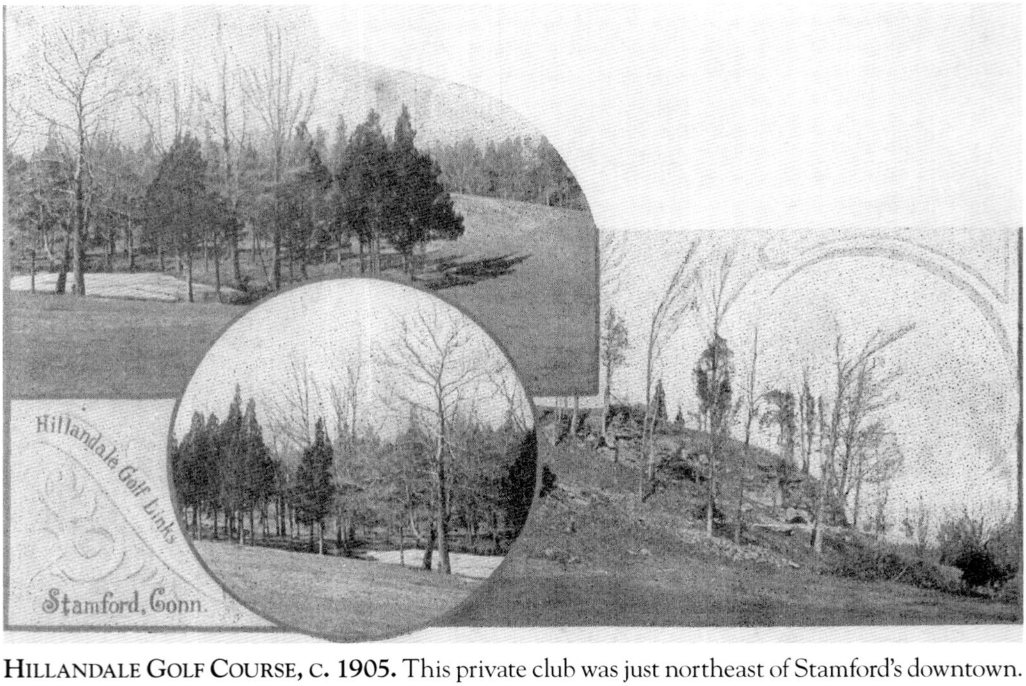

HILLANDALE GOLF COURSE, C. 1905. This private club was just northeast of Stamford's downtown. Initially populated mainly by the affluent, the area, including the golf course, is now a middle-income residential neighborhood.

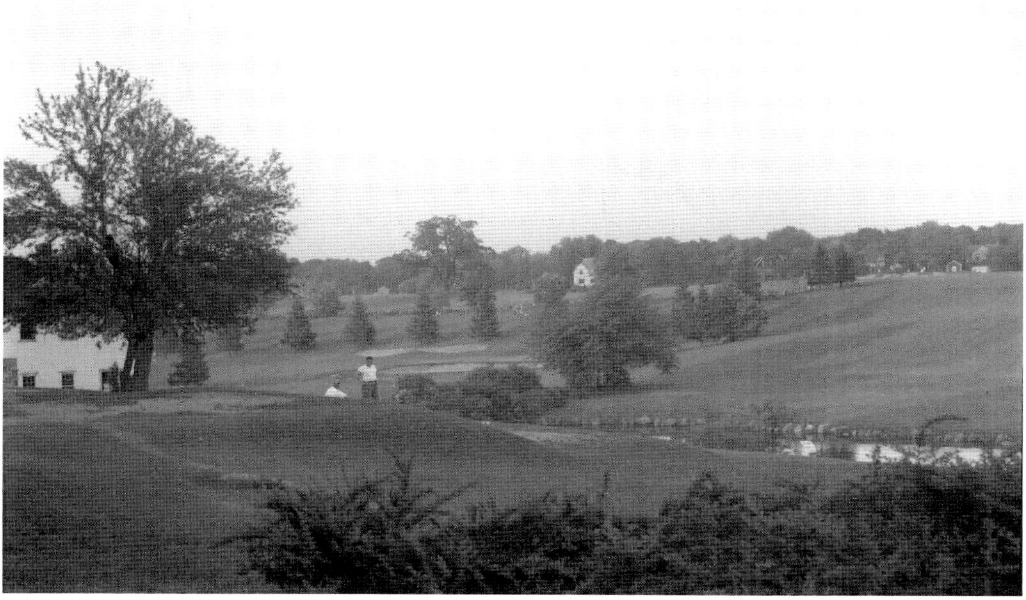

HUBBARD HEIGHTS GOLF COURSE, c. 1950. Originally a farm owned by the Hubbard family, Hubbard Heights opened as a private golf course in the late 1920s. It became a public course in 1949 and is now named the E. Gaynor Brennan Public Golf Course, although locals still refer to it as Hubbard Heights. The course is seen above, and the clubhouse is below.

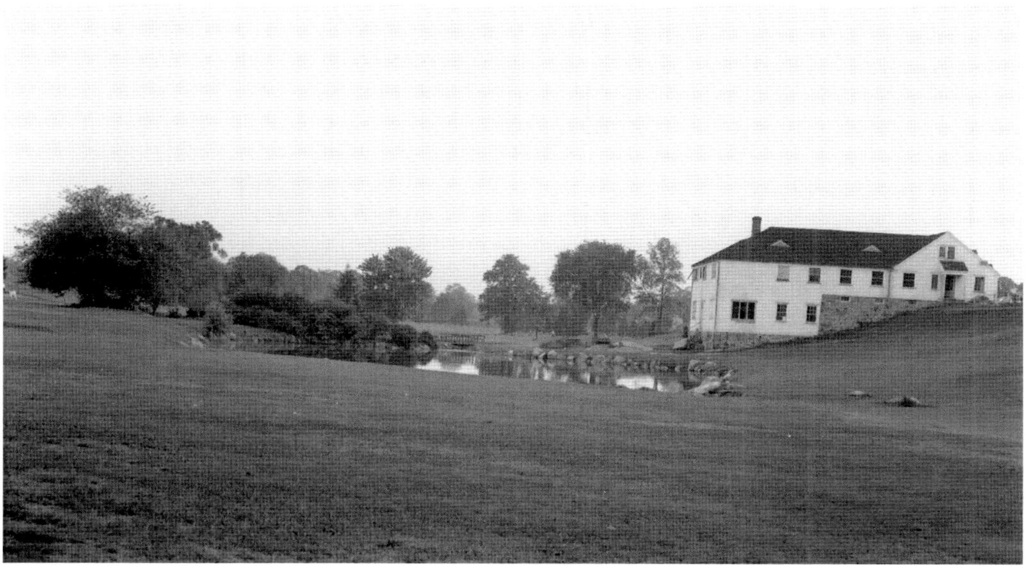

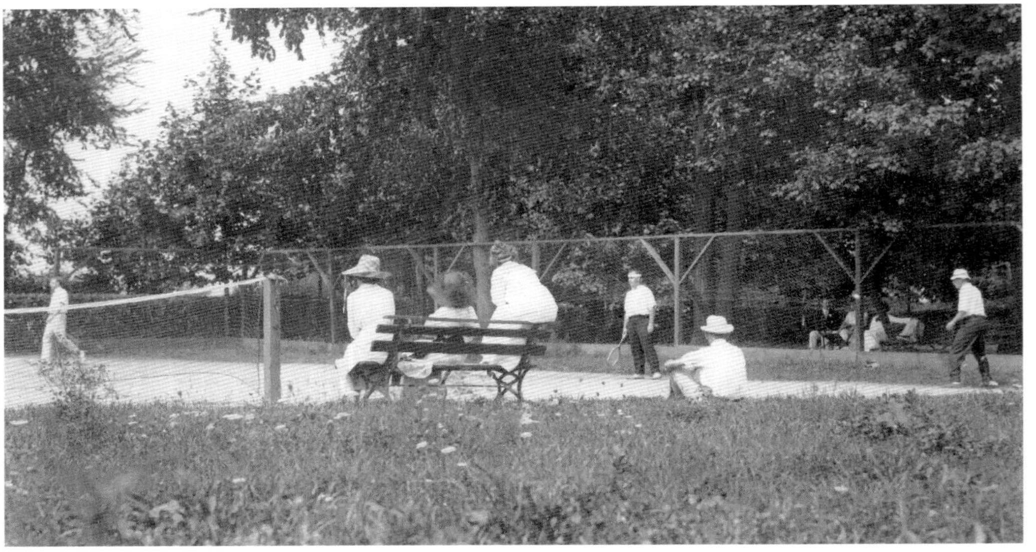

SHIPPAN TENNIS COURTS. This photograph was included in a photograph album created to sell real estate to Stamford newcomers. Shippan is an area of land on a peninsula of the Long Island Sound on the east side of Stamford. The area is home to a number of parks and clubs as well as businesses and residences.

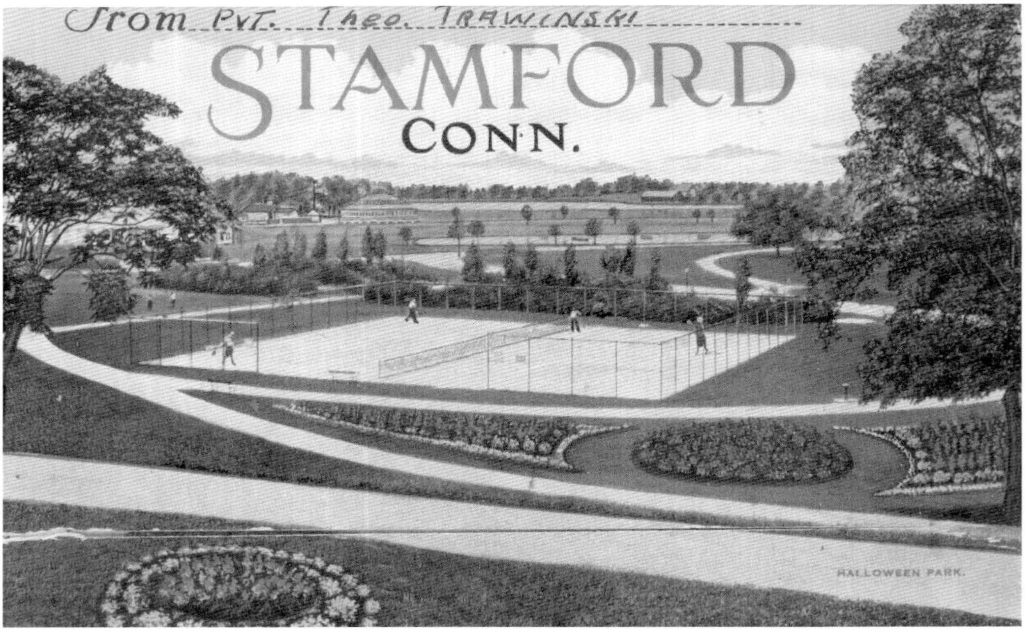

HALLOWEEN PARK, 1924. This cover of a postcard booklet shows not only the public tennis courts but also the spacious playing fields behind it. Inside the cover is a description extolling the virtues of this growing "gateway of Western New England" with its "excellent harbor, a fine yacht club, good private and public schools, 100 acres of parks, social parks, and a modern Chamber of Commerce."

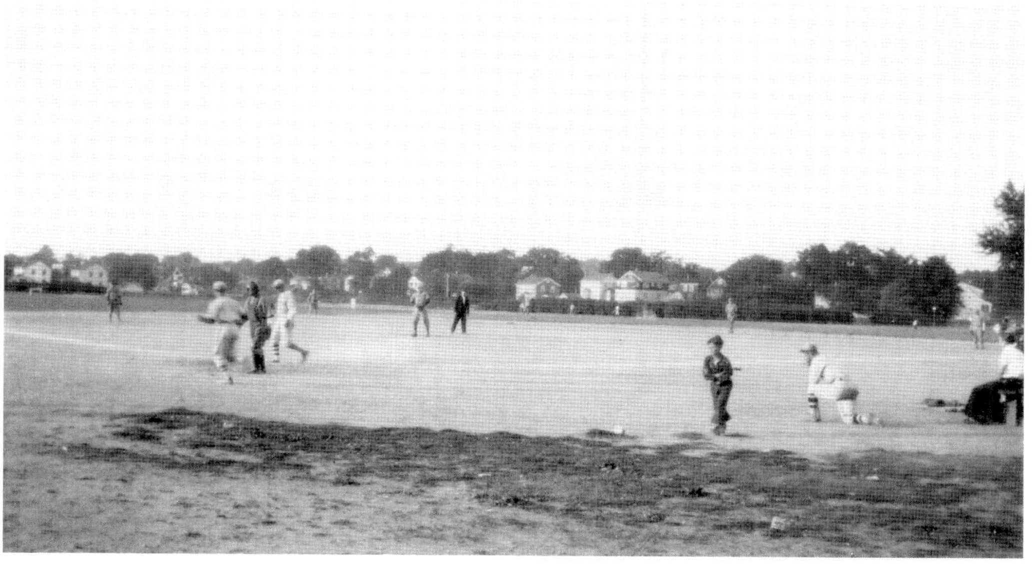

HALLOWEEN PARK BASEBALL FIELD, C. 1926. Every section of Stamford had its ball field; in Shippan, on the coast, the field was in Halloween Park. Later renamed Cummings Park, it featured this baseball field, tennis courts, and a large, popular beach. The playing fields were used heavily by many ethnic communities in the south and east ends.

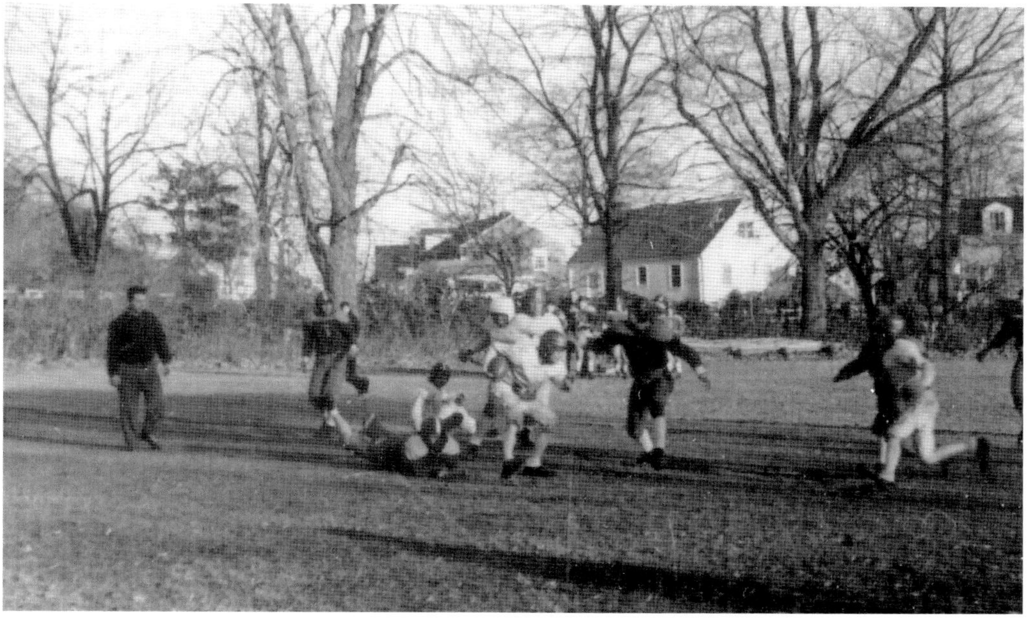

DAYCROFT SCHOOL FOOTBALL FIELD. The Daycroft School was a private Christian Science–based school that moved to Stamford in 1935. Most of Stamford's private schools maintained playing fields, and many were used by both school teams and by teams in the community.

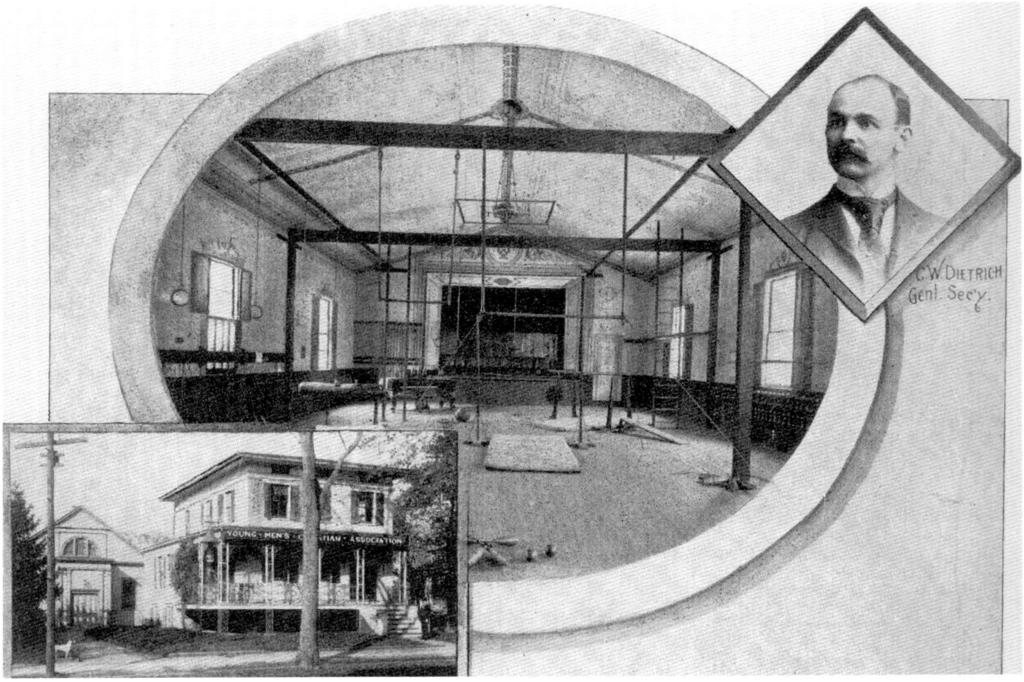

YMCA, 1892. This print shows the gymnasium of the original Stamford Young Men's Christian Association (YMCA) and the exterior buildings. The YMCA was established in 1882 and used this building until the 1950s, when a new facility was constructed at the corner of Washington Boulevard and Bell Street.

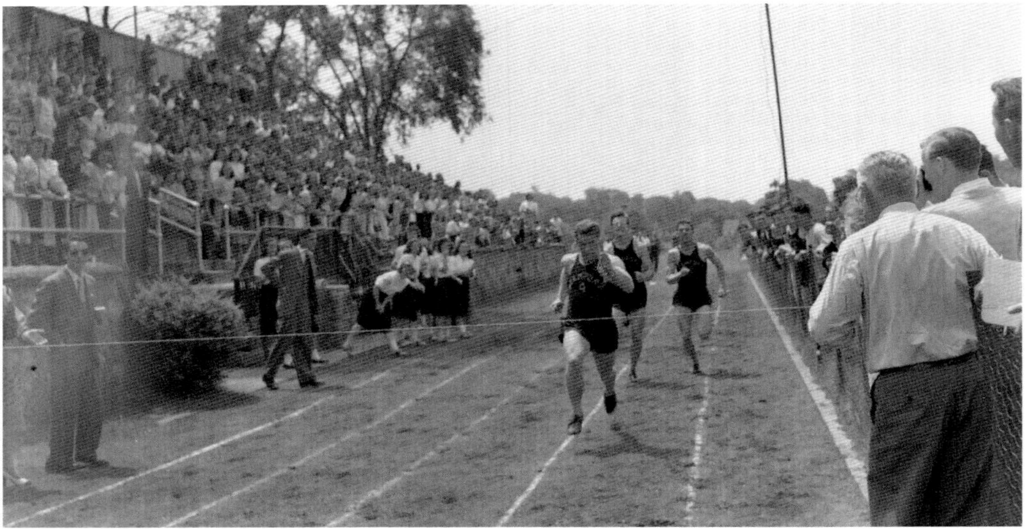

STAMFORD HIGH TRACK MEET, 1948. Boyle Stadium at Stamford High School was completed in 1942, a successful construction project of the Works Progress Administration (WPA). The stadium included facilities for track and field events, including this track as well as space and equipment for pole vaulting and long jump.

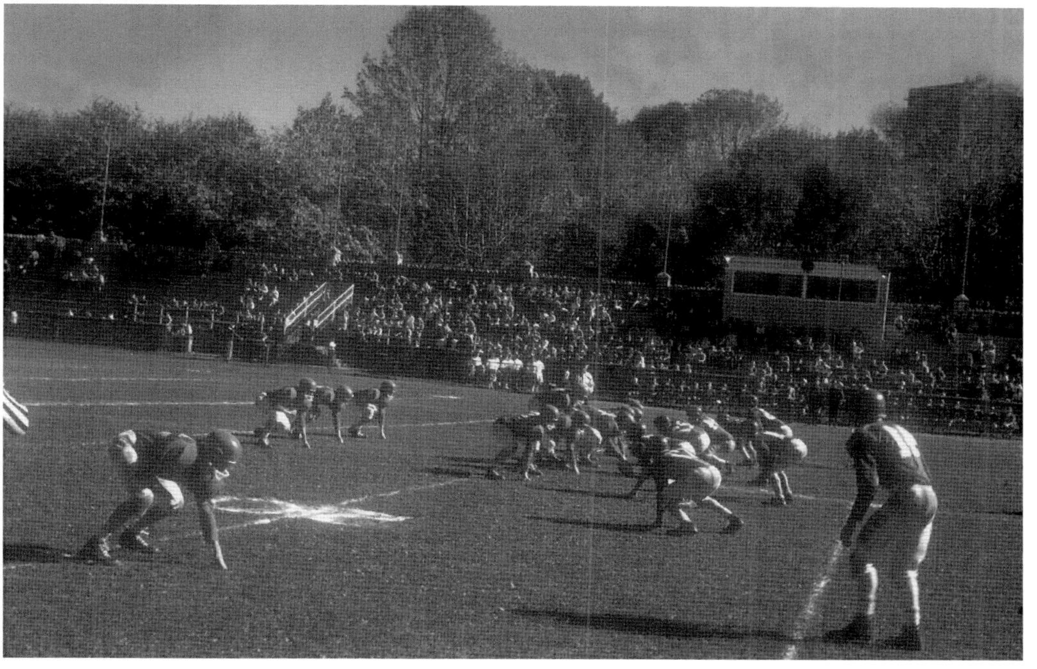

DOLAN JUNIOR HIGH SCHOOL FIELD. In the 1960s and 1970s, middle schools began to offer interscholastic football and other sports to their students. This is a photograph of Dolan Junior High School's field on a beautiful New England fall day.

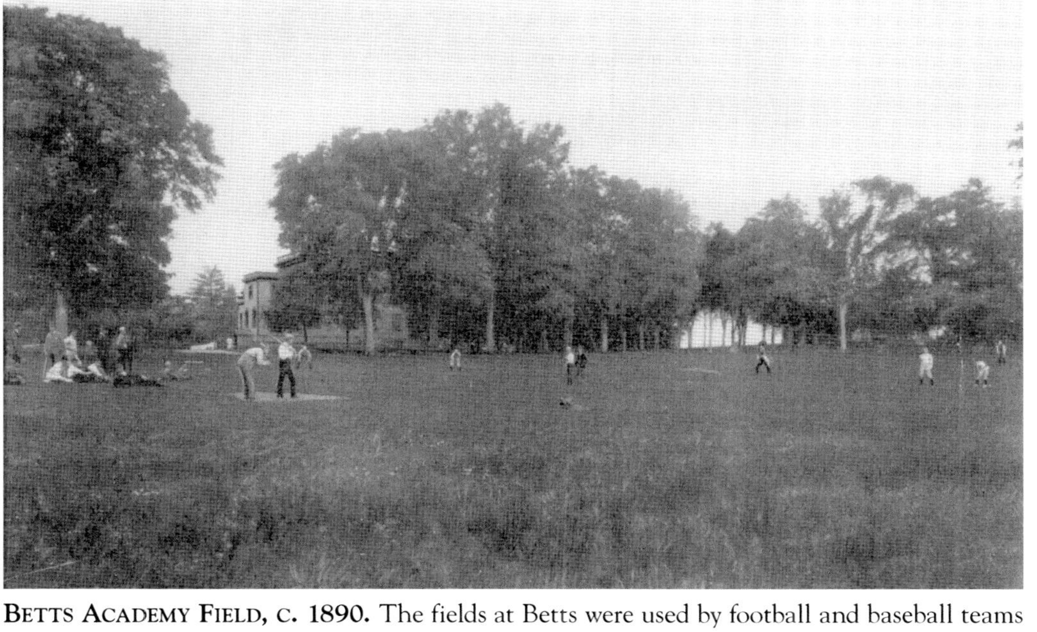

BETTS ACADEMY FIELD, C. 1890. The fields at Betts were used by football and baseball teams from all over Stamford throughout the early years of both sports.

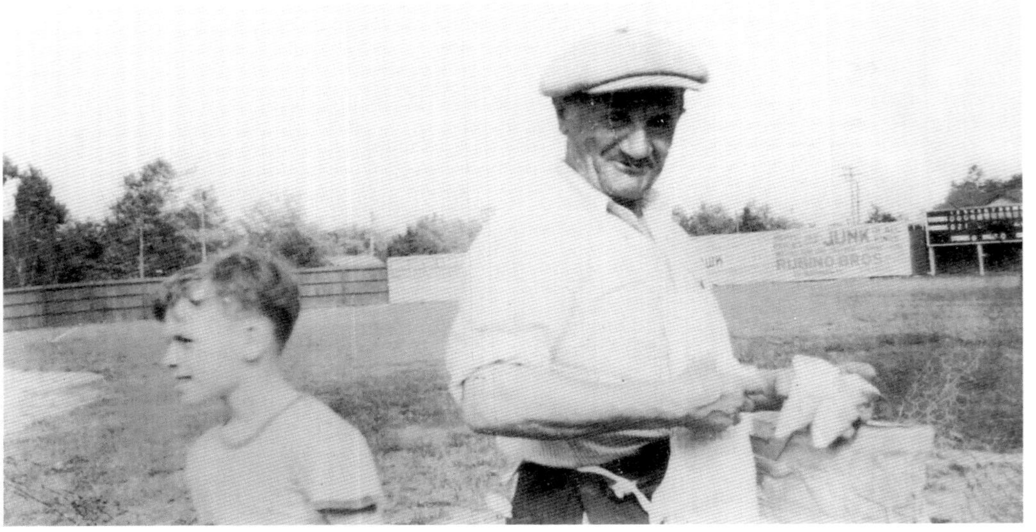

PEANUT VENDOR AT MITCHELL FIELD. Mitchell Field was originally a baseball diamond in the Shippan area of Stamford. John Connelly later led a group of investors who purchased the property and converted it into Stamford's first enclosed sports venue. Mitchell Stadium was not only used heavily for baseball, but was also used for many other sporting events, including boxing and wrestling. A number of professional baseball teams, including Negro League teams and the St. Louis Cardinals, came to play at Mitchell.

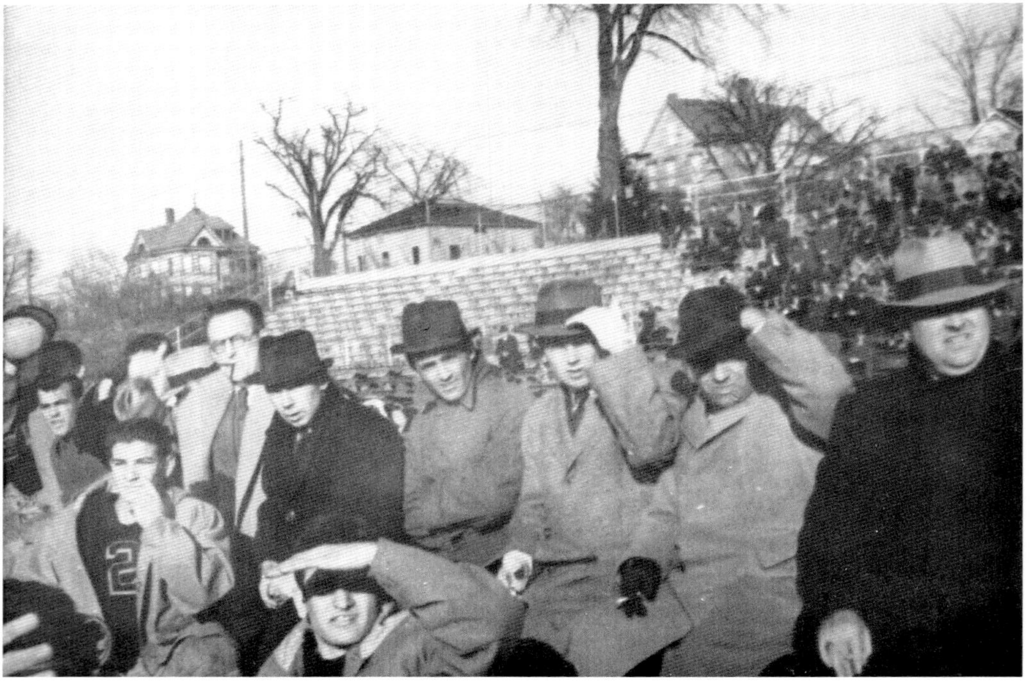

STAMFORD HIGH SCHOOL FOOTBALL BENCH. The Stamford High football players and coaches watch a game from the bench.

4

ON THE DIAMOND

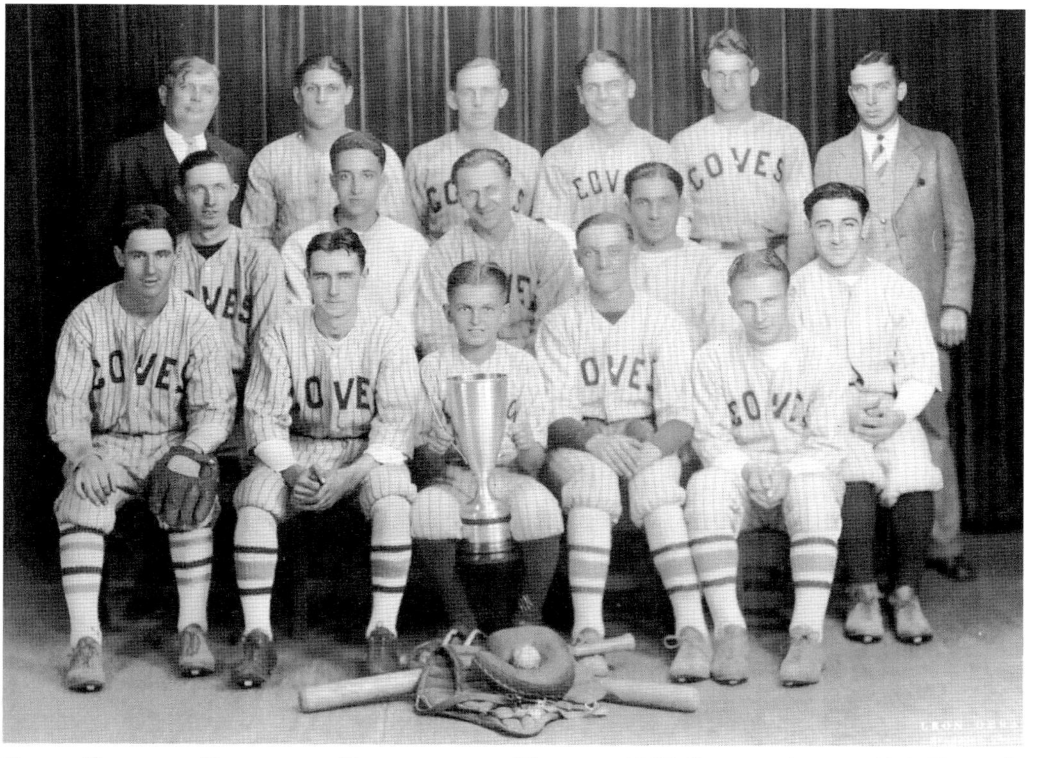

COVES BASEBALL CLUB WITH CHAMPIONSHIP TROPHY, 1927. Sports columnist Bob Kennedy has identified the period from 1917 to 1948 as the "golden age of Stamford baseball." In 1916, the Industrial League was founded, featuring teams from Stamford's industrial powerhouses: Yale & Towne, Pitney Bowes, Stamford Rolling Mills, and the New Haven Railroad, among a great many. Yale & Towne alone sponsored an eight-team, in-house league. The period also saw a growing number of club teams, most of them organized by athletic clubs and competing for the city championship. The 1920s also saw the rise of Stamford High School baseball, which groomed soon-to-be-stars like pitcher Paul Kuczo and infielder John Scalzi and was coached by the legendary Mike Boyle. In the 1930s, Ed Hunt, a Stamford recreation superintendent, established recreational teams for Stamford's youth, ultimately paving the way for the Little League teams of the 1950s. Finally, Stamford supported two professional teams during the era: the Pioneers, established in 1941; and the Bombers, established in 1947.

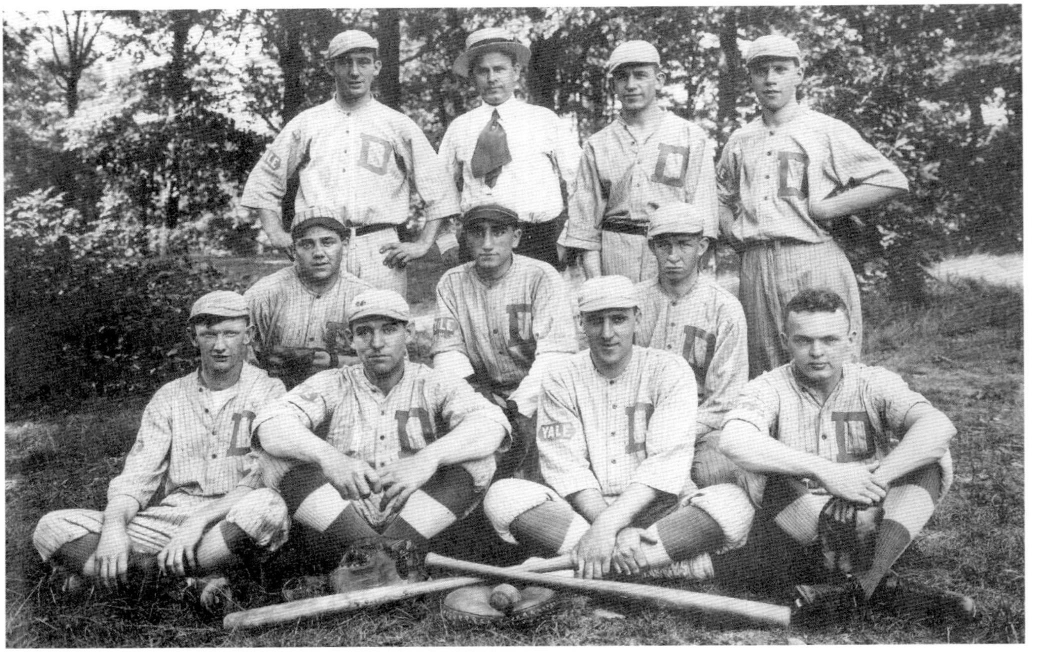

YALE & TOWNE DODGERS, 1919. Yale & Towne's eight in-house baseball teams were all named after major-league teams, including the Dodgers, the Red Sox, the White Sox, the Tigers, and the Giants. The company supported athletic teams of all kinds, including volleyball, basketball, and bowling. This photograph was taken at Woodside Park.

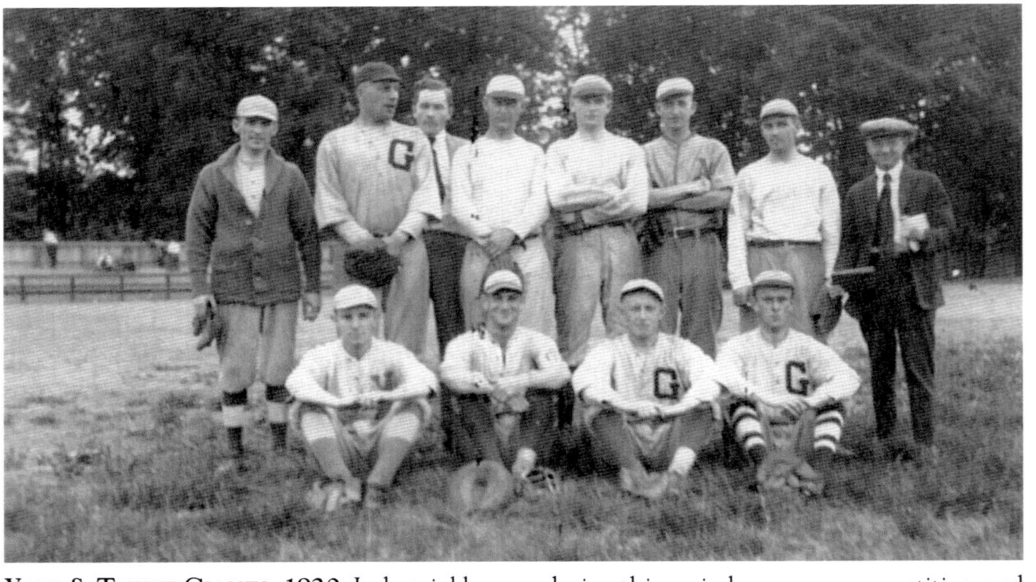

YALE & TOWNE GIANTS, 1920. Industrial leagues during this period were very competitive, and it was not uncommon for companies to hire workers based on their baseball ability. Many players belonged to several clubs. It is well known that George Bowman, Stamford's first police chief, was originally enticed to come to Stamford to play ball for Yale & Towne.

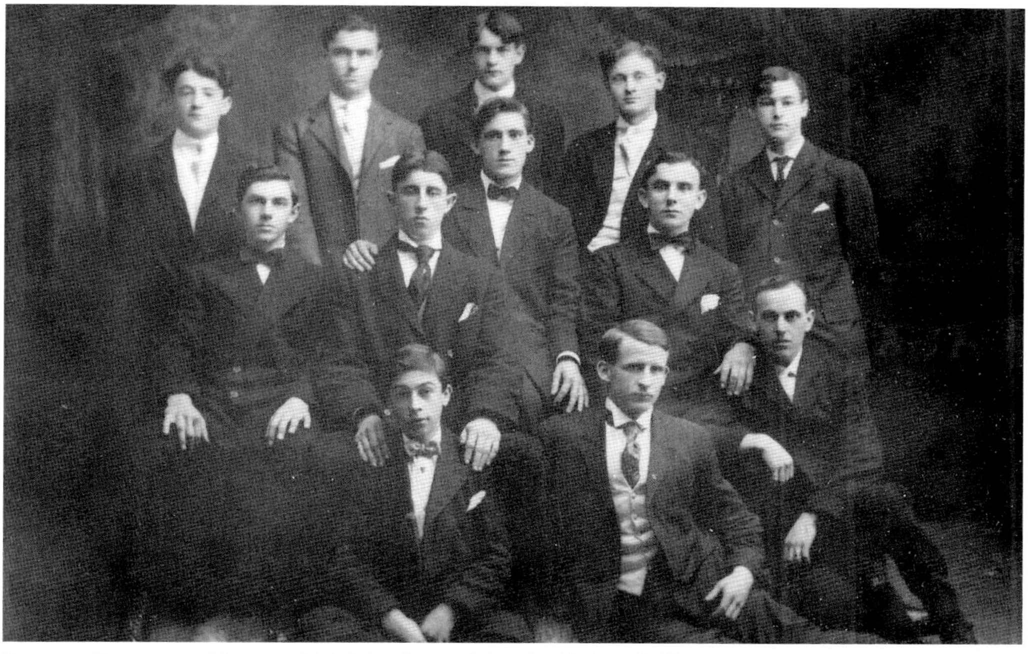

SCULLY BASEBALL CLUB, 1919. Members of the Scully baseball team were part of a private club. This is a unique photograph, as it is the only one known from the period where the members are not posing in their uniforms.

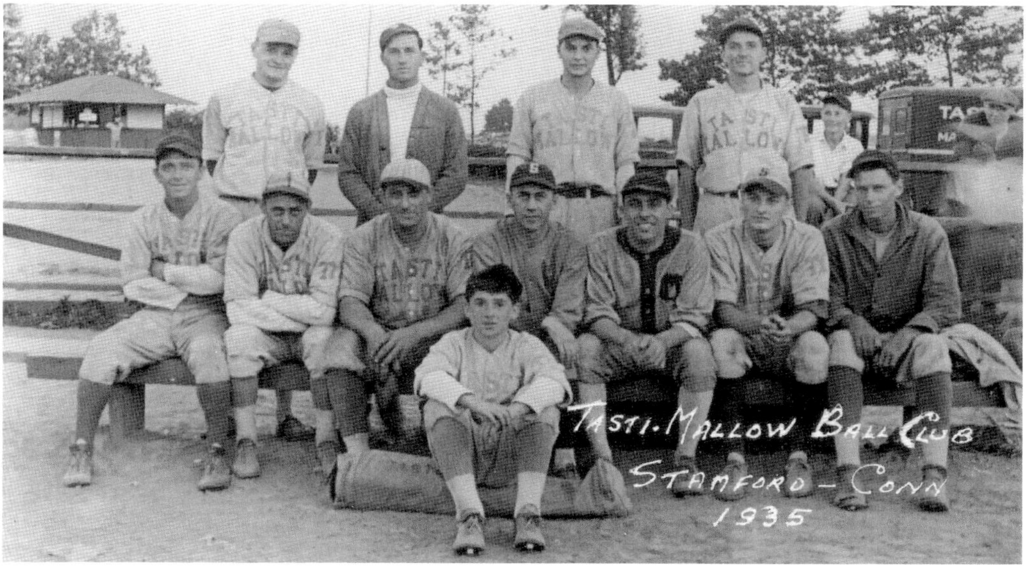

TASTI-MALLOW BALL CLUB, 1935. This was one of the original five teams in the Twilight League, founded in 1932. The other four teams were the University Club, Stamford Gas and Electric Athletic Club, the West Side Athletic Club, and the Stamford All-Stars. A May 27, 1931, article in the *Norwalk Hour* mentions that five of the members were the Magliola boys, the sons of Emil Magliola, the owner of the Tasti-Mallow Company.

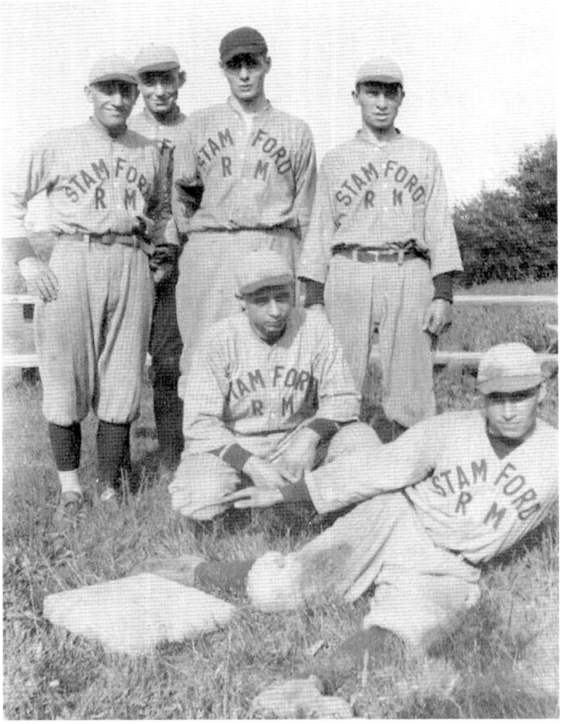

STAMFORD ROLLING MILLS TEAM, 1919. The Stamford Rolling Mills were one of the largest concerns in Stamford, with two mills employing 1,500 workers in 1917. Like many industries in Stamford, they often hired their baseball talent—with good results. They dominated Stamford baseball in the 1910s after hiring standout players like, from left to right, (first row) Anthony "Tony" Marruco and Edward "Ed" Hunt; (second row) Felix LiVolsi, Matthew "Matty" Douglas, Edward "Ed" Greany, and Ralph Williams.

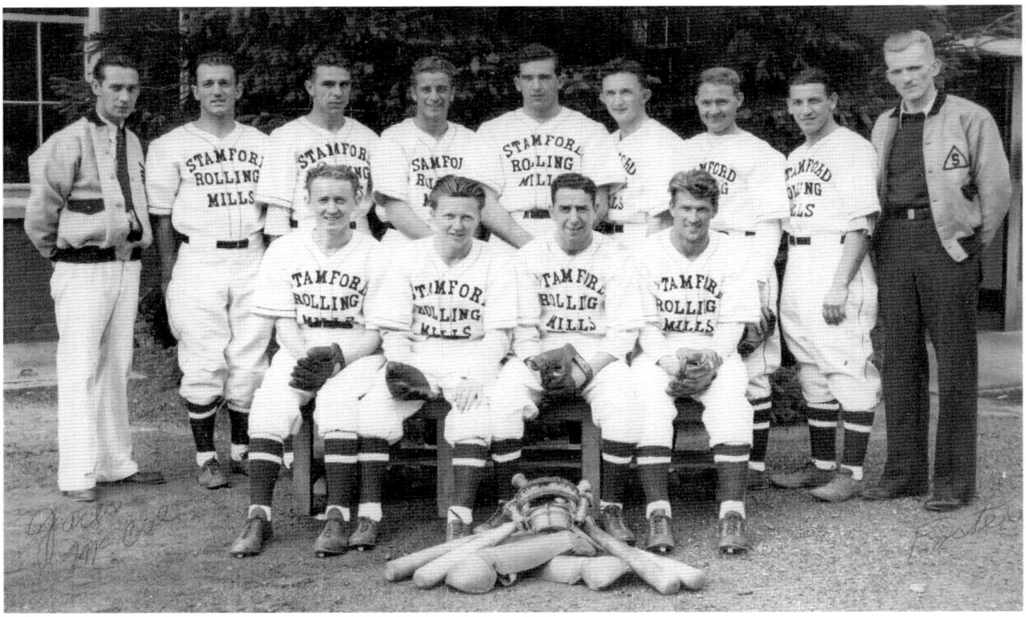

STAMFORD ROLLING MILLS BASEBALL TEAM, 1930S. Though not as dominant as they were in the 1910s, the 1930s Stamford Rolling Mills teams nevertheless continued to field competitive teams in the Industrial League. The gentleman on the left in this photograph is identified as Jack McCue, and the one on the right is identified only as Foster.

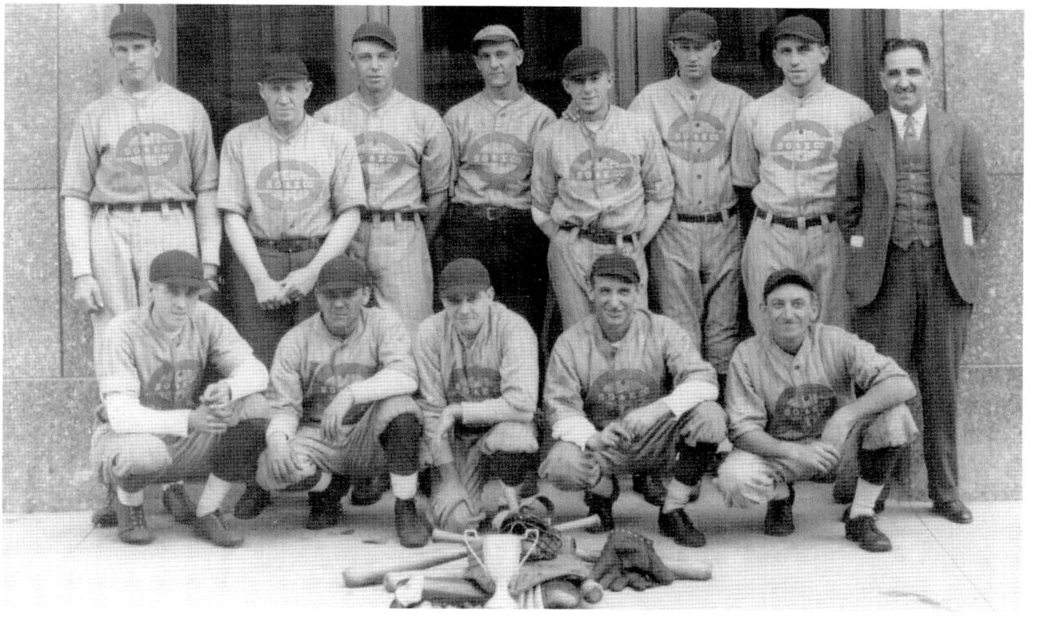

STAMFORD GAS AND ELECTRIC BASEBALL TEAM, C. 1930. The team is seen here when it played in the Industrial League, which it completely dominated in the early 1930s. Between 1930 and 1935, the team won four league titles and three Connecticut state titles. As Yale & Towne and Stamford Rolling Mills had done before them, Stamford Gas and Electric hired the best ballplayers they could find to create their winning teams.

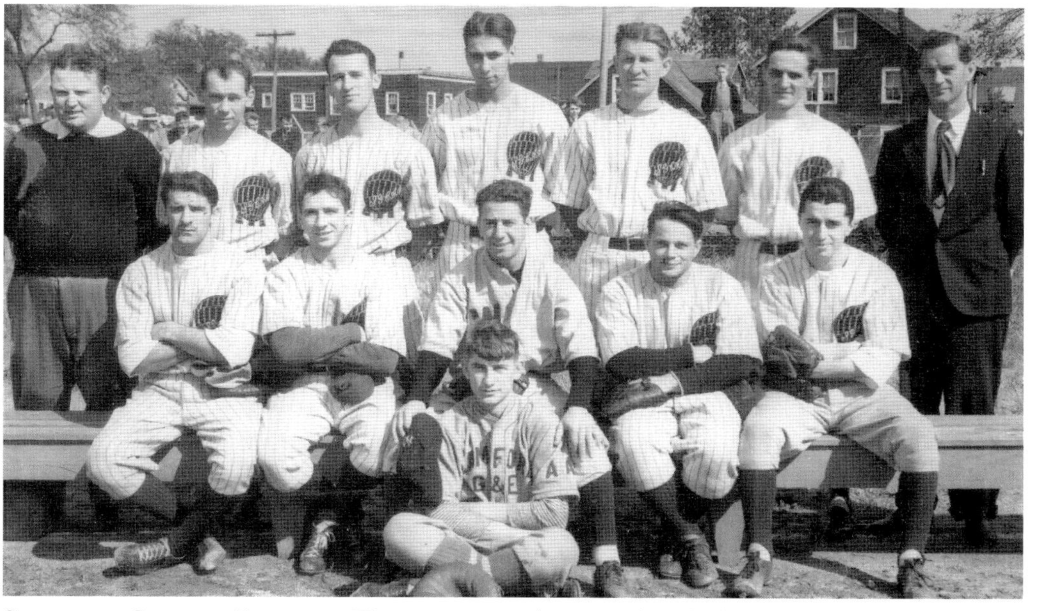

STAMFORD GAS AND ELECTRIC. These team members are identified as, from left to right, (front) Kociniac; (first row) Koproski, Montagnino, Deleo, Romaniello, and Rinaldis; (second row) Accosta, Kuczo, Yeager, Spiers, Kotos, Martin, and Bottomley.

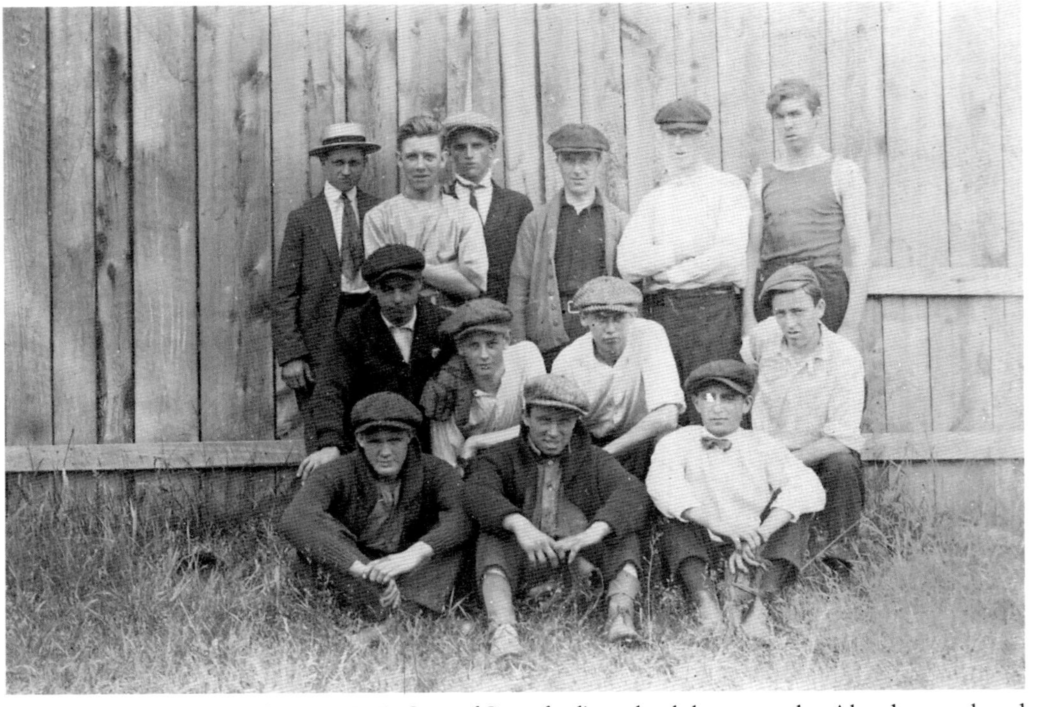

ABERDEENS BASEBALL CLUB, 1915. One of Stamford's early club teams, the Aberdeens, played at the West End diamond, where this photograph was taken. The men in the first row are unidentified, and the rest are identified as, from left to right, (second row) Engel, Trippie Williams, and Dinacola; (third row) "Dad," unidentified, Ray Joyce, and Mitchell.

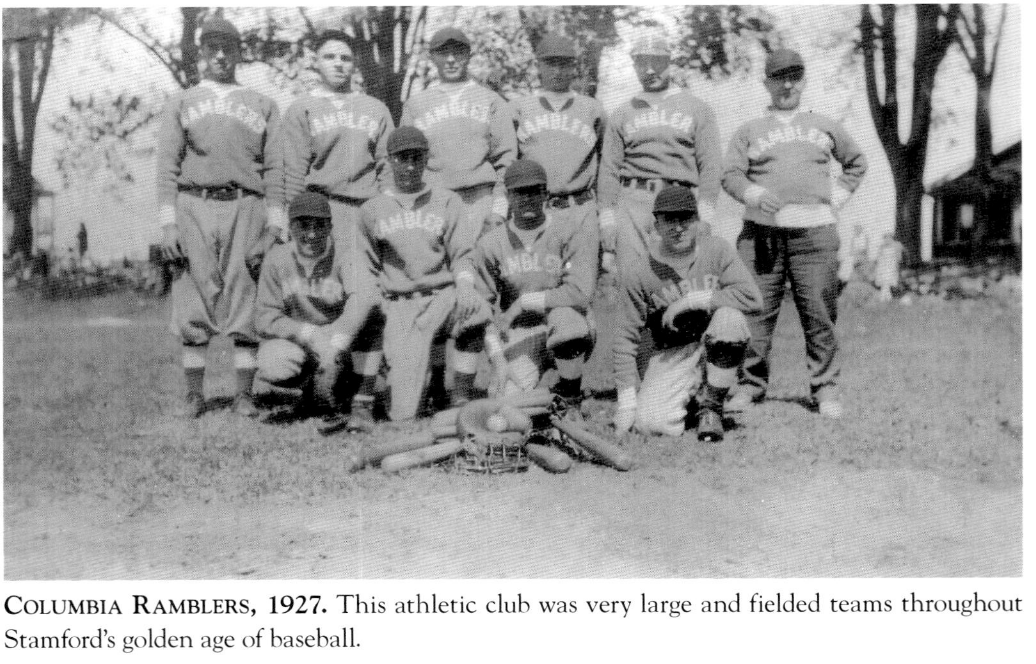

COLUMBIA RAMBLERS, 1927. This athletic club was very large and fielded teams throughout Stamford's golden age of baseball.

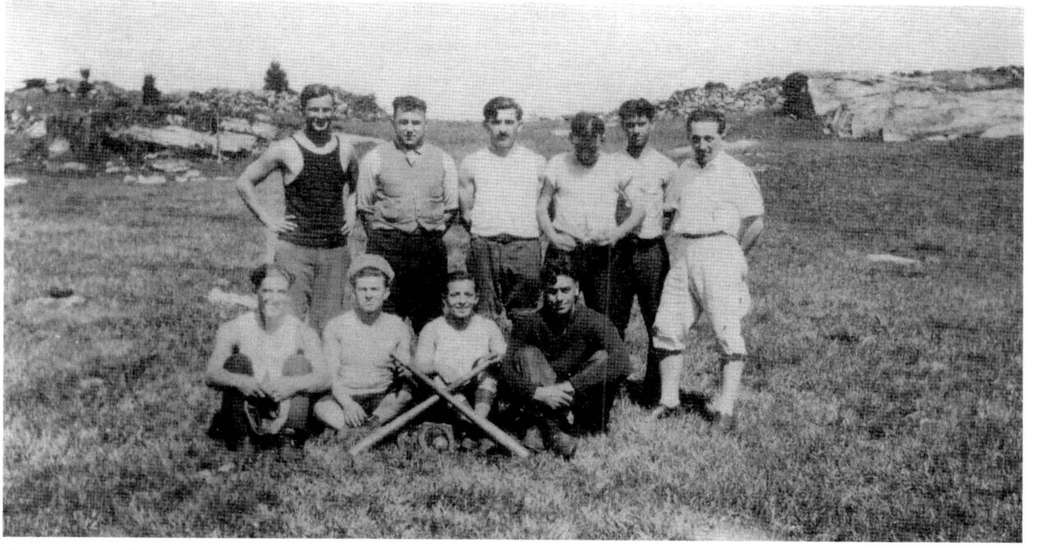

Columbia Ramblers, 1925. A group of Ramblers pose during an outing at Miller's Farm in Bedford, New York. Like many of the larger clubs, the Ramblers sponsored an outing for its members every year. The most common outing in Stamford was a clambake, something the Old Timer's Athletic Association did each year starting around 1945.

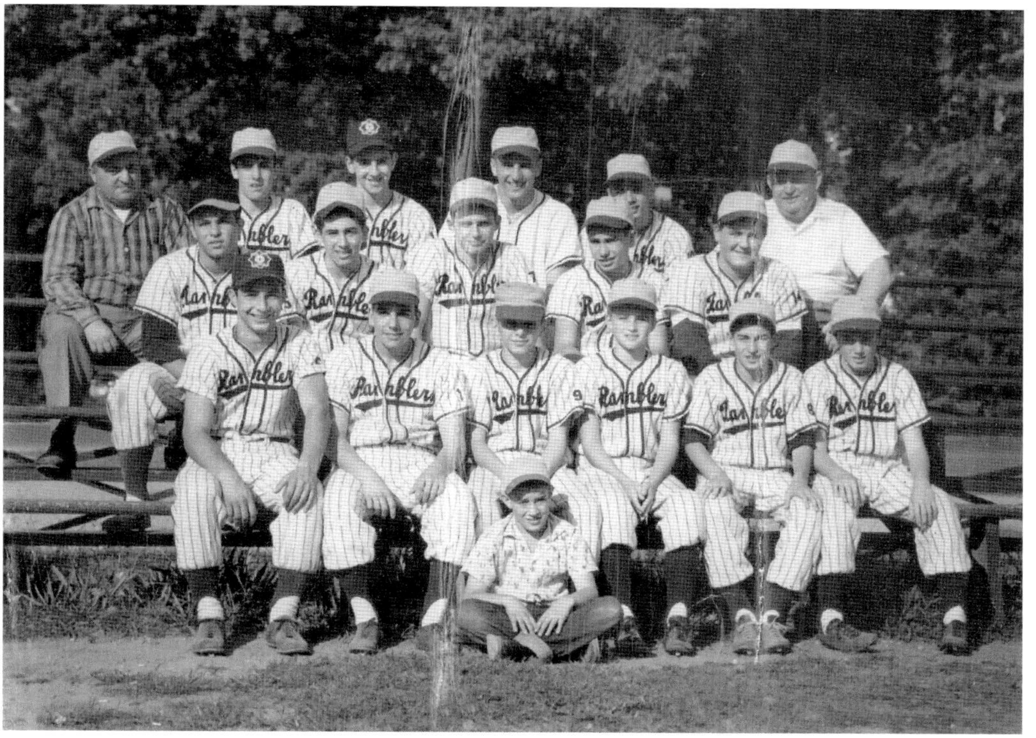

Ramblers Little League Team. Although the large club leagues slowly phased out during World War II, the Ramblers name carried on as a Little League team.

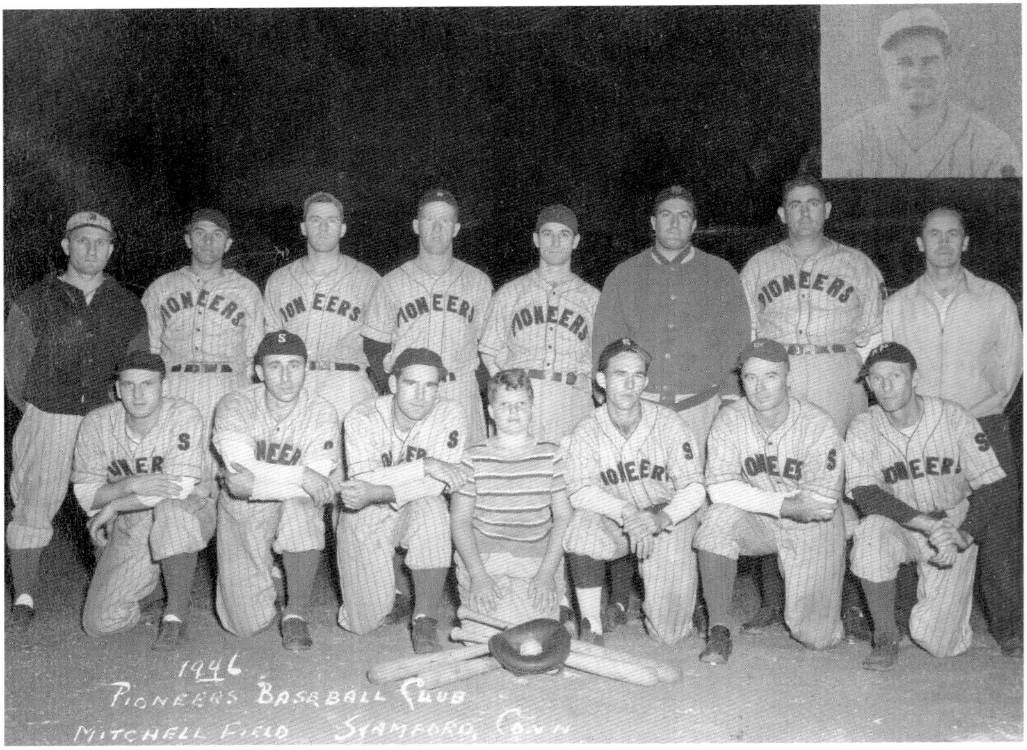

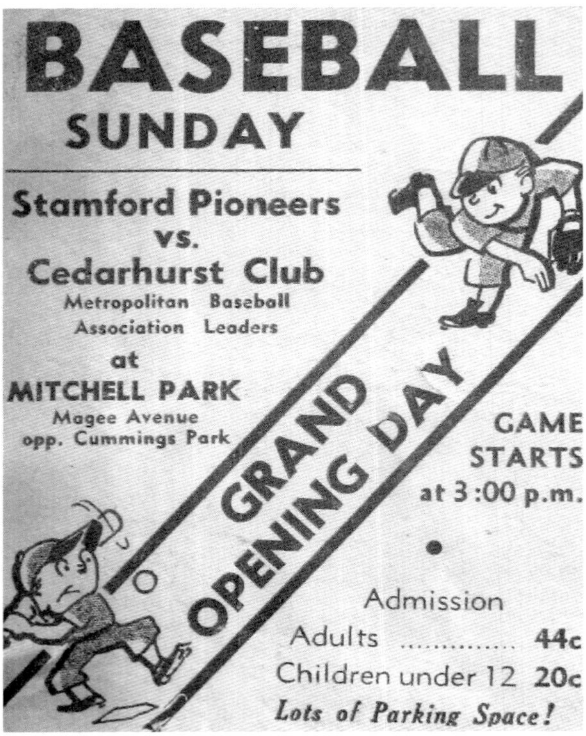

PIONEERS BASEBALL CLUB, 1946. The Pioneers were organized as a semiprofessional club in 1941 and played at Mitchell Field. They were such a strong team that in 1941 they defeated the National League's St. Louis Cardinals. Seen above are, from left to right, (first row) John Potts, Nick Lemone, "Scotty" Koproski, Bobby Scalzi (mascot), Jackie Tyler, Roy Tarr, and Tim Adams; (second row) John Scalzi (manager), Vito DeVito, Jim Sheehan, Ed Sheehan, Wally Signer, Vinnie Ventura, John Synnott, and John Connolly (business manager). The inset in the top right is a newspaper cutout of Bill Salamone that was glued to the photograph. At left is an advertisement in the *Stamford Advocate* for the club's opening day, in 1941 at Mitchell Field.

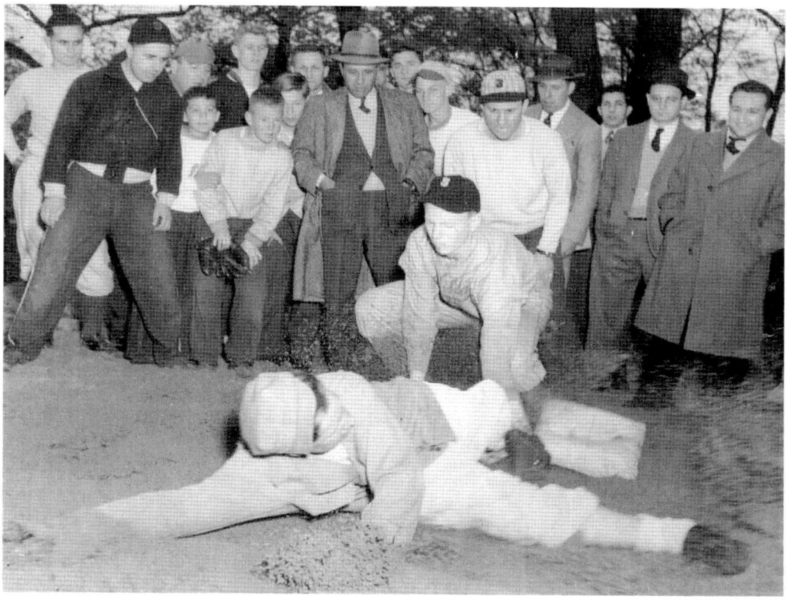

West Side Club Baseball School, 1940s. This is a great photograph of an unidentified serviceman sliding into "home." The staged photograph was taken at a baseball school sponsored by the West Side Baseball Athletic Club. The catcher is Dave Wise.

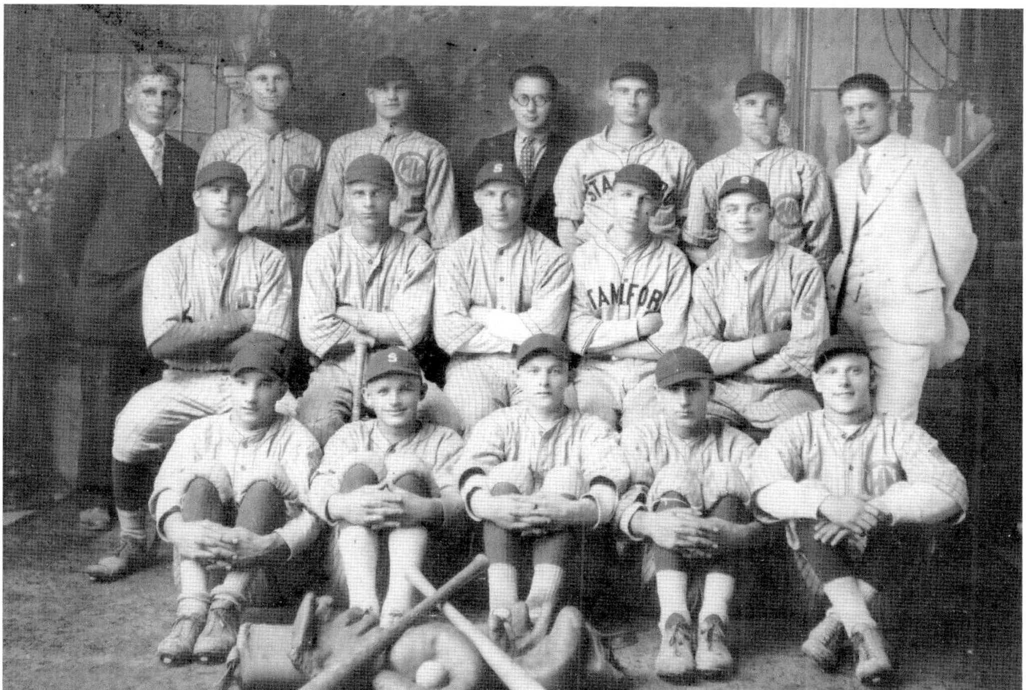

Holy Name Athletic Club, 1920s. Holy Name was an athletic club founded in 1925 and supported by Stamford's large Polish community. It remains today as a private social club for Polish Americans. The men in this photograph are identified as, from left to right, (first row) Niczabitowski, Byczyaka, Czescik, Koproski, and Duda; (second row) Koproski, Wilks, Bujolous, Milne, and Dombroski; (third row) Mrus, Parker, Klica, Lenczycki, Bella, Waskiewicz, and Steamer.

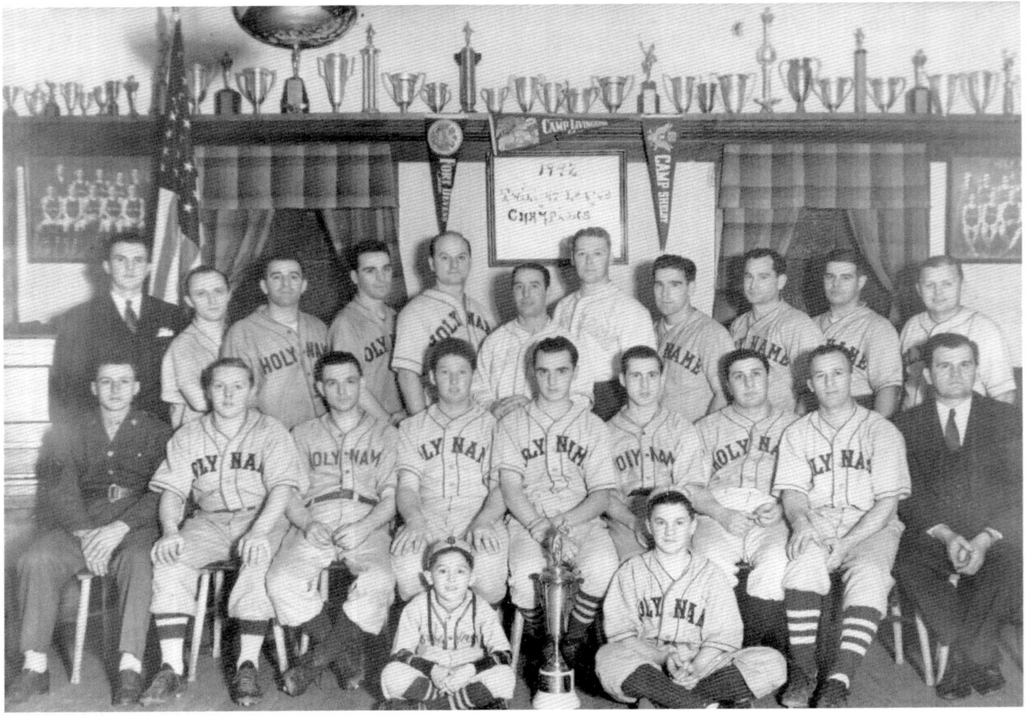

HOLY NAME BASEBALL, 1942 TWILIGHT LEAGUE CHAMPIONS. The 1942 league champs pose in front of a formidable row of the club's previous trophies. The Twilight League, founded by ballplayer and the head of Stamford recreation Edward Hunt in 1932, was active for 75 years.

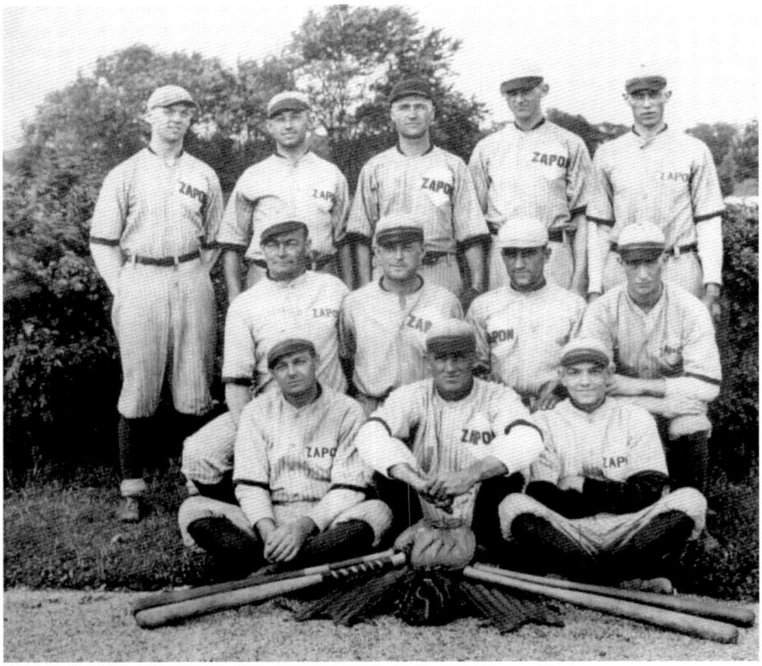

ZAPONS. The Zapon Leather and Cloth Company fielded the Zapons in the Industrial League in the 1920s. The team was nicknamed the Zaps and was one of the more powerful ball clubs in Stamford at the time. In 1921, they threatened the mighty Yale & Towne dynasty in a close game for the city championship, going down 4-2 at Halloween Park.

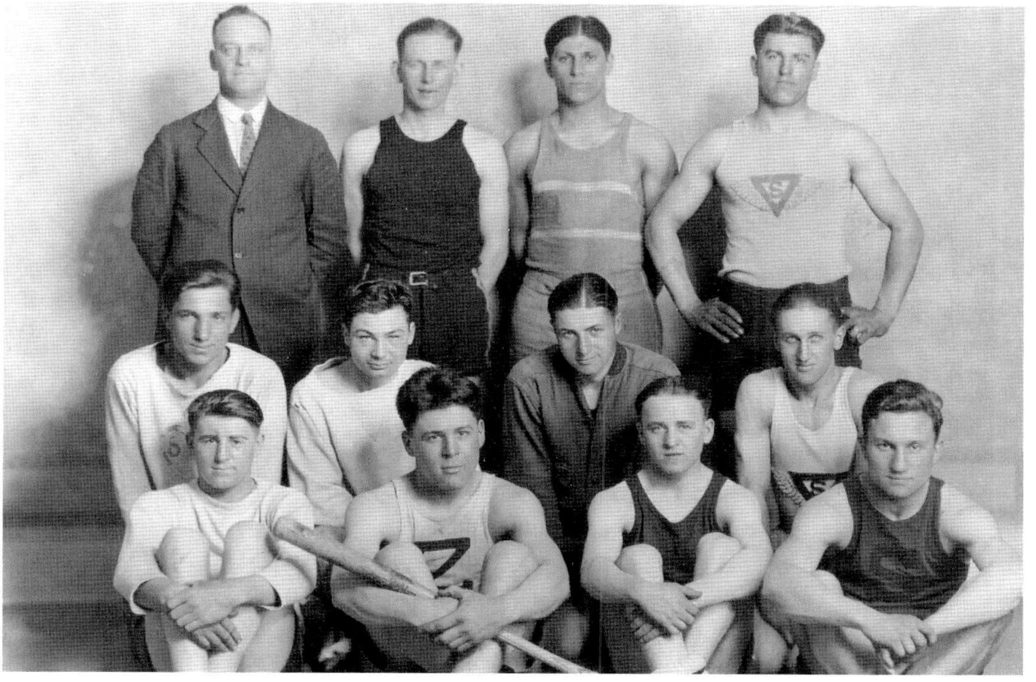

YMCA BASEBALL TEAM, C. 1925. Al Koproski Sr. (third row, far right) played on and organized several baseball teams in the 1920s. He is seen here as a young man playing for the YMCA, which was active in Stamford from the late 1800s.

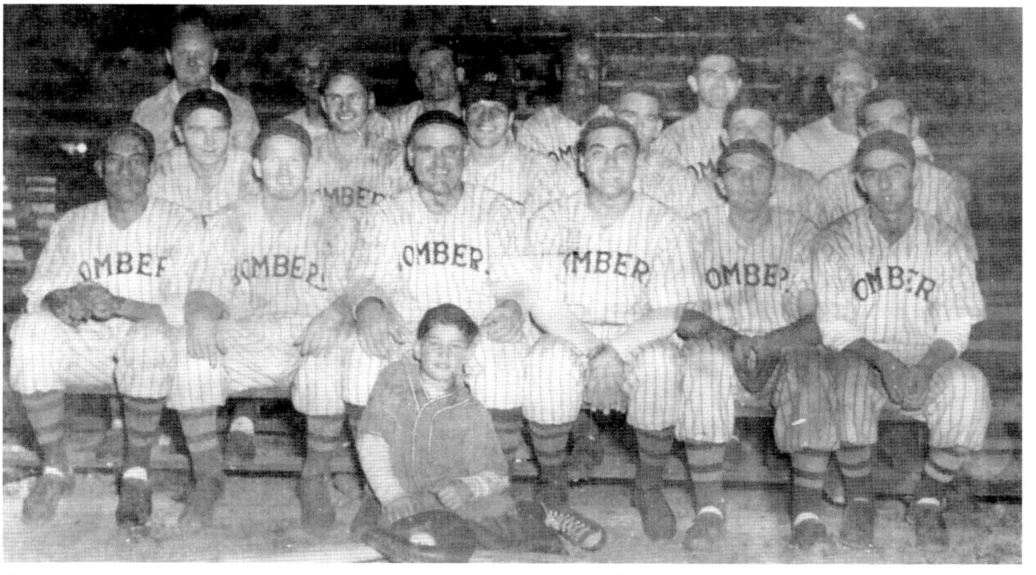

STAMFORD BOMBERS. The Bombers, Stamford's first professional team, were one of the minor league teams formed in the 1940s to play in the short-lived Colonial League. In 1947, the team included six black players, a fact particularly significant because there were only 17 black players among the thousands of players in the minor leagues. (Courtesy of Joseph Deleo Jr.)

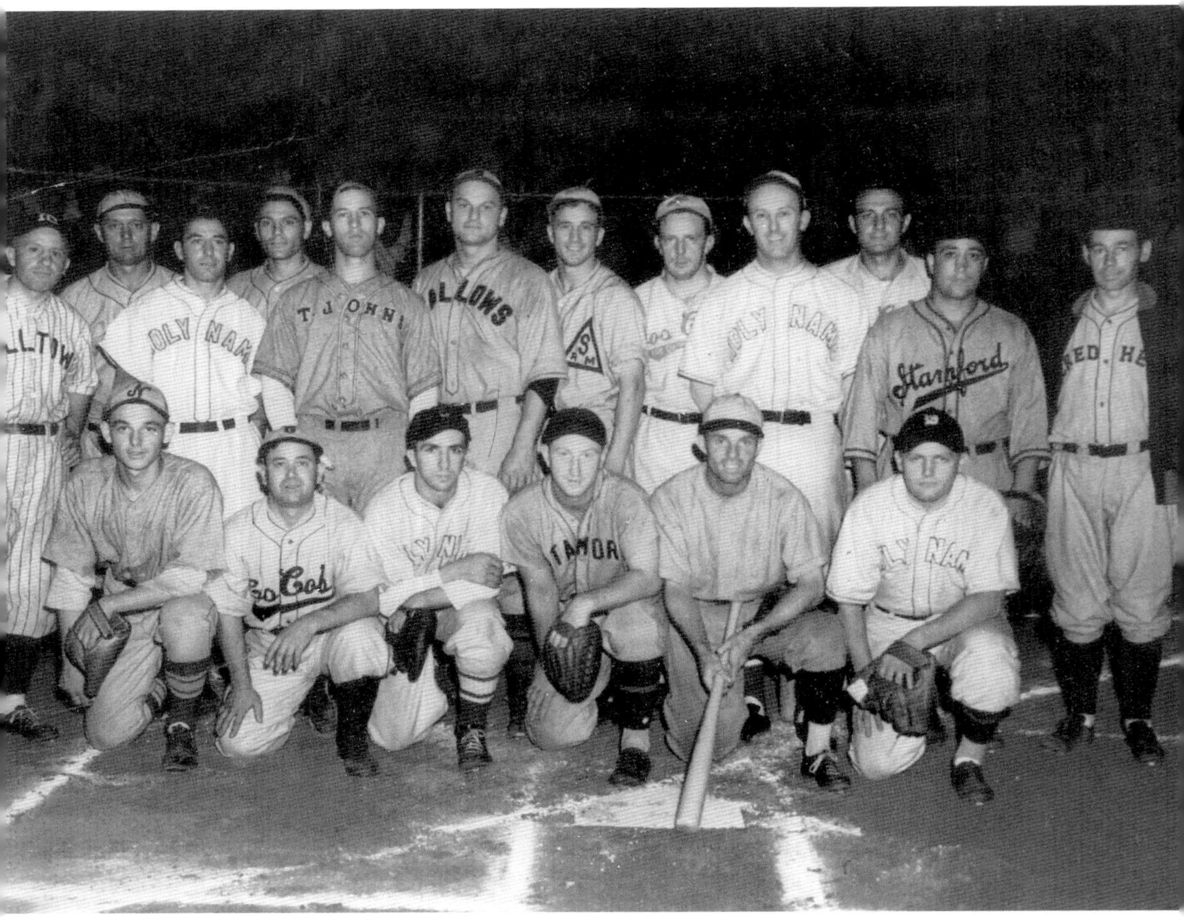

STAMFORD ALL-STAR TEAM. The Twilight League All-Star team poses at Belltown field, where they faced off against the St. Louis Cardinals. The team included members from Holy Name, Belltown, Sacred Heart, Cos Cob, Stamford, Stamford Rolling Mills, and the Mallows. These men are identified, from left to right, as (first row) Dudas, Bolgna, Montagnino, Carmen, Holshan, and Byczajka; (second row) Felix LiVolsi (manager), Stanley, Deleo, Yeager, Magliola, Dimizianno, Burnes, O'Grady, DeLuca, Lione, and Kuczo.

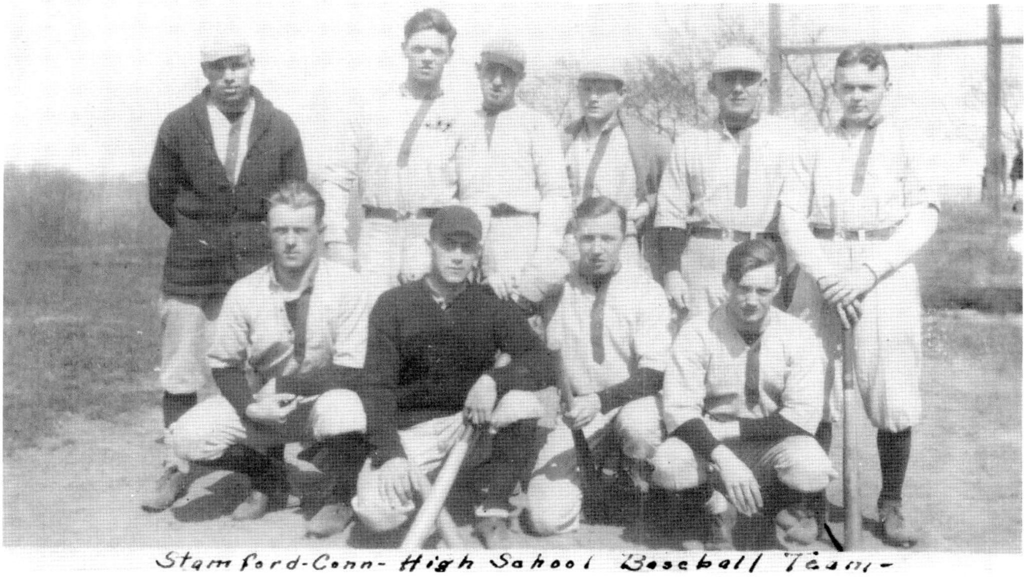

STAMFORD HIGH BASEBALL TEAM, 1919. In the 1920s, Stamford High School's baseball team began to win notoriety with star players like pitcher Paul Kuczo and infielder John Scalzi. The 1923 and 1924 seasons were high points for the team, which posted 19 wins and 5 losses over those two seasons. Kuczo went on to pitch on winning Villanova teams before returning to Stamford High to become an assistant coach to Mike Boyle. Scalzi played at Georgetown and was hired upon his graduation by the professional Boston Braves.

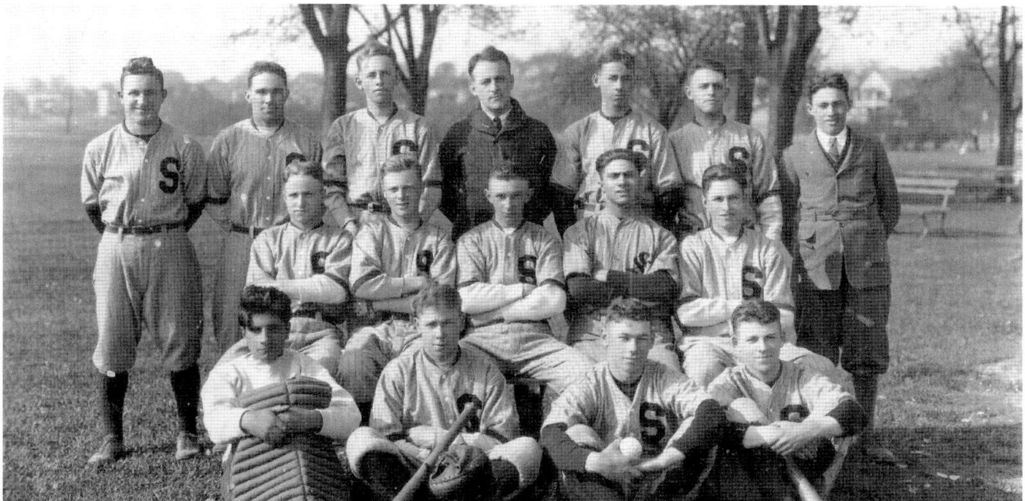

STAMFORD HIGH BASEBALL TEAM, 1922. This squad had an outstanding season this year, posting a record of nine wins and two losses. The team included, from left to right, (first row) ? Fusaro, Moon Mullins, Paul Kuczo, and Jack Harrison; (second row) Bill Telesco, Charles Connelly, Frank Brincil, Johnny Franchina, and ? Cummings; (third row) Johnny Scalzi, ? Kelly, "Corny" O'Connell, coach Mike Boyle, Bill Connelly, Allen Ungemack, and Hack Wolfson.

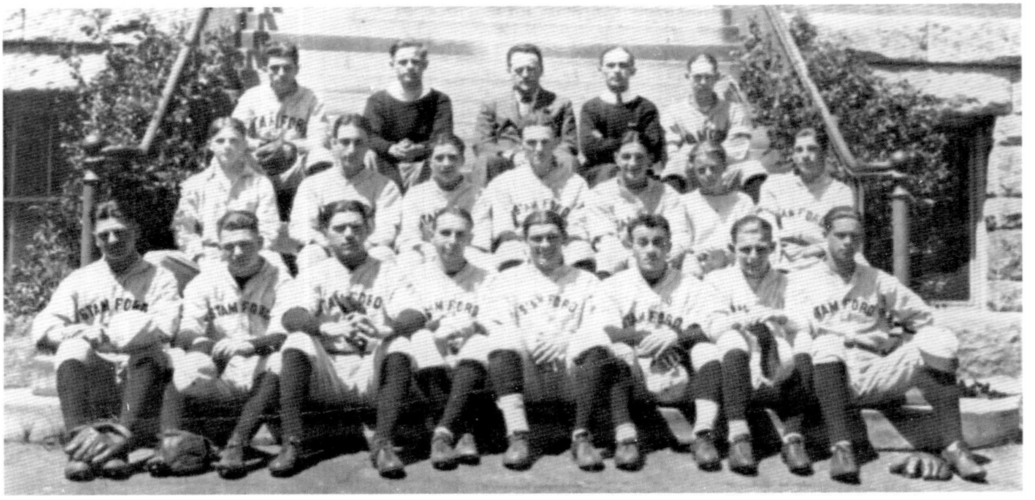

Stamford High Baseball Team, 1926–1927. The 1926 team went undefeated, with 7 wins and 0 losses. The team included, from left to right, (first row) Gus Wennerberg, Paul Bratton, Gus Karukas, Toby Malin, Eddie Bella, Mike Bellos, ? Lynch, and Paul Jarrett; (second row) Dick Holahan, Mickey Lione, Louis Montagnino, Ed Wynn, Chris Pachiog, Tommy Clear, and Dave Mackler; (third row) Bill Dolan, Douglas Hemming, coach Mike Boyle, Harold McDonald, and Pierce Mullen.

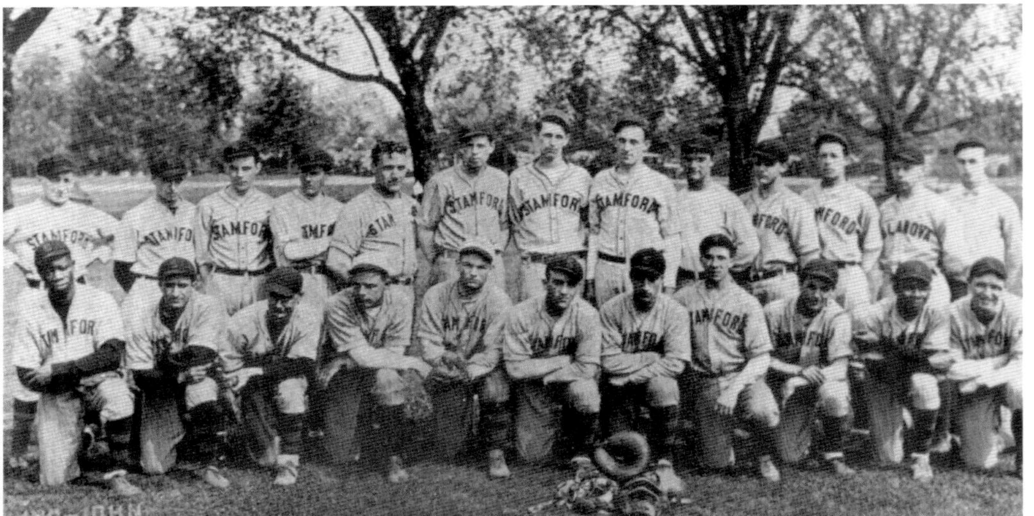

Stamford High Baseball Team, 1929. This was the first year that African Americans played on the team. One reason coach Mike Boyle's team was so formidable was that he recruited solely based on talent. From left to right are (first row) McKeithen, Thomas Telesco, Fred Blundell, Franci Lynch, Wilmer Bratton, Michail Bellos, Michael Lione, Louis Montanino, Jams Romanos, Rod Henderson, and John Best; (second row) Mike Laureno, Harry Rinaldi, Charles Farrell, Edward Ryan, Franci Moyes, Rube Quintard, Leo Pantas, Edward Wynne, ? Ladas, John Lohn, Roger Hart, Paul Kuczo, and Walter Kennedy.

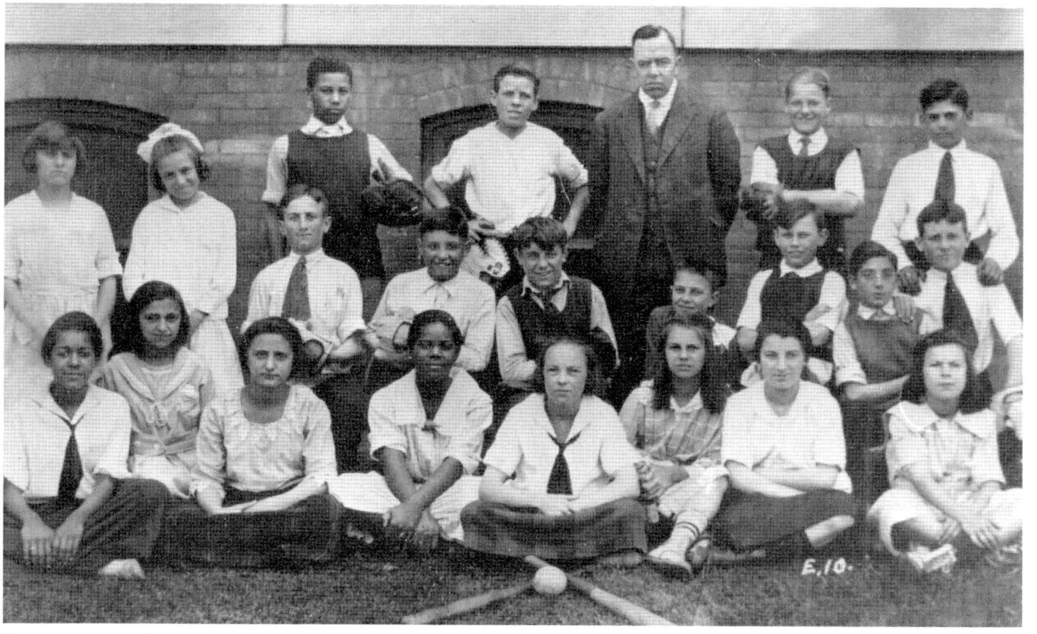

Elm Street School Baseball Team. Prior to the introduction of Little League play in 1950, Stamford's elementary schools, churches, and athletic organizations sponsored youth teams, who competed from the 1920s through the 1940s. Public schools were unique in this environment, as youngsters of both genders learned to play on ethnically and racially mixed teams. In contrast, the teams sponsored by churches and athletic clubs tended to be much more homogenous and were typically built around a single ethnic community. (Courtesy of Andrew Dzamba.)

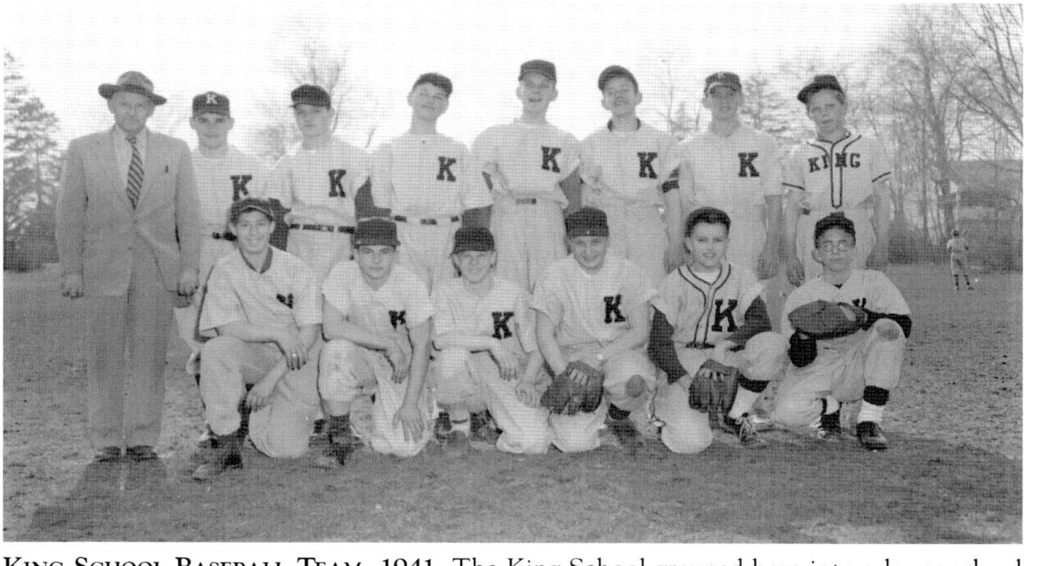

King School Baseball Team, 1941. The King School grouped boys into a lower school (grades 5 and 6), upper school (grades 7 and 8), and a high school (grades 9–12). Each school had its own athletic teams; this photograph shows the 1941 upper school team.

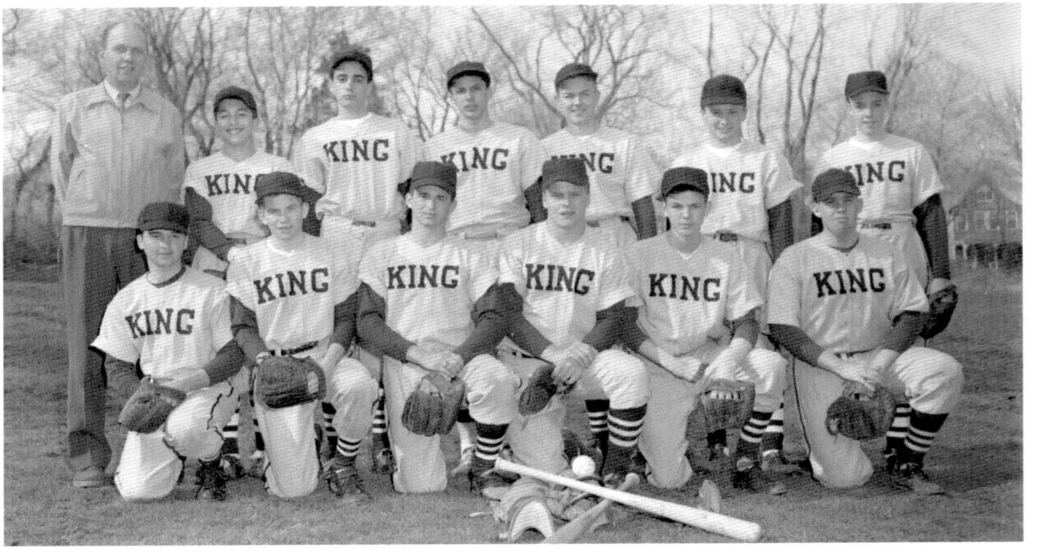

KING SCHOOL BASEBALL TEAM, 1956. The King School varsity high school team had an excellent season in 1956, with six wins and two losses. Their key player was pitcher Fred Willis, who pitched three one-hitters and one no-hitter. The team included, from left to right, (first row) Richard Lace, Stanley Rothenberg, Fred Willis, Ron Sebra, Jack Chesney, and Abbot Scwebe; (second row) Coach Olson, Stephen Hane, Jim Kweskin, Andy Robsky, Gordon Dancy, Francis Dolgrove, and Carl DuBois.

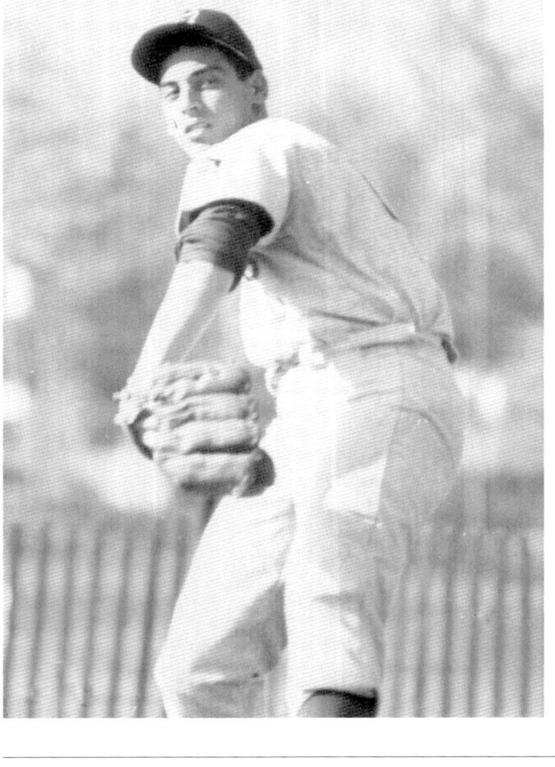

RIPPOWAM PITCHER FRANK COSENTINO, 1967. Rippowam opened as a second high school in 1961 and operated as such until 1983. The 1967 team, known as the "Rip Nine," posted an 18-6 record and included future Major Leaguer Bobby Valentine.

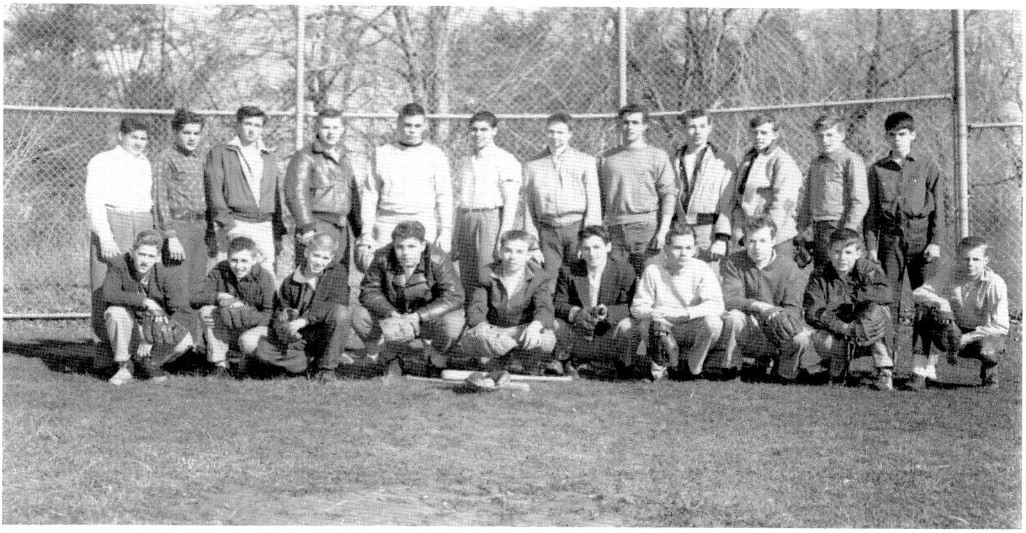

UNIDENTIFIED STAMFORD BASEBALL TEAM, C. 1950. This image of a team posing out of uniform provides the opportunity to see the boys in a wide variety of period fashion, from oxford shirts and pleated trousers to six-inch jean cuffs and leather jackets.

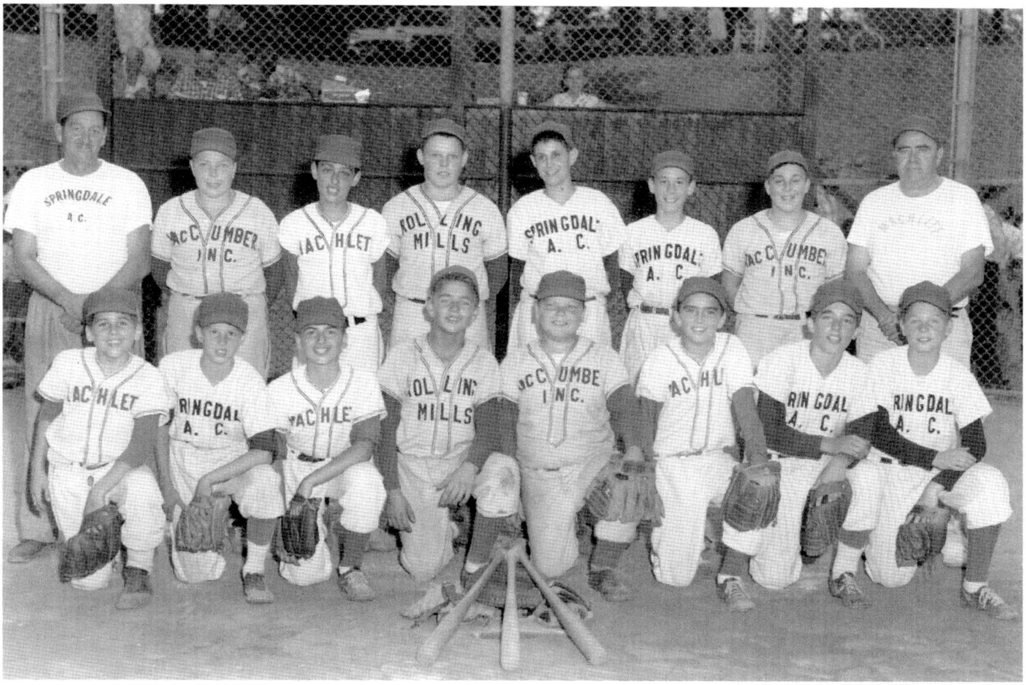

SPRINGDALE LITTLE LEAGUE, 1958. After World War II, Stamford began to evolve from an industrial center to a hub for corporate headquarters. This helped in large part to bring about a shift from adult baseball to youth baseball. Industrial leagues waned, but little leagues blossomed. This photograph of the Springdale Little League team shows that the same organizations and businesses that had sponsored adult teams were now sponsoring youth teams.

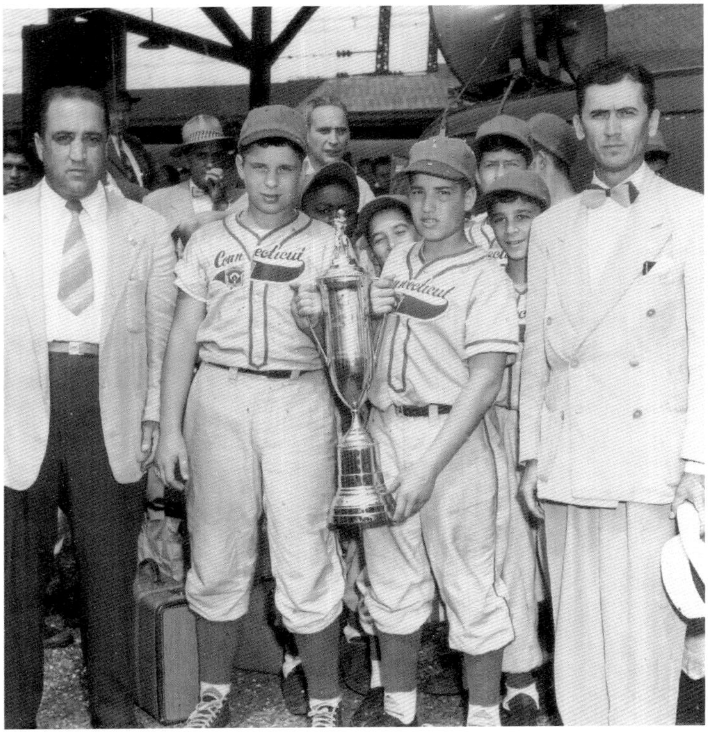

BABE RUTH 1953 CHAMPIONS WITH TROPHY. Micky Lione (left), who founded the Little League, poses with his national championship Little League team and their trophy. (Courtesy of Gerry Lione.)

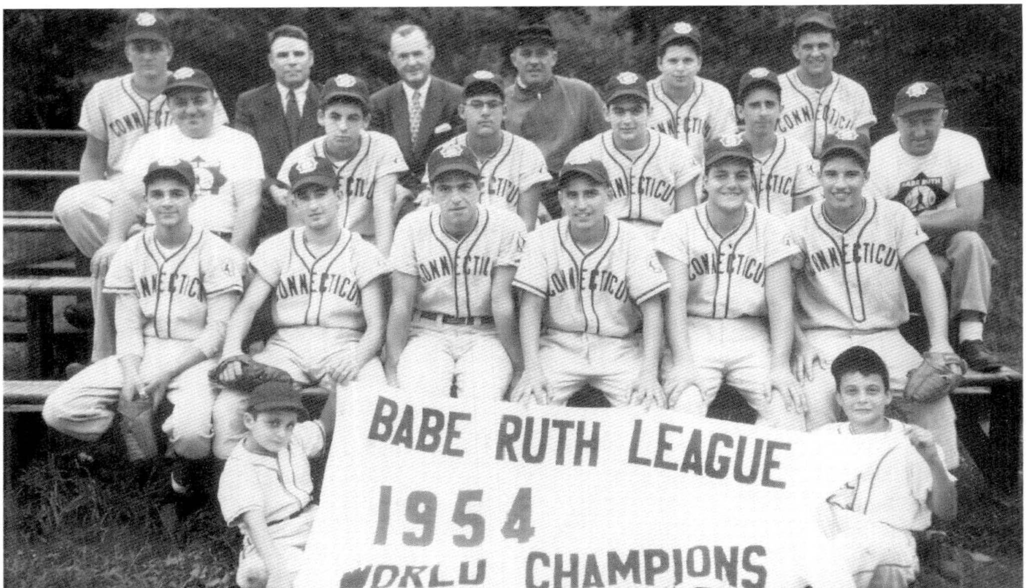

BABE RUTH LEAGUE WORLD CHAMPIONS, 1954. In 1952, the Stamford Recreation League created a Little Big League to provide older youth the opportunity to continue playing Little League ball. The first three years saw Stamford winning the Little Big League National Championship, in 1952 and 1953, and the Babe Ruth League World Championship in 1954.

DELEO BROTHERS, 1950. Joseph "Junie" Deleo (right) poses with his cousins Abbe (left) and Buffy Deleo (center) in front of the Deleo Bros. truck, all sporting uniforms from different Little League teams. The Deleo brothers owned a general contracting business in Glenbrook. This photograph was taken at the Vine Road ball field during the first year of Stamford Little League. (Courtesy of Joseph Deleo Jr.)

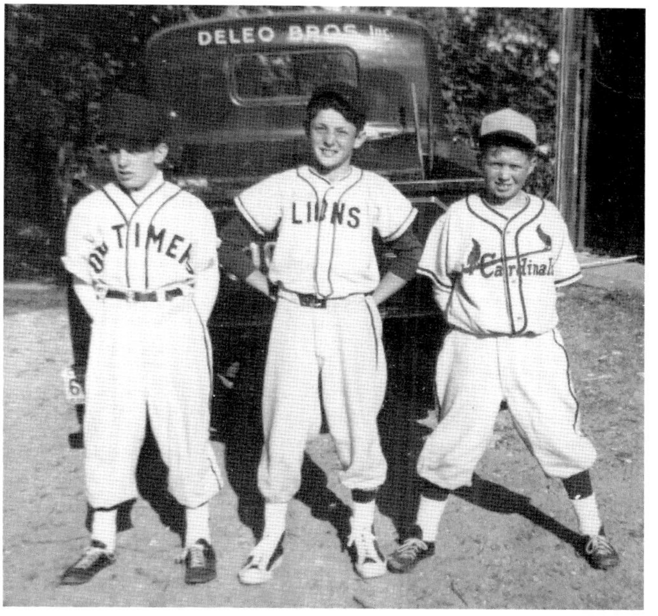

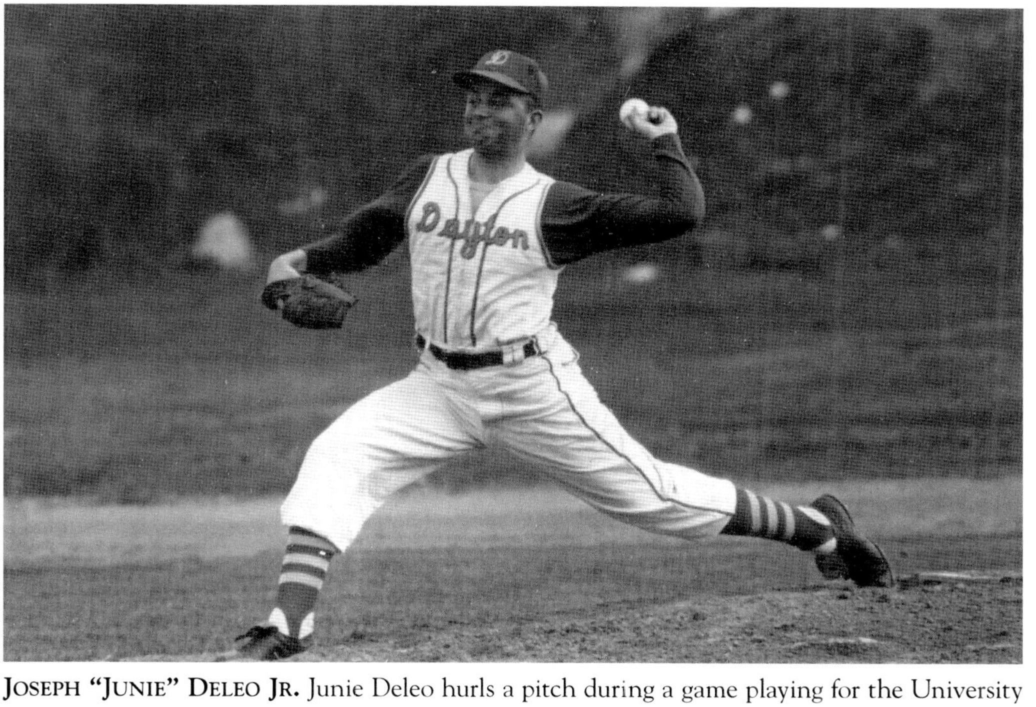

JOSEPH "JUNIE" DELEO JR. Junie Deleo hurls a pitch during a game playing for the University of Dayton in 1963. Junie, short for Junior, played on the 1957 championship American Legion team and spent a year with the New York Mets after college. He began coaching the Clairol Little League team in 1967 and is still coaching the team in 2012, despite the fact that Clairol packed up and left Stamford several years ago. Team parents help pay the registration fee to retain the Clairol name for the team. (Courtesy of Joseph Deleo Jr.)

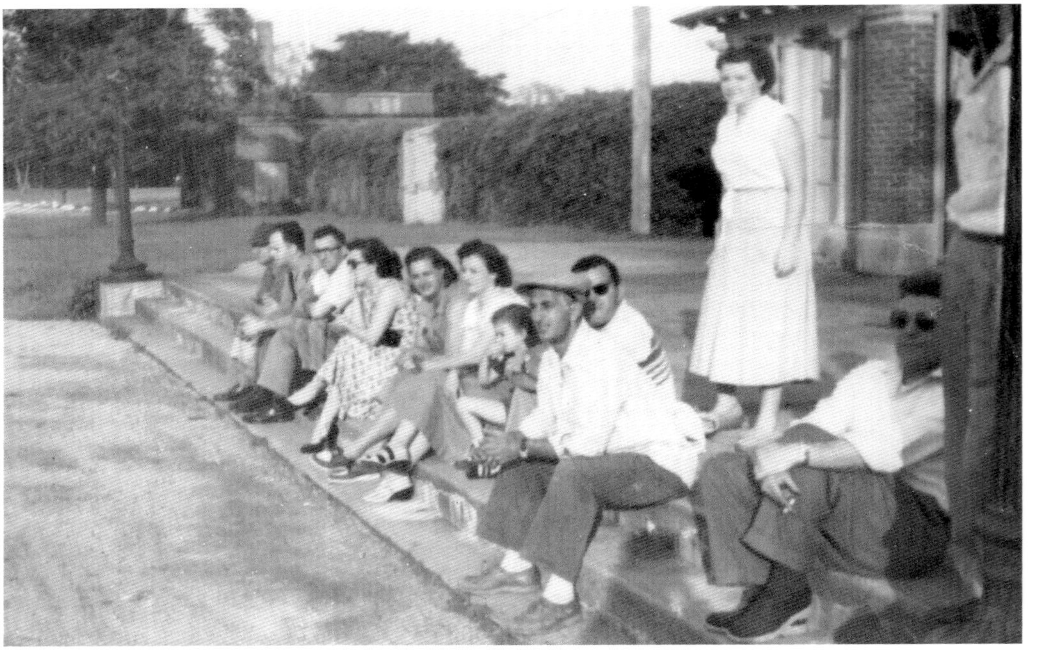

LITTLE LEAGUE SPECTATORS, C. 1955. A group of parents watches a Little League game at the Vine Road field in the Turn of the River neighborhood. (Courtesy of Joseph Deleo Jr.)

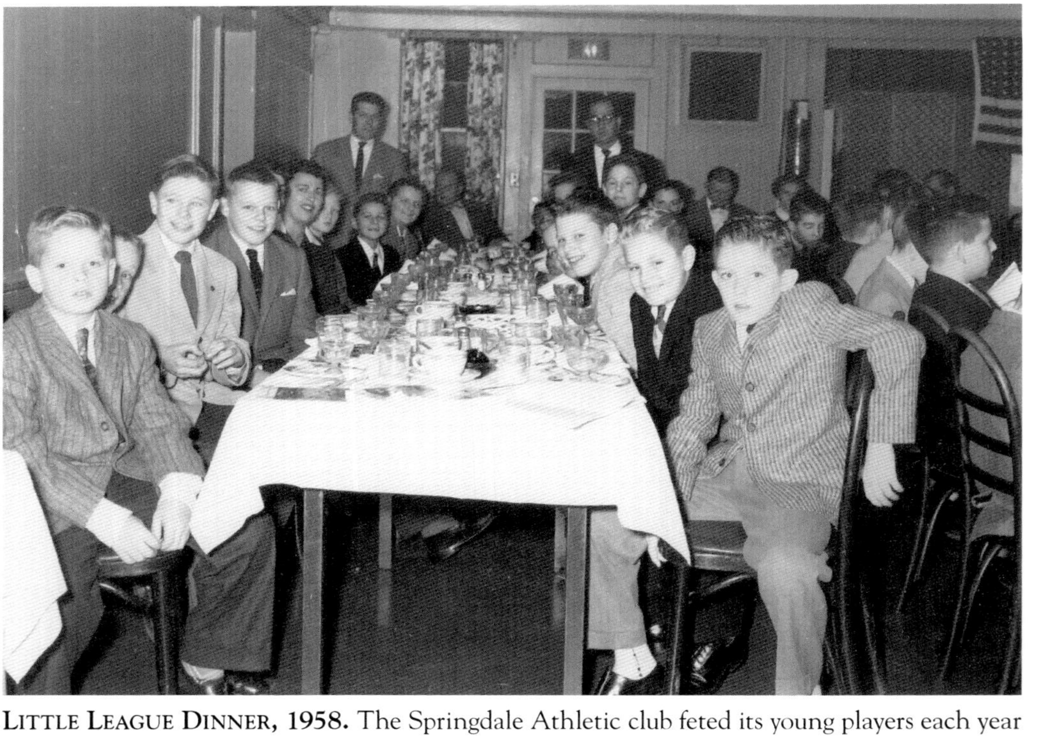

LITTLE LEAGUE DINNER, 1958. The Springdale Athletic club feted its young players each year at its annual awards dinner.

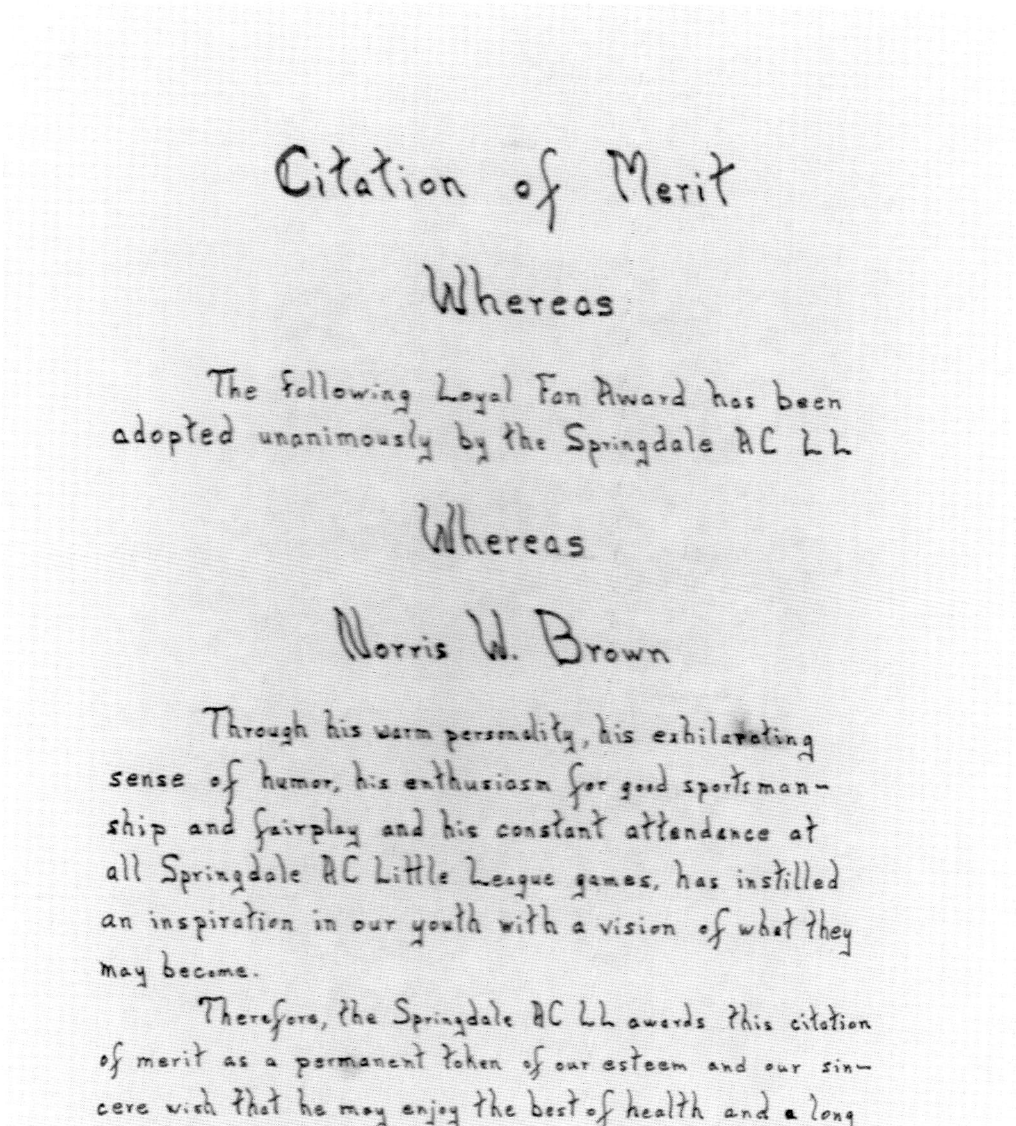

Citation of Merit

Whereas

The following Loyal Fan Award has been adopted unanimously by the Springdale AC LL

Whereas

Norris W. Brown

Through his warm personality, his exhilarating sense of humor, his enthusiasm for good sportsmanship and fairplay and his constant attendance at all Springdale AC Little League games, has instilled an inspiration in our youth with a vision of what they may become.

Therefore, the Springdale AC LL awards this citation of merit as a permanent token of our esteem and our sincere wish that he may enjoy the best of health and a long happy life.

Sam Guarino — President

November 13, 1965

Jerry F. Cacace — Secretary

LITTLE LEAGUE AWARD, 1965. The Springdale Little League shows its appreciation to a loyal fan, Norris W. Brown, with this handwritten Citation of Merit.

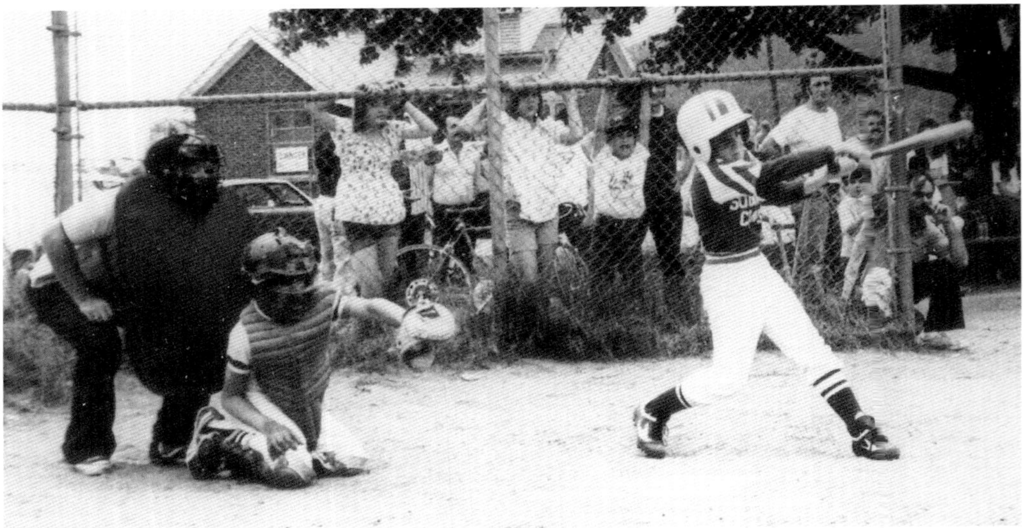

SHIPPAN SPORTS AND SOUNDVIEW CONSTRUCTION. Carl Lobozza was a well-known and prolific Stamford photographer as well as a photograph historian. He has provided an extensive photographic record of Stamford, including its sports life. Lobozza volunteered at the Stamford Historical Society for many years, and his immense contributions have become a sizeable part of the photograph collection. Both these photographs were snapped during Little League games in 1975. Carl's son James is the batter for Soundview Construction in the photograph above.

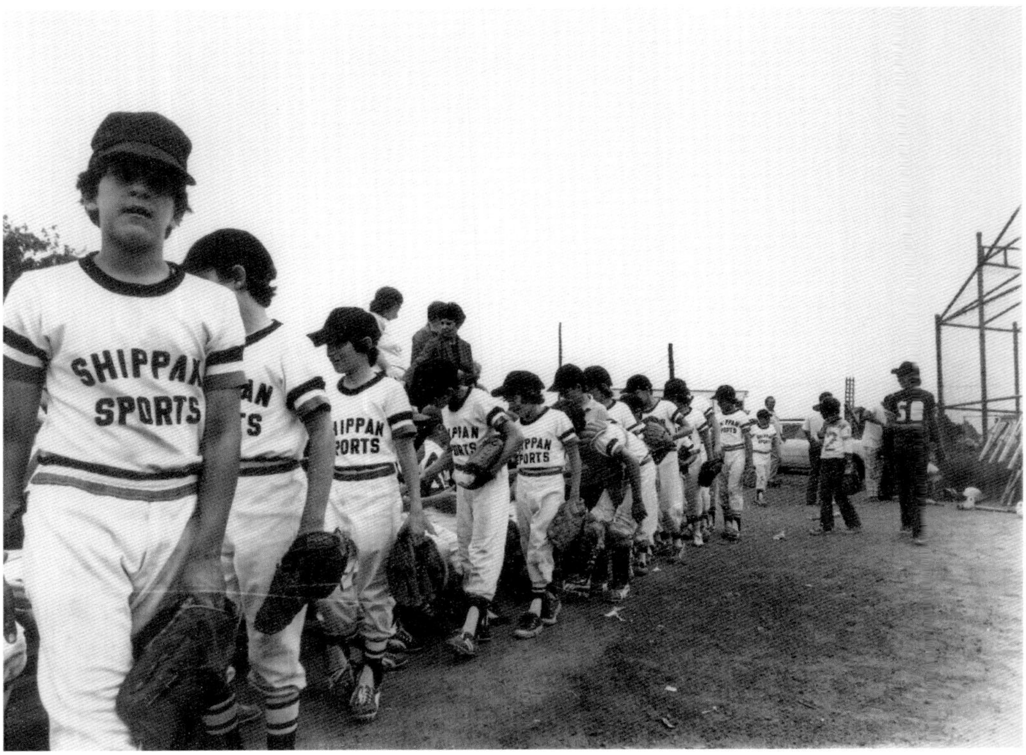

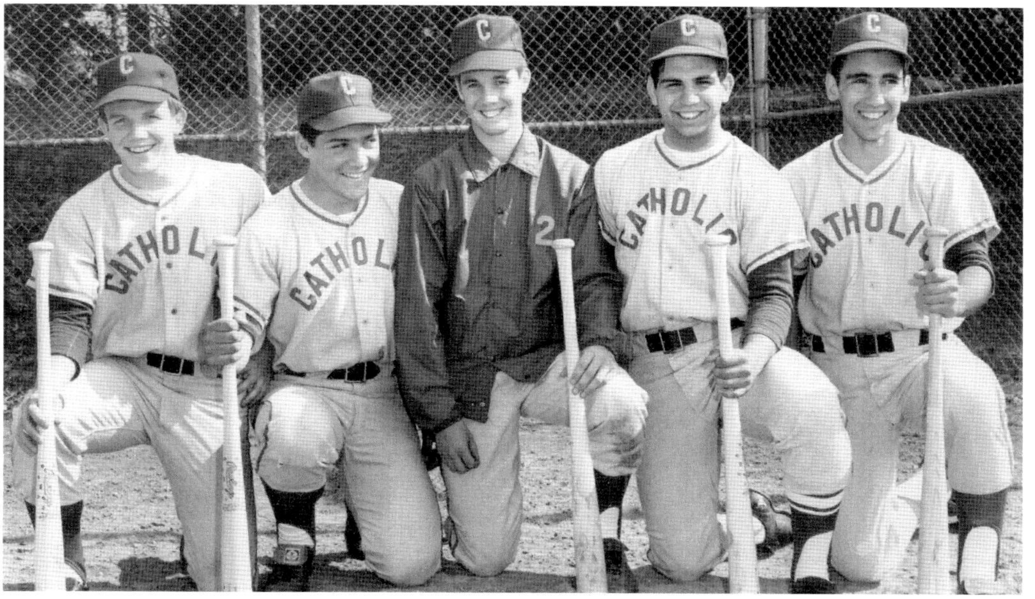

STAMFORD CATHOLIC BASEBALL PLAYERS, 1968. Stamford Catholic High School, which opened in 1959, was a relatively small school drawing its student population from the many Catholic neighborhoods around town. The Polish, Irish, Italians, and Hungarian communities were all able to support their own Catholic parishes. Stamford Catholic provided new opportunities to bring these communities together through education—and sports. Seen here, from left to right, are James Tully, Thomas Vitti, Mark Feeley, Rocco Possidento, and Dominic Carlucci.

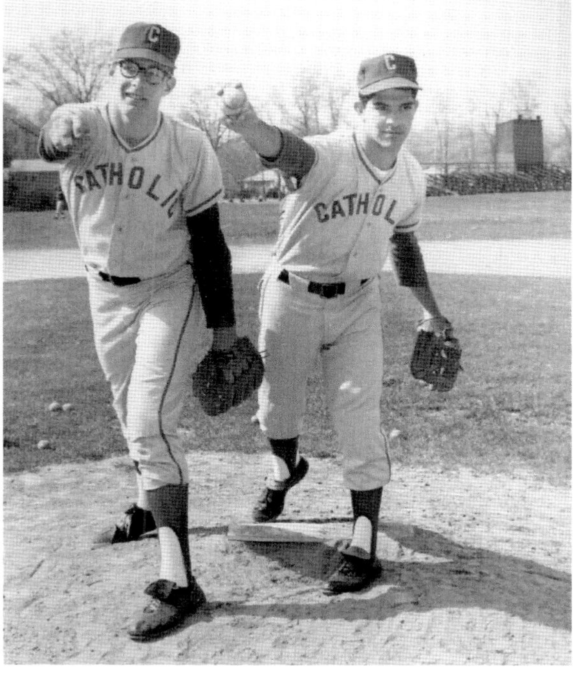

STAMFORD CATHOLIC PITCHERS, 1968. Larry Jost (left) and Bennett "Ben" Salvatore throw out pitches for the photographer. Salvatore played baseball and football for Stamford Catholic, winning all-state honors, and went on to become a longtime referee in the National Basketball Association (NBA).

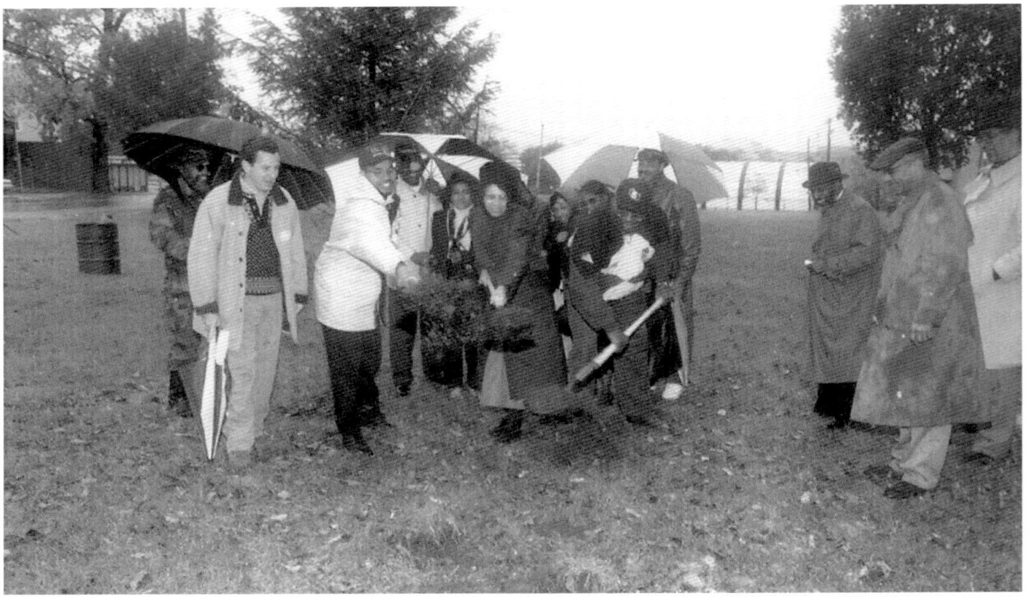

JACKIE ROBINSON PARK DEDICATION, 1996. Jackie Robinson lived in Stamford for more than 20 years. In 1996, the city honored him with the Jackie Robinson Park of Fame. His daughter, Sharon Robinson (center, with shovel), is seen here at the ground-breaking and dedication ceremony.

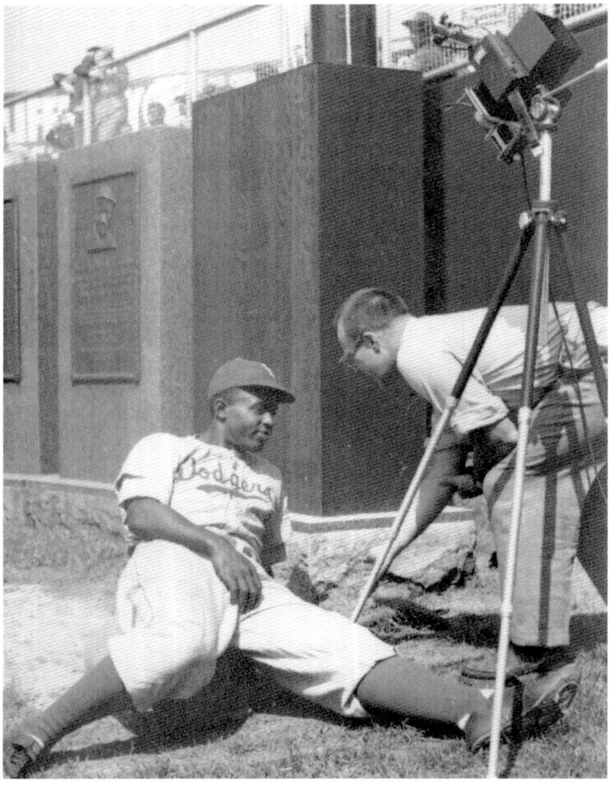

OZZIE SWEET POSES JACKIE ROBINSON "SLIDE." Stamford-born photographer Oscar "Ozzie" Sweet gets Jackie Robinson ready for a posed "action shot," set up by Stamford's Nick Scutti. Sweet and Scutti worked together to photograph many famous athletes. In this photograph, taken at the original Yankee Stadium, Scutti placed a metal lift under Jackie to give the appearance of a true slide. (Courtesy of Nick Scutti.)

5

IT GETS HOT ON THE GRIDIRON

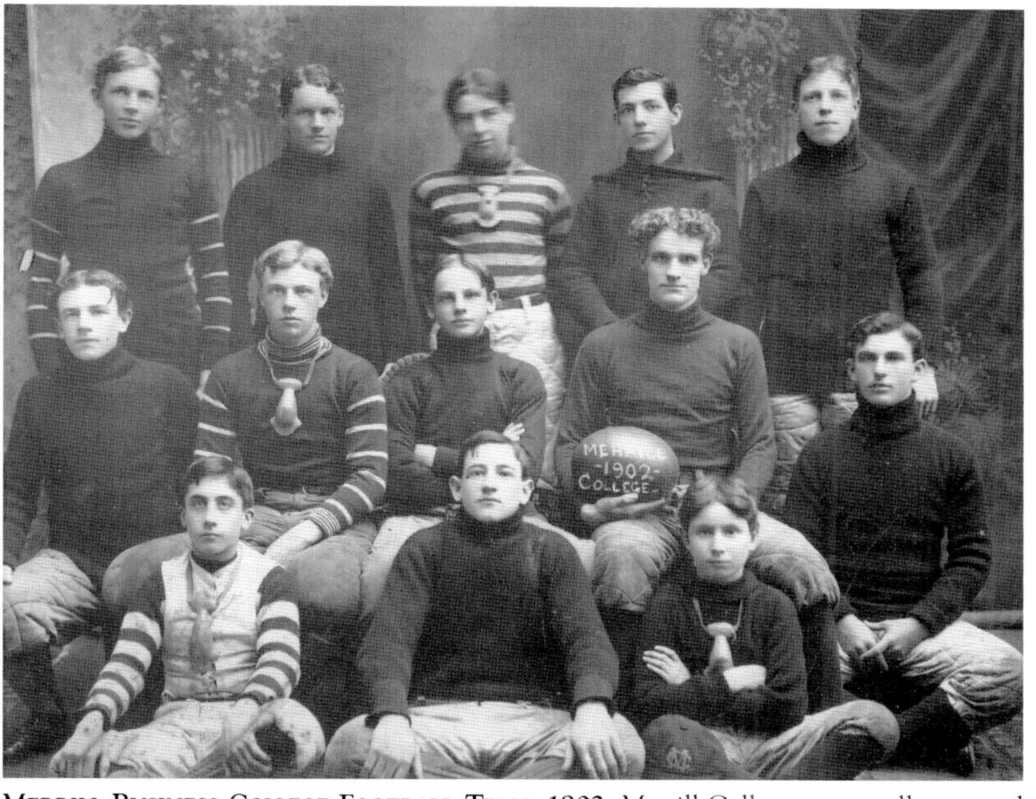

MERRILL BUSINESS COLLEGE FOOTBALL TEAM, 1902. Merrill College was a well-respected local business school with an equally respected football squad. The photograph donor's father, Bartow Ayres, is identified as being second from the left in the second row, or "the blond with the nosepiece." In the very early 1900s, football could be excessively brutal, and its rules were constantly being revised to make the game less violent but retain its excitement. The public perception of football as being too violent nearly led to its being dropped from Stamford High athletics in 1906. In the end, the principal, Mr. Avery, decided to retain the team, a good decision considering the outstanding teams Stamford High would produce under head coach Mike Boyle beginning in 1907.

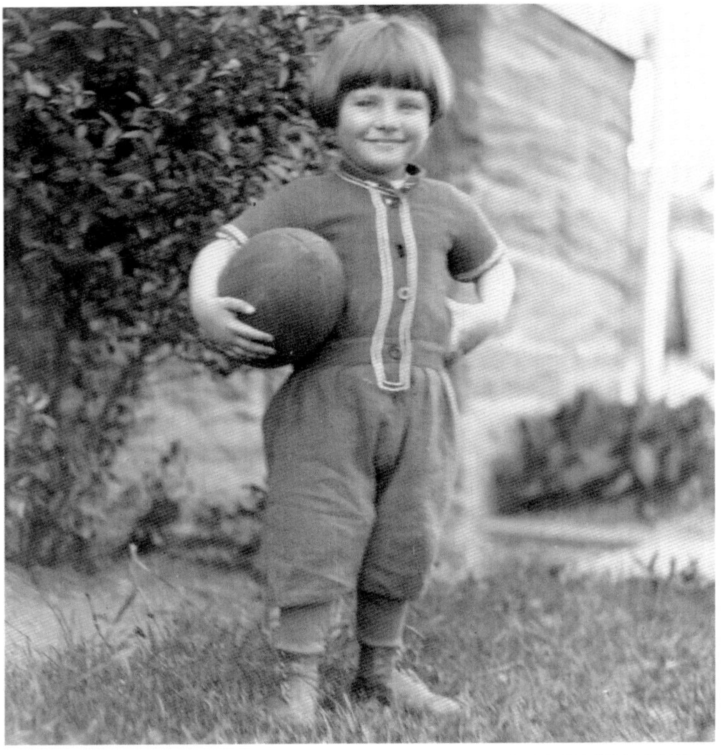

RUSSELL HAFF, c. 1915. This young man dreaming of future gridiron glory is Russell Haff, the son of German parents who lived on Washington Avenue (now Washington Boulevard). The image speaks to the popularity of the sport with first-generation immigrants, who in all likelihood had not played the game in their native countries. Haff served as a private in the US Army during World War II, suffering wounds to both of his legs in Normandy, for which he was awarded the Purple Heart.

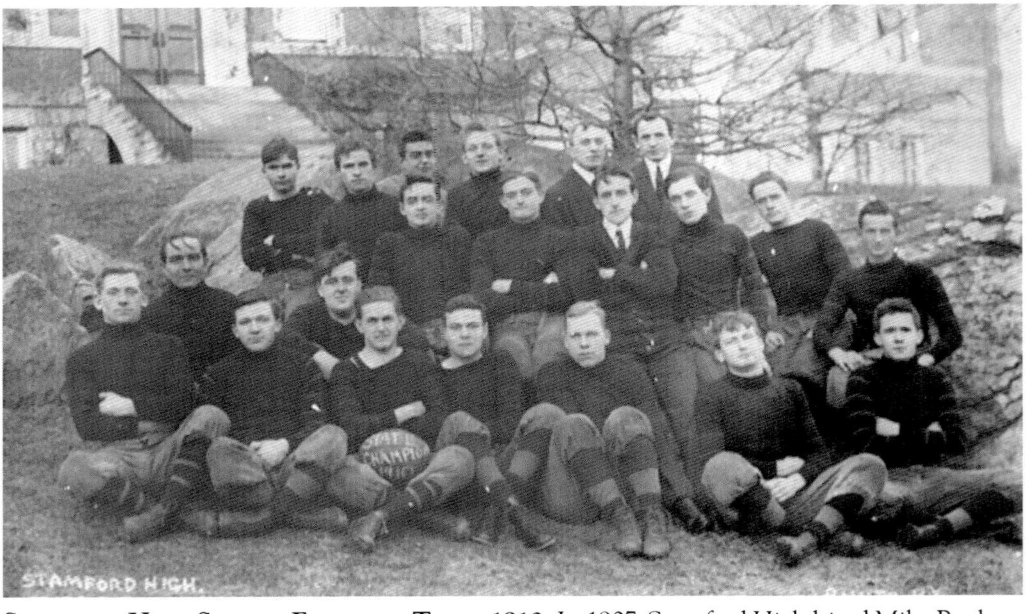

STAMFORD HIGH SCHOOL FOOTBALL TEAM, 1910. In 1907, Stamford High hired Mike Boyle as head coach, and a 31-year football dynasty began. Boyle is seen here with an early team, in the center with a tie. In the 31 years that Mike Boyle coached football, Stamford had eight undefeated seasons and an overall winning percentage of .809.

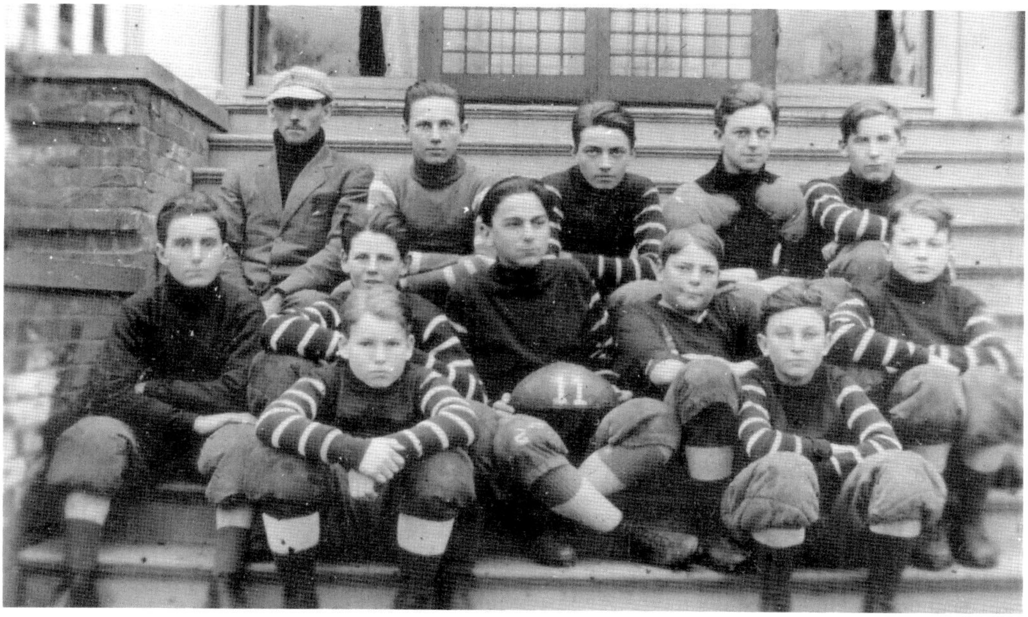

MANOR SCHOOL FOOTBALL SECOND TEAM, 1911. The Manor School was a major football force in Stamford, providing other top-tier teams, such as Betts Academy and the King School, with their fiercest competition in the early days of the game.

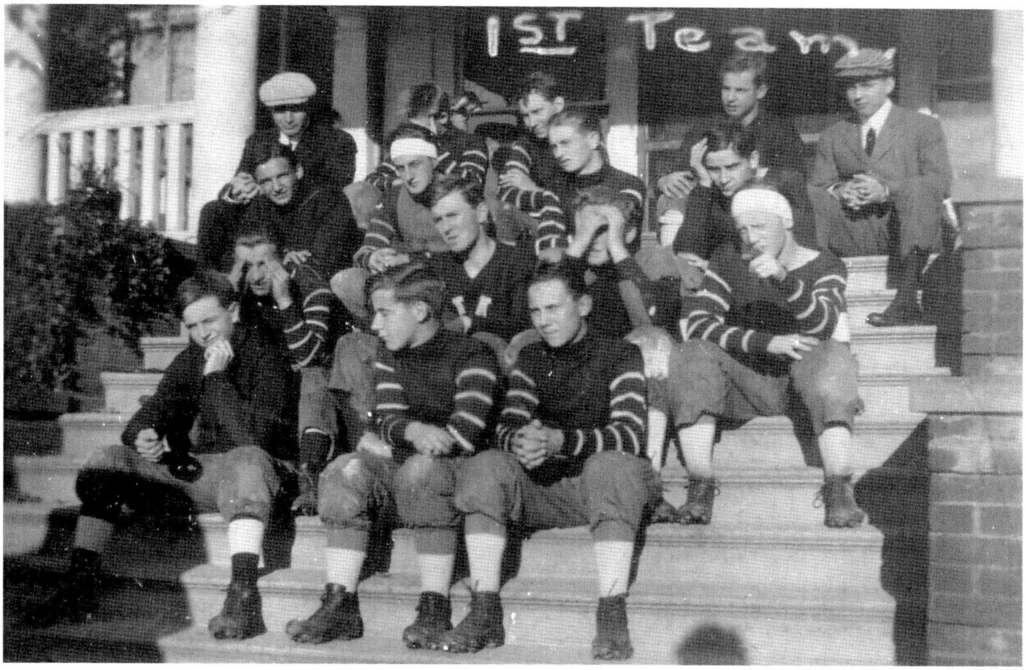

MANOR SCHOOL FIRST TEAM, 1911. The first team, seen here, is much older and more intimidating than the second team seen above. The player on the right wearing a white headband and pointing at the camera looks especially intimidating.

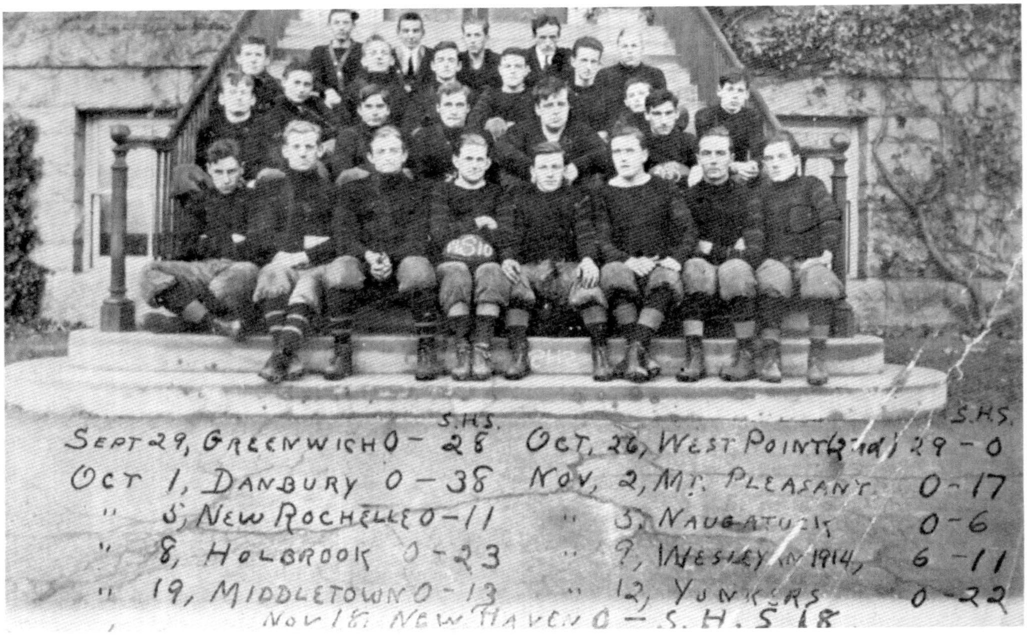

STAMFORD HIGH SCHOOL FOOTBALL TEAM, 1910. This photograph, complete with the handwritten season record, was distributed as a postcard. Coach Mike Boyle is in the fourth row on the far right, looking especially dour. This year, they got trounced by the West Point second team but beat the Wesleyan squad.

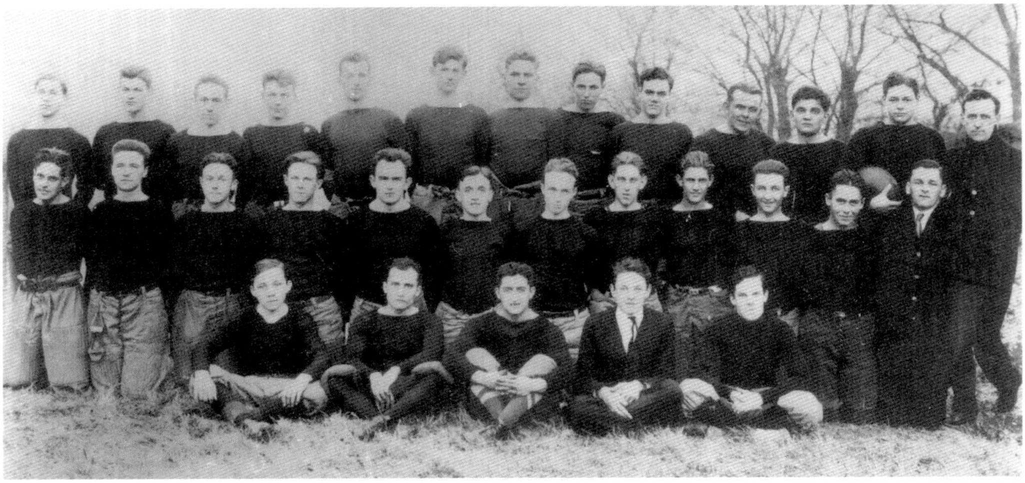

STAMFORD HIGH SCHOOL FOOTBALL TEAM, 1916. The 1916 squad had an impressive record of five wins, one loss, and two ties. The team included, from left to right, (first row) Dan Graf, Larry DeMott, Nick Colucci, Fleming Rutledge, and Paul Poole; (second row) Walter Foster, Dave McGoury, Clarence Weed, John Dora, unidentified, Sam LaGuardia, ? Conwell, unidentified, Leslie Lewt, Edgar Charleson, Peter McManus, John Connelly, and Charles Leonard; (third row) unidentified, Ben Zwart, Paul Rosa, Bill Baster, Sam Wolfson, T. Thompkins, Frank Graf, William Foster, George Burns, Barney O'Toole, Mike Luciano, Brainerd Embree, and Mike Boyle.

FRANK GRAF, 1918. A member of the 1916 Stamford High football team (opposite page), Frank Graf was all-American guard at the University of Pennsylvania, where he is seen here in 1918. He died from injuries related to his professional football career in 1933.

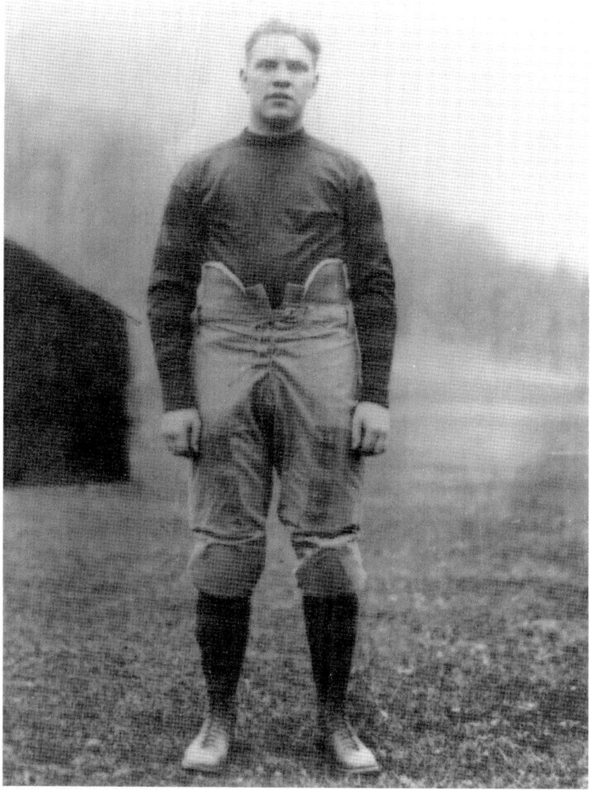

STAMFORD HIGH SCHOOL FOOTBALL SQUAD, 1926–1927. The players below are identified as, from left to right, (first row) Bella, Wynne, Duffy, Karukas, Condos, Scalzi, Konspone, Roles, Malin, Connelly, Coppola, and Pachios; (second row) coach Mike Boyle, Lenczycki, Sherman, Brooks, LiVolsi, Strauss, Bellos, Cuddy, Hemming, Mantell, Mosey, and Lubelsky; (third row) Pedersen, Pachiso, Westermann, Wennerberg, Birmingham, Judson, Chicatell, and Donohue.

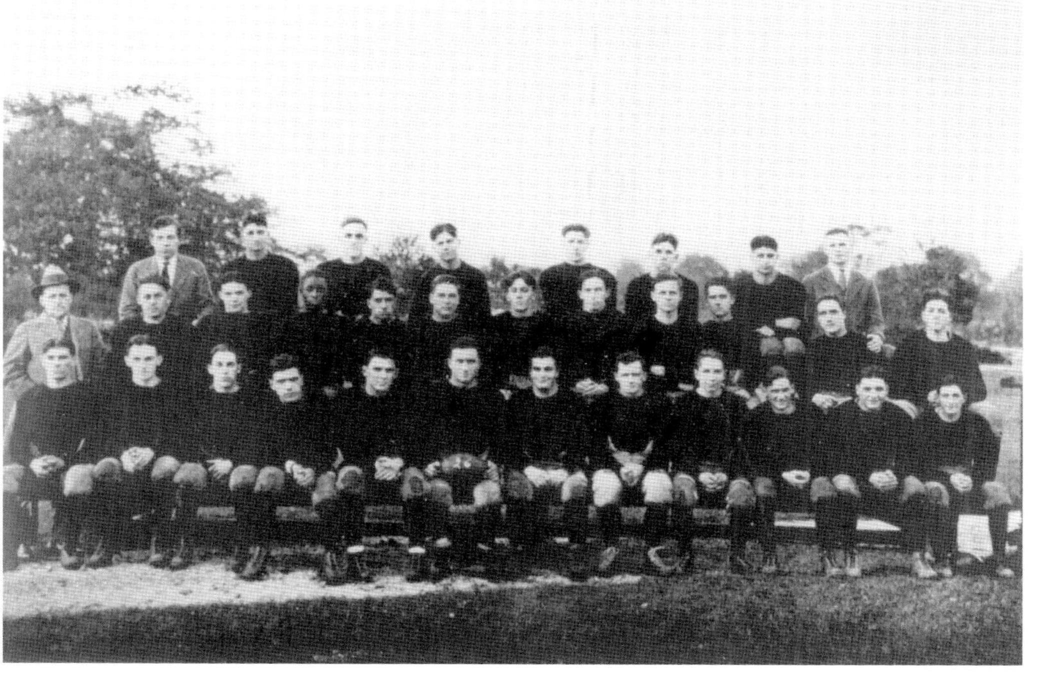

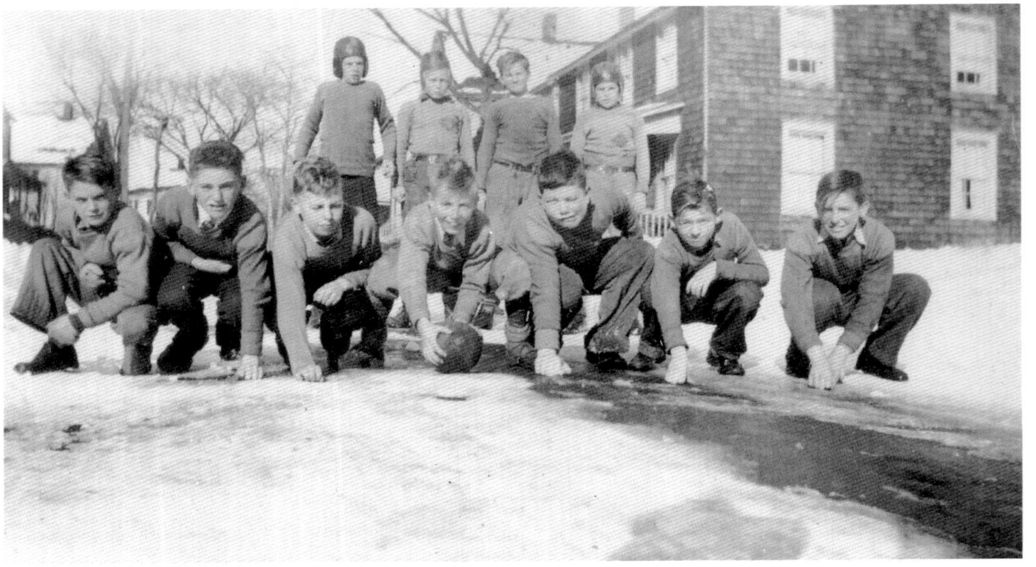

St. John's Boys' Brigade, 1938. Sponsored by St. John's Roman Catholic Church, the boys' brigade junior league football team was very successful in the late 1930s and early 1940s. At the time of this photograph, the team was in its third straight year of going undefeated and untied.

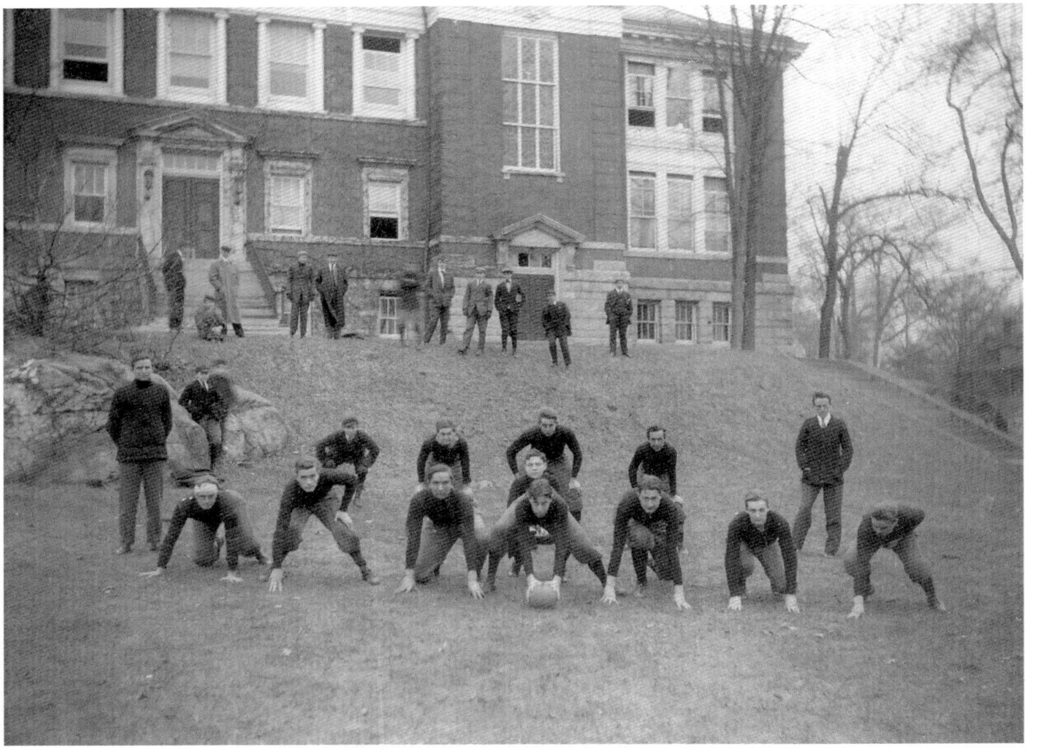

Stamford High School Football Squad, c. 1920. The team poses in formation on the school grounds on Forest Street. Coach Mike Boyle is on the right, wearing a tie.

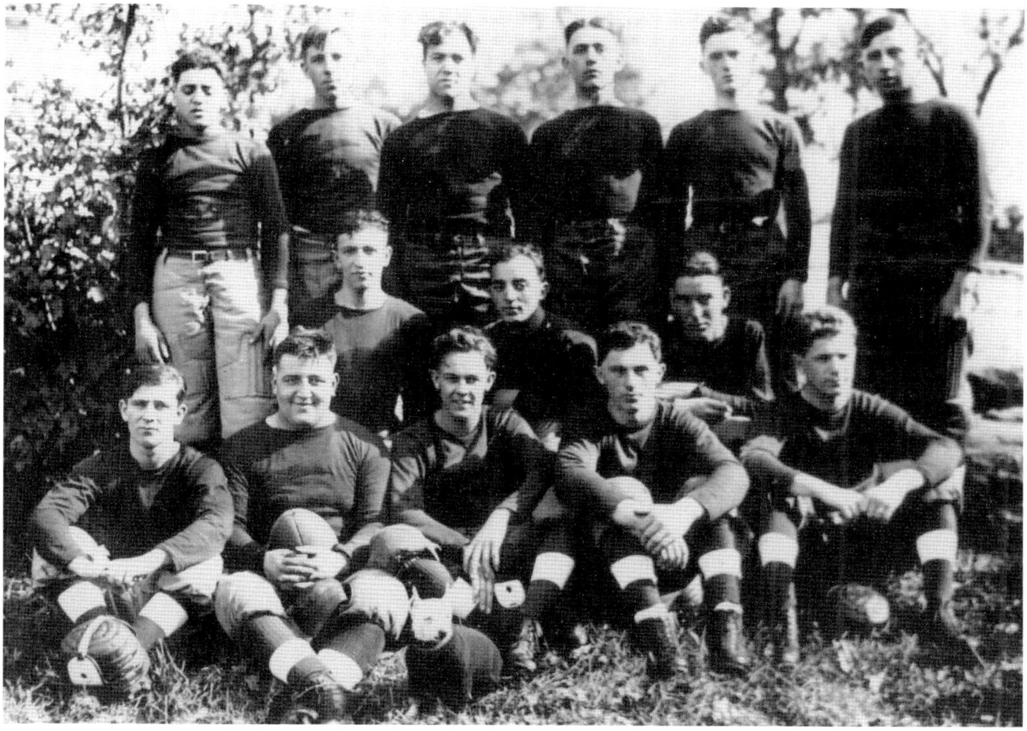

CRESCENT FOOTBALL TEAM, 1918. Note the small dog in the football sweater in front of the team, which included, from left to right (first row) Herman Kaelin, Dominick "Happy" Mazza, Tom Richardson, Abe Wossey, and Martin Levitan; (second row) Max Levine, Alphonse Vacca, and William Miller; (third row) Sidney Altman, Joe Mrus, Joe Bochicchio, Mike DeVito, Harry O'Meara, and Abe Alswanger. The burly, smiling "Happy" Mazza was the team's center.

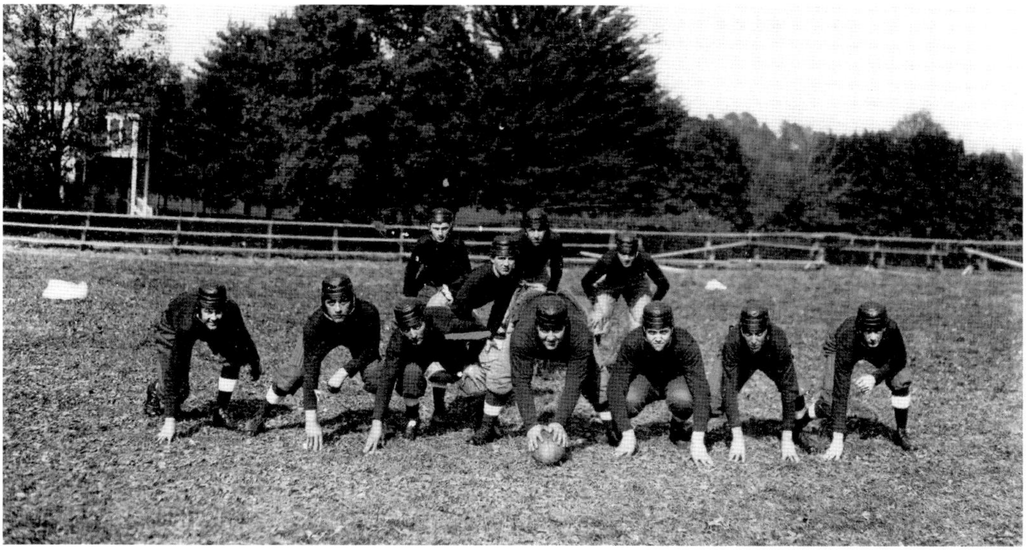

CRESCENT FOOTBALL TEAM, 1918. The Crescents are seen here lined up in formation.

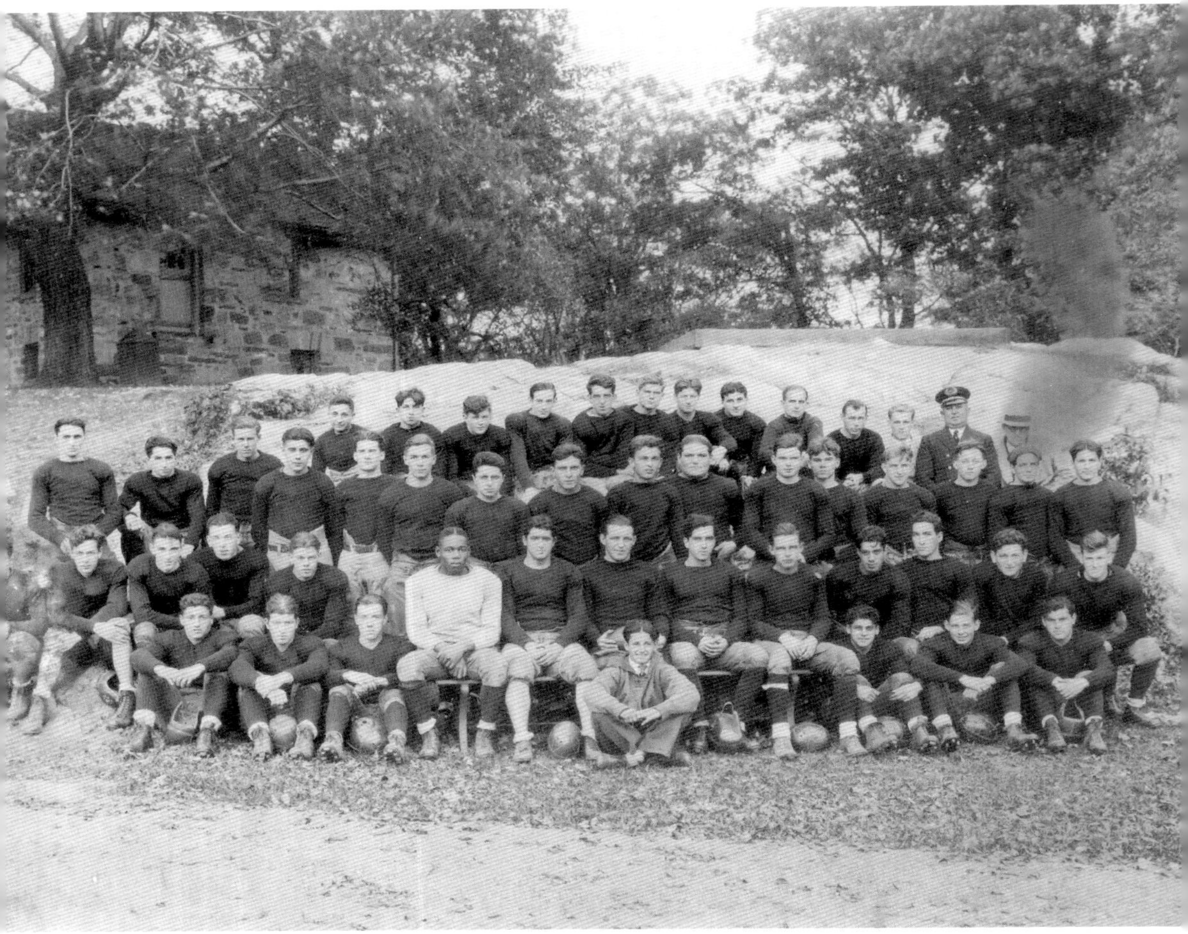

STAMFORD HIGH SCHOOL FOOTBALL TEAM, 1930. After a state championship in 1929, this squad had a very short season, only four games, in which to rebuild. With so few games, the season was probably the worst on record for coach Mike Boyle: two wins, one loss, and one tie. The team members are identified, from left to right, as (first row) Fabrizzio, Grabenstein, Coughlin, Bello, Besh, Shannon, Lynch, Chicatell, Yaderiski, and Blais; (second row) Grimaldi, Rose, Viola, Maher, Carlin, Lopiano, Santtesino, Sussman, and Walker; (third row) Condos, Alonzy, Black, Umile, Birmingham, Saunders, Rinaldi, Vitti, Zhoyan, Pitnie, Herman, Kochis, Wajeck, Celotto, Betz, and Ogera; (fourth row) Scalzi, Kunes, Lanis, White, Fuller, Holowink, Caputo, Good, Kuczo, Crain, Brennan, and Boyle.

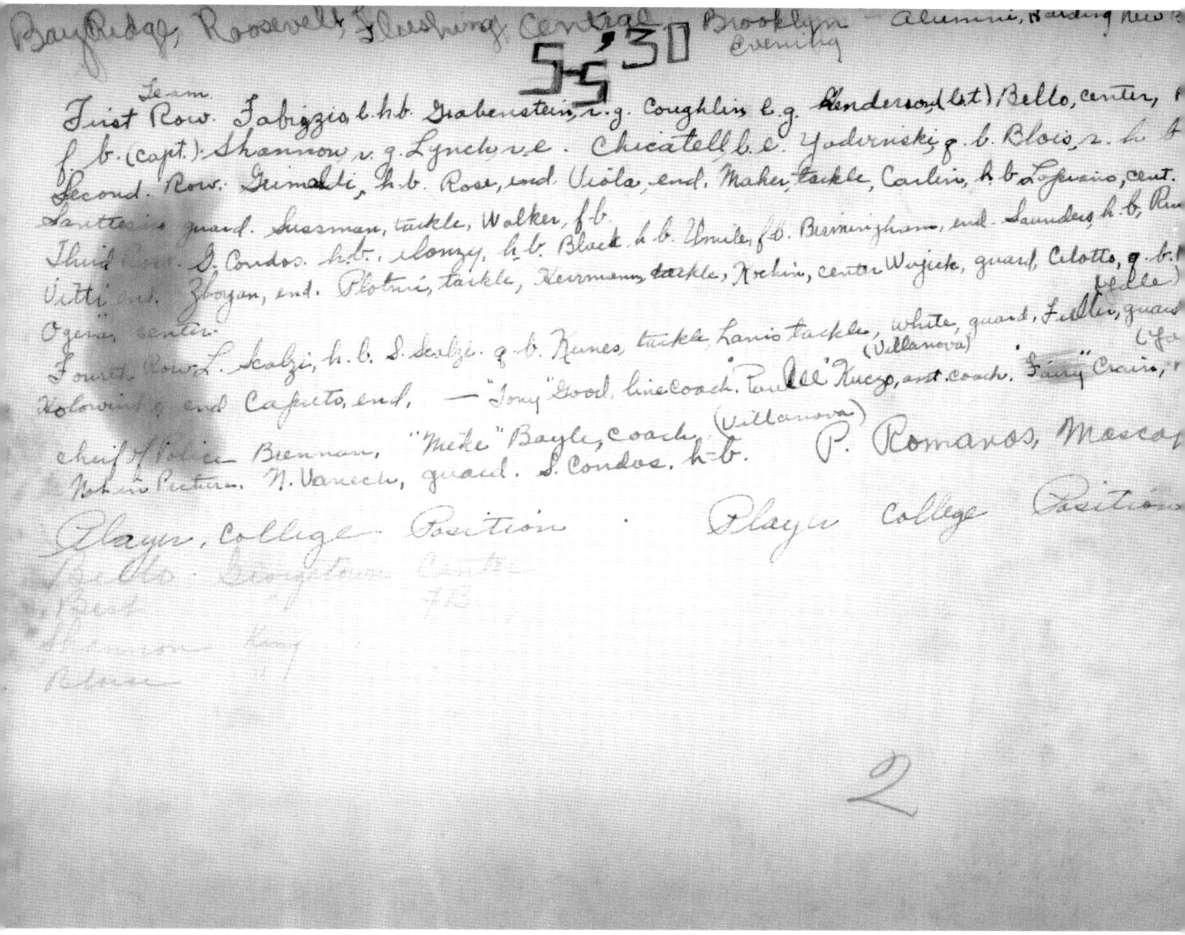

STAMFORD HIGH SCHOOL FOOTBALL TEAM, 1930. This is the back of the photograph on the opposite page, including player names, positions, nicknames, and other information about the players and coaches. Listed across the top are the other teams they played that season.

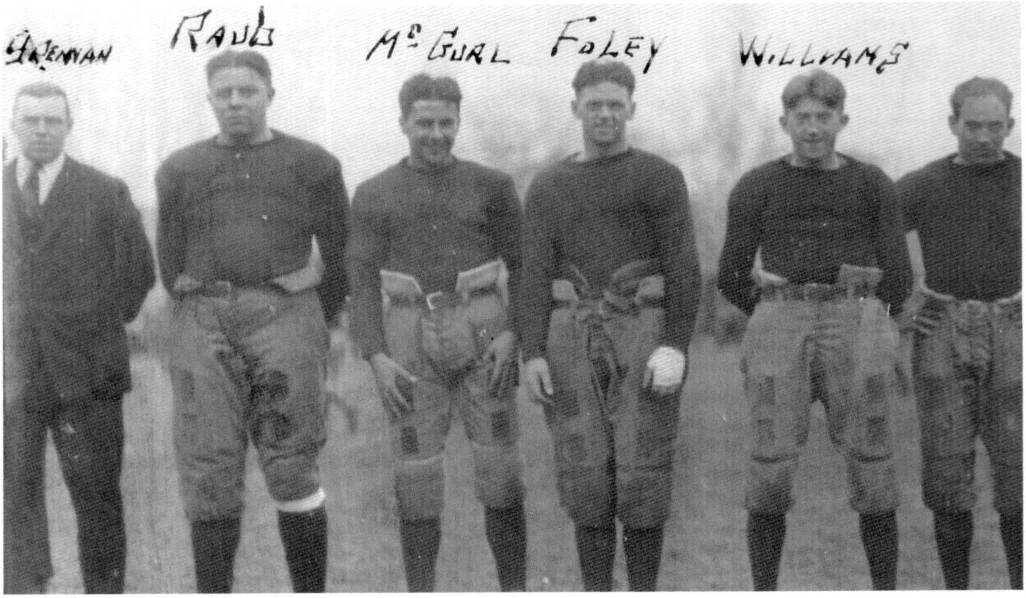

STAMFORD ALL-STARS, C. 1925. This photograph shows literally half of the squad—only the left side of the photograph has been recovered. The All-Stars were Stamford's first semiprofessional team. They were later taken over by Felix Livolsi and became the Stamford Pros, and then later the Golden Bears. At the far left is coach William Brennan, who played for Stamford High from 1917 to 1920.

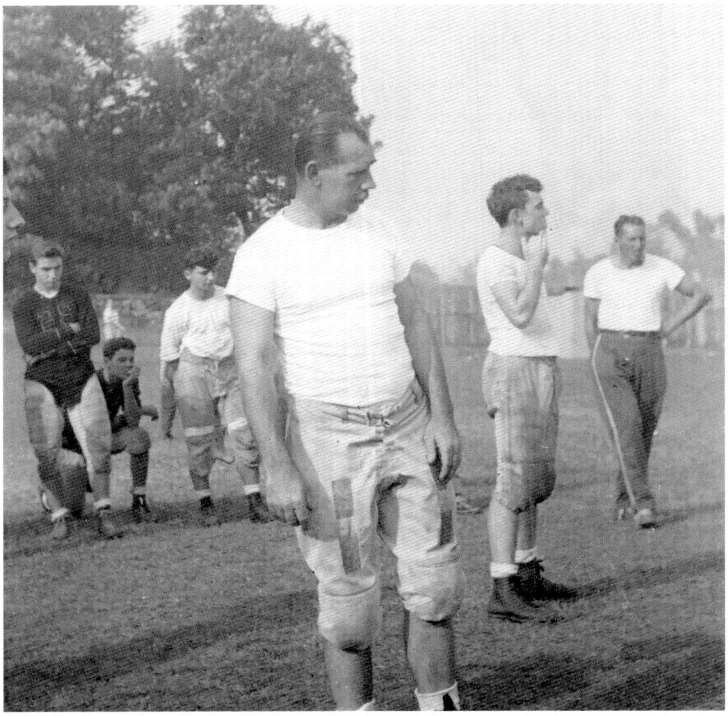

COACH PAUL KUCZO. Players look on as Coach Kuczo watches the Stamford High School team during practice. Kuczo began as an assistant coach under Mike Boyle and went on to lead the team as head coach until 1957.

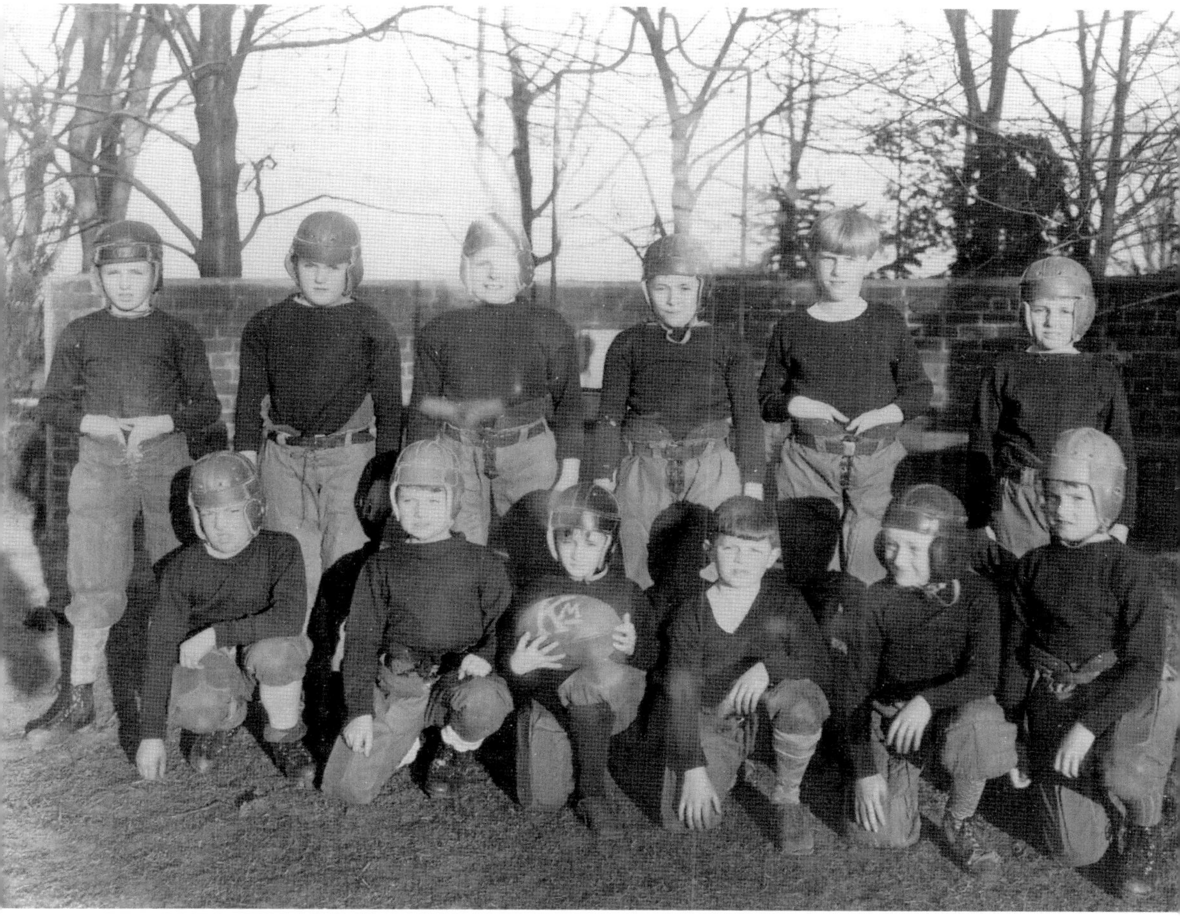

KING SCHOOL FOOTBALL PLAYERS, C. 1931. The lower school team (fifth-graders and sixth-graders) from the King School poses for their team photograph. The King School, a boys' preparatory school, has been fielding football squads since the earliest days of the game in the late 1800s.

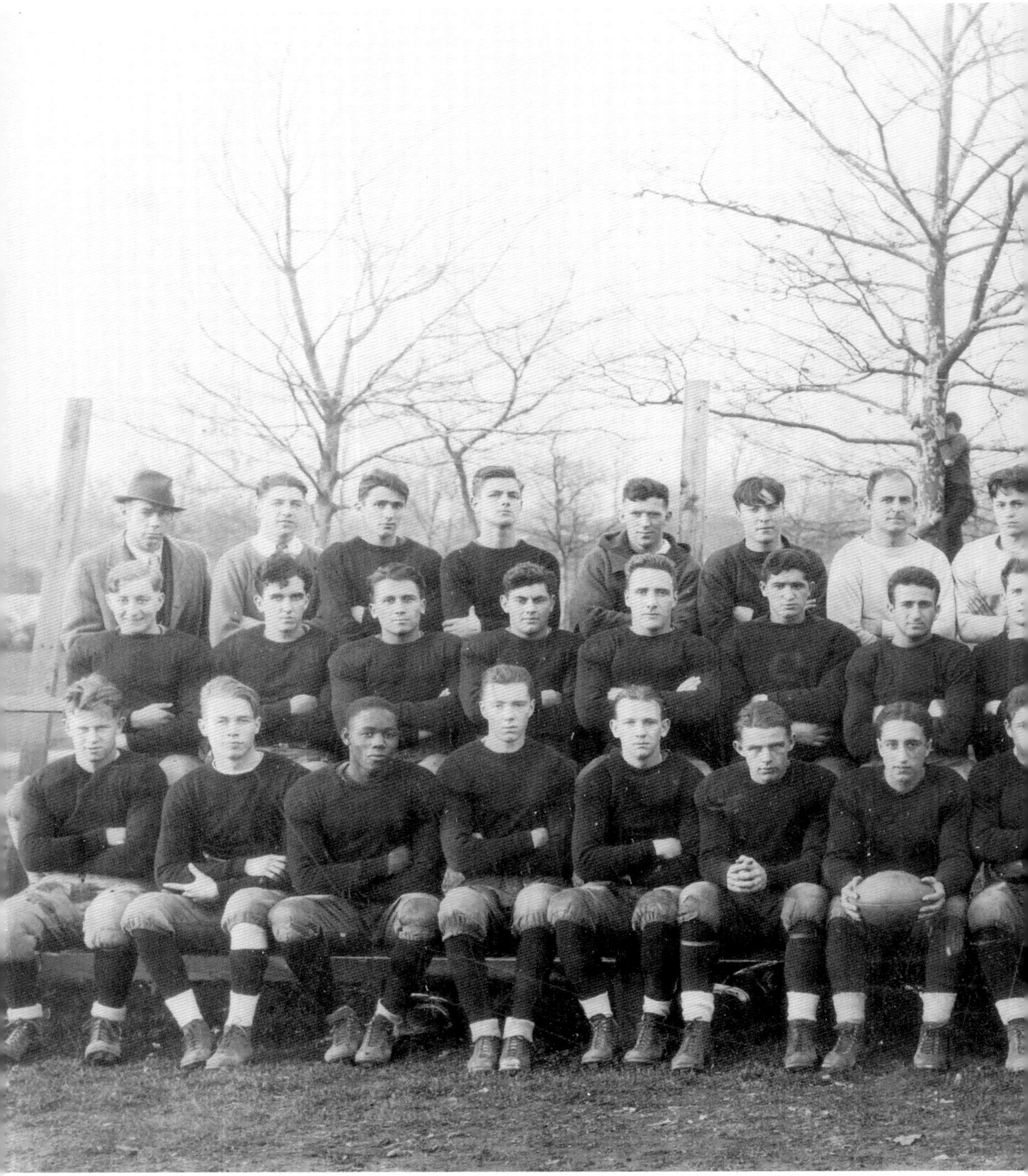

STAMFORD HIGH SCHOOL FIRST TEAM, 1929 STATE CHAMPIONS. This squad brought home the state championship and included the first African American on a Stamford squad. Coach Mike Boyle is near the center of the third row, wearing a fedora; Paul Kuczo, who took over for Boyle as coach, is on the far left of the third row, also wearing a hat. Some of the players were identified

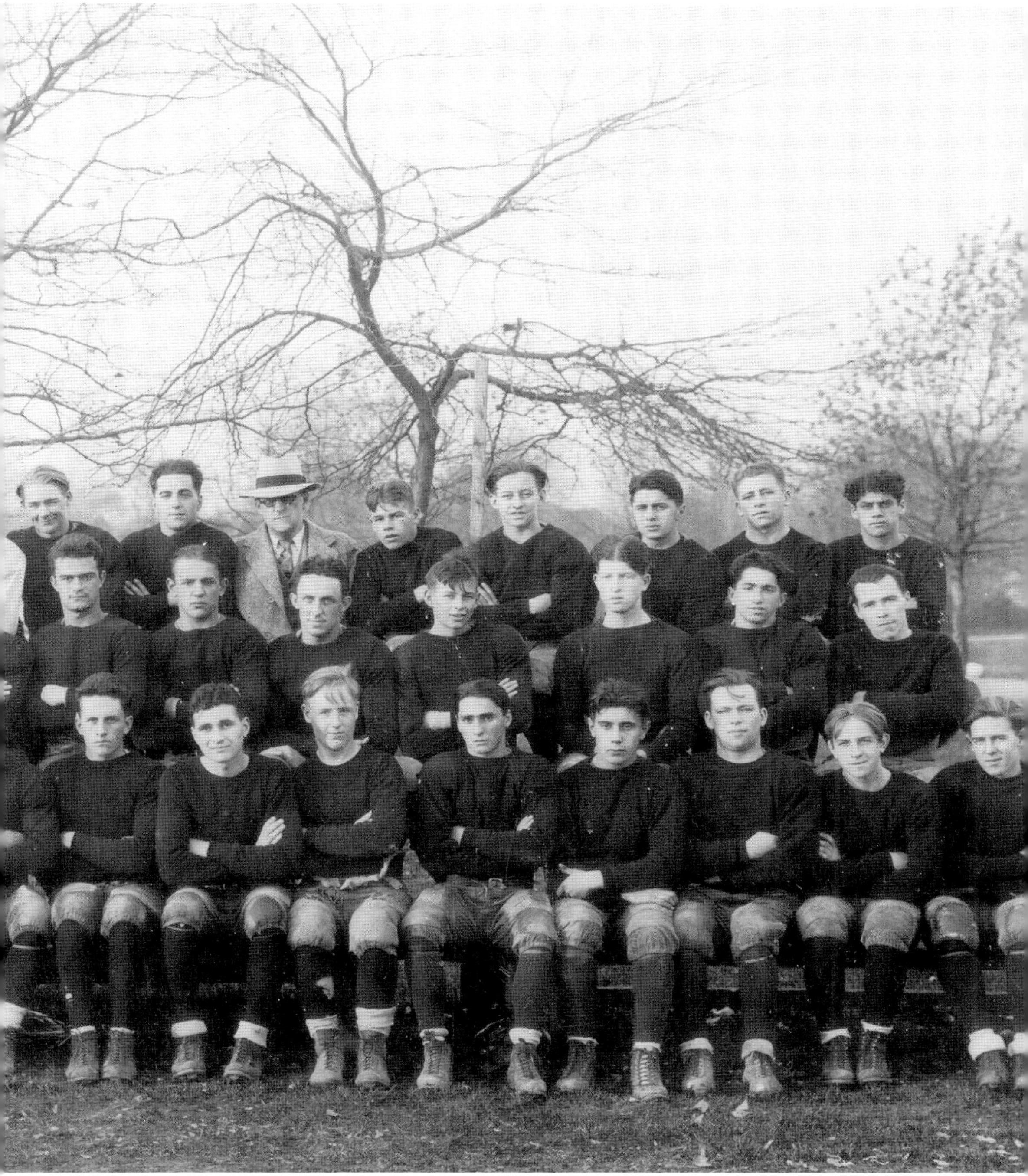

by position on the back of the photograph. They are Tom Page, end; Frank Moyes, tackle; Soc Lada, guard; "Riggo" Bello, center; Bud Shannon, guard; Dzamba, tackle; Lynch, end; Telsco, left halfback, Hanrahan, right halfback; Best, fullback; and Mike Lione, quarterback.

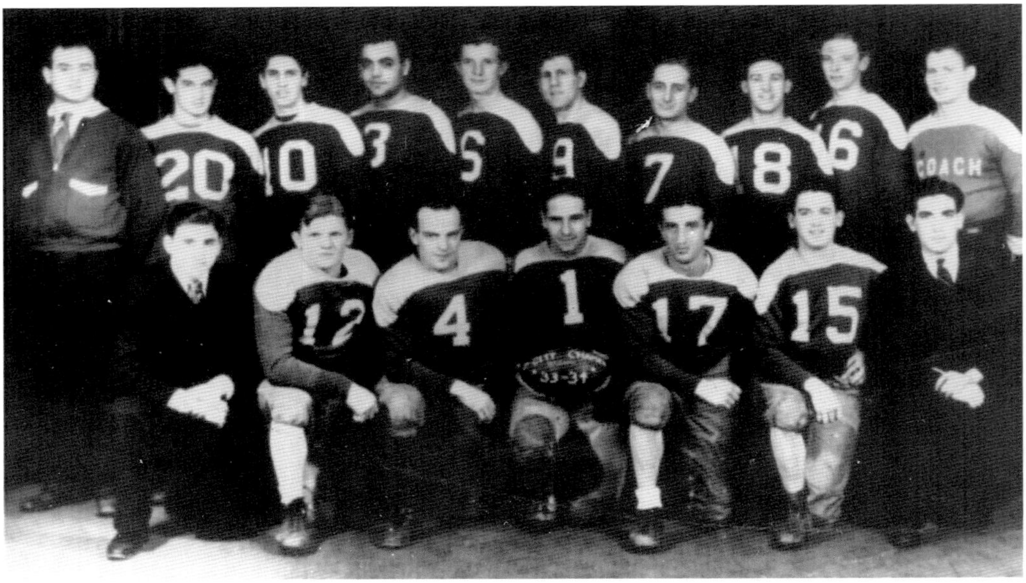

ST. MARY'S ATHLETIC CLUB FOOTBALL TEAM, 1933–1934. Founded in 1910 by Joseph Leonard, the St. Mary's Athletic Club sponsored semiprofessional football and baseball teams. Above, the 1933–1934 city champion football club poses for a photograph. The team included, from left to right, (first row) Pat Morelli, Joe Ballo, T. Givins, Louis Fuda, H. Umile, William Yeager, and Sebastian Interlandi; (second row) Moses Morelli, Ed Umile, Daniel Morelli, Frank Baldassare, ? Reynolds, William Valenti, Sal Suttile, S. Yeager, J. Zboyan, and Abe Morelli. In the photograph below, William Valenti poses in stance.

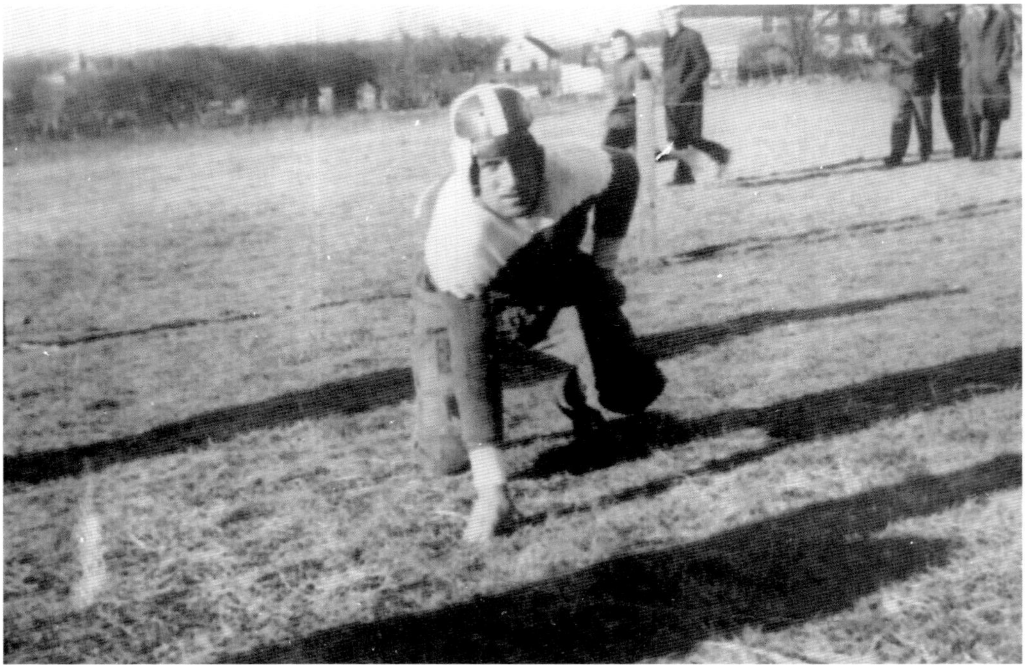

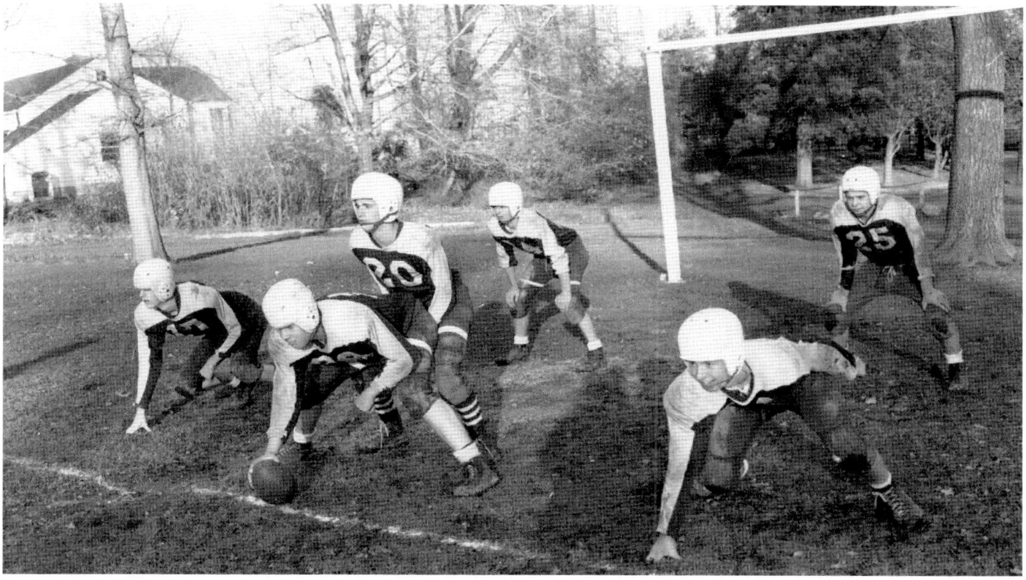

King School Varsity Football Players, 1955. According to the King School yearbook, the 1955 team "was not the eleven man game played by the school for the past years, but was now a more rugged and open-field game called six man football." Six-man football was created in 1934 by a Nebraska high school coach named Stephen Epler, who developed the game as an alternative for small high schools. The members of the 1955 team, some of whom are seen here, were Ron Sebra, Fred Willis, Clark Varnum, Abbot Schwebel, Kevin Foster, Francis Colgrove, Jack Chesney, Clifton Reynolds, Stanley Rothenbergy, Robert Barnes, Jim Kweskin, and Dick Castles.

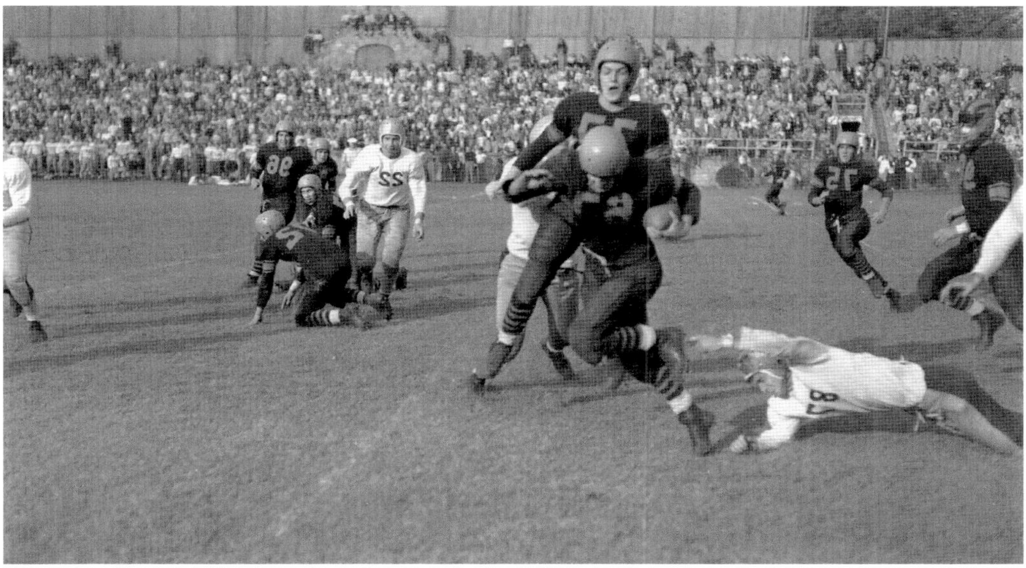

Stamford High School Player Running the Ball, c. 1952. In the 1940s and 1950s, high school football was the biggest spectator sport in Stamford. Here, in 1952, the stands were packed as people from all over the city came to cheer on the Stamford 11.

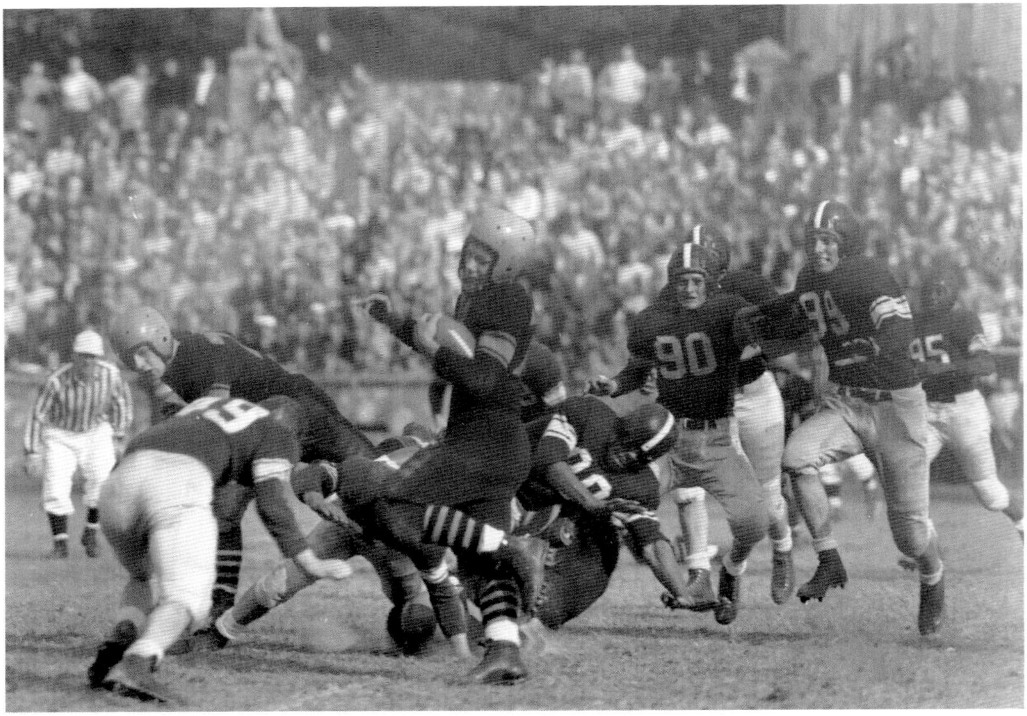

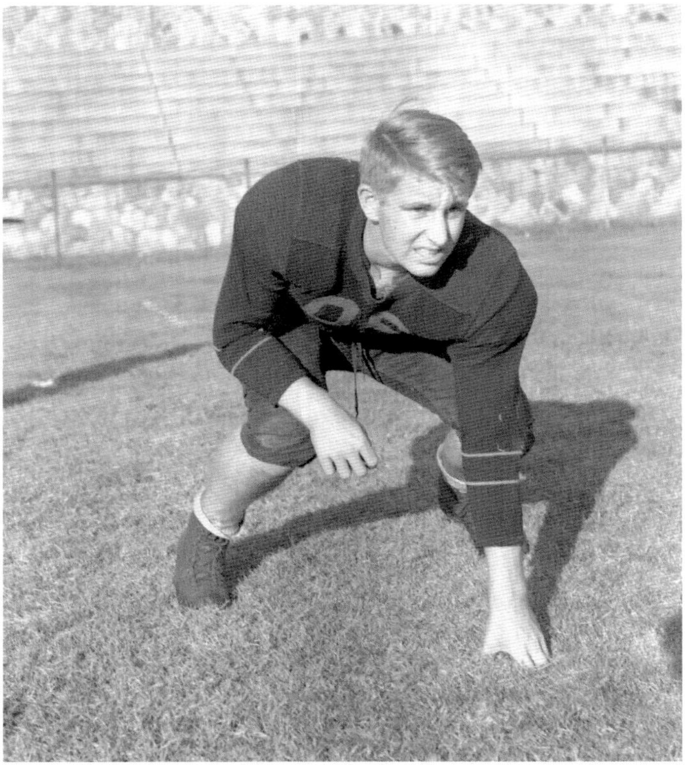

STAMFORD HIGH SCHOOL FOOTBALL GAME, C. 1952. The face of the Stamford player above shows that he is quite aware that he is surrounded by opponents.

STAMFORD HIGH SCHOOL LINEMAN, 1948. An unidentified player for the Stamford squad takes his lineman stance.

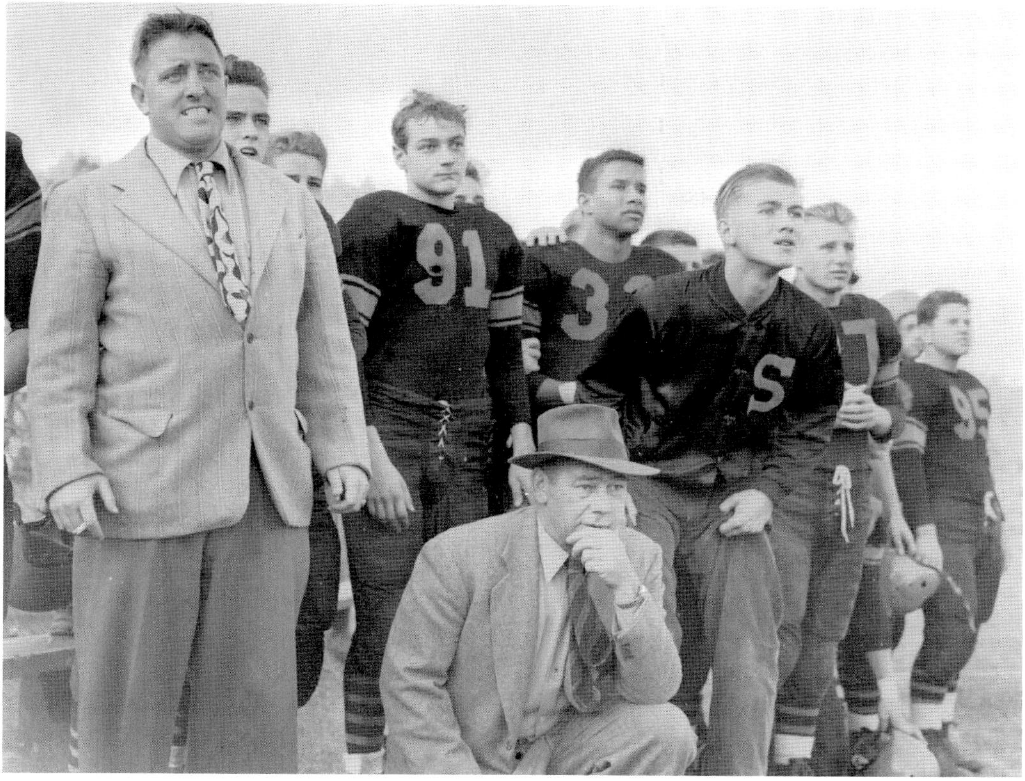

STAMFORD HIGH BENCH AND COACHES, 1948. The Stamford High School bench and coaches Jack Lockery (left) and Paul Kuczo (left) watch anxiously during a close game.

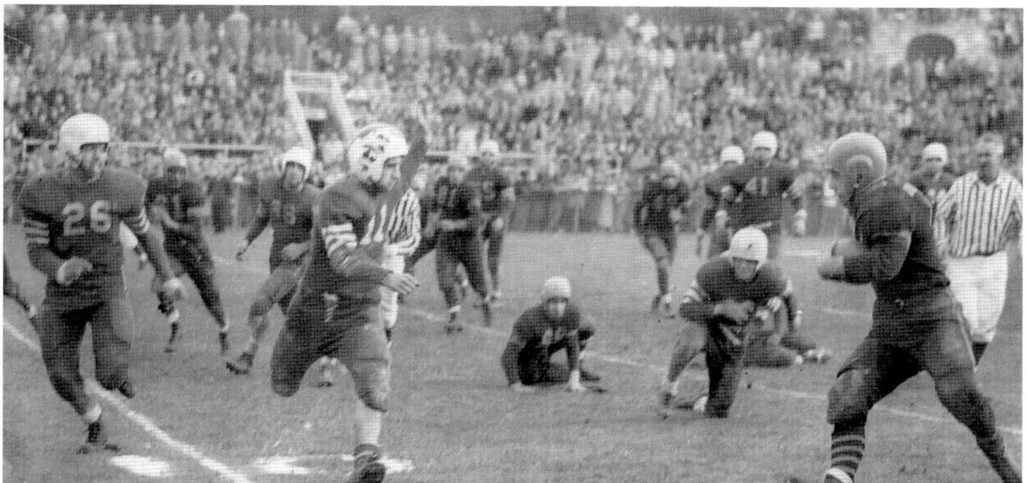

STAMFORD HIGH SCHOOL FOOTBALL GAME, 1952. In this game, Stamford High faces off against Fairfield Preparatory School. This 1952 squad won the Connecticut state championship. The players seen here are identified, in no particular order, as Duarte, Samuel, and Butkaresky.

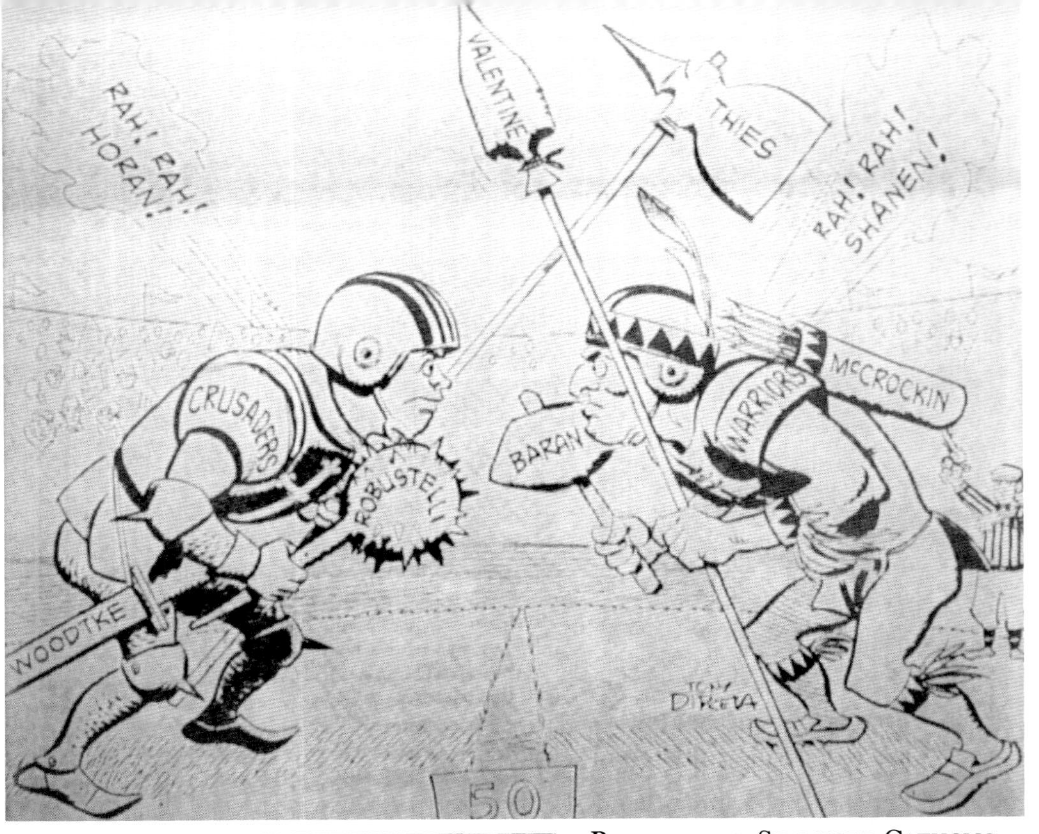

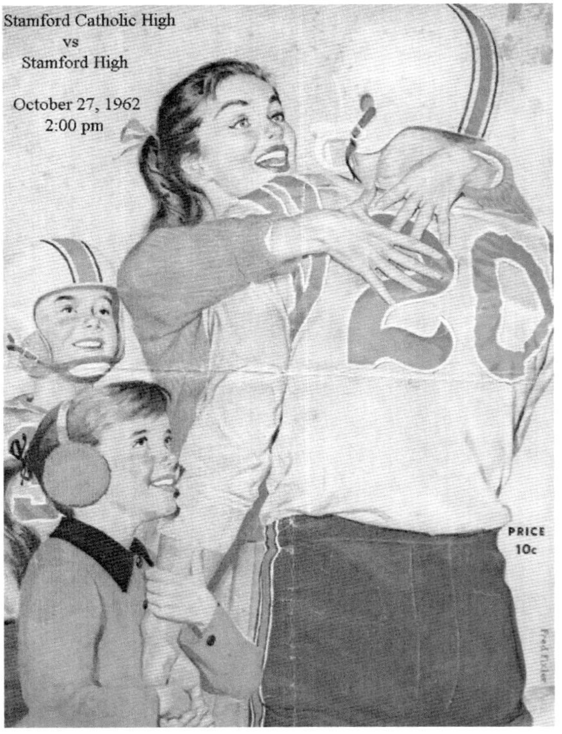

RIPPOWAM VS. STAMFORD CATHOLIC CARTOON. Stamford cartoonist Tony DiPreta, known for his Joe Palooka cartoon strip, drew this cartoon portraying an upcoming championship match between the Stamford Catholic High School Crusaders and the Rippowam Warriors. The two undefeated teams collided in the first ever Fairfield County Interscholastic Athletic Conference (FCIAC) championship game. DiPreta's cartoons were featured in Stamford publications throughout his life.

PROGRAM COVER, 1962. This program cover drawing was created for the 1962 game between Stamford Catholic and Stamford High. While it is certainly cheesy, it is indicative of the adulation star players received at the time.

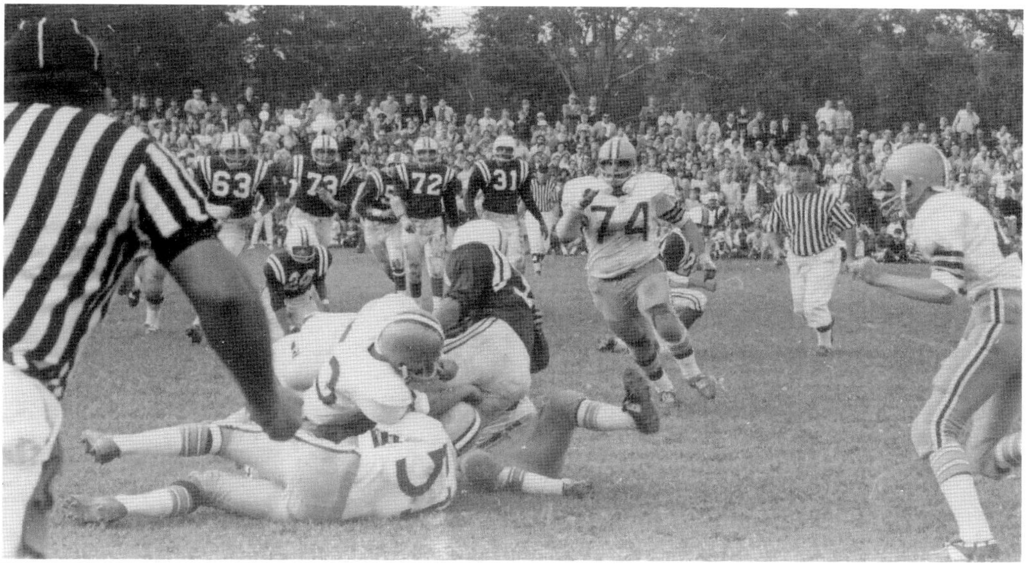

Rippowam vs. Stamford Catholic, 1967. With a student body of less than 800, Stamford Catholic was David taking on the Goliaths of Connecticut football, including in-town giants like Rippowam and Stamford High.

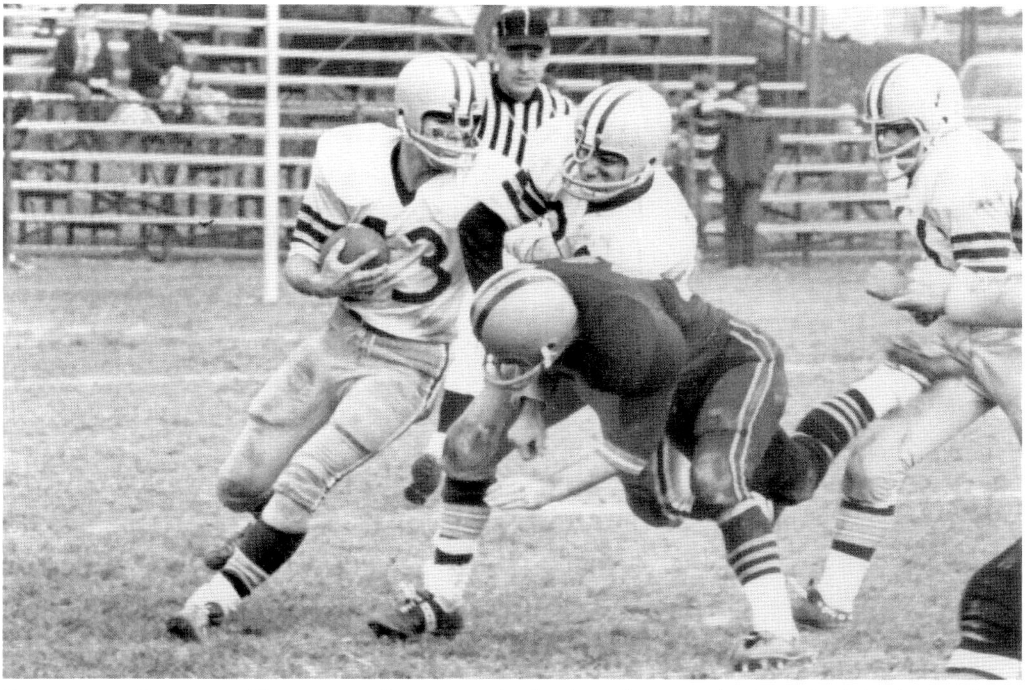

Stamford Catholic Football Game, 1967. In this photograph, Stamford Catholic player Tom Doyle goes around the left end against Stamford High. The 1967 Stamford Catholic team featured a number of outstanding players, including Chris Leone, Rocco Possidento, and Rick and Bob Robustelli, the sons of all-time Stamford great Andy Robustelli.

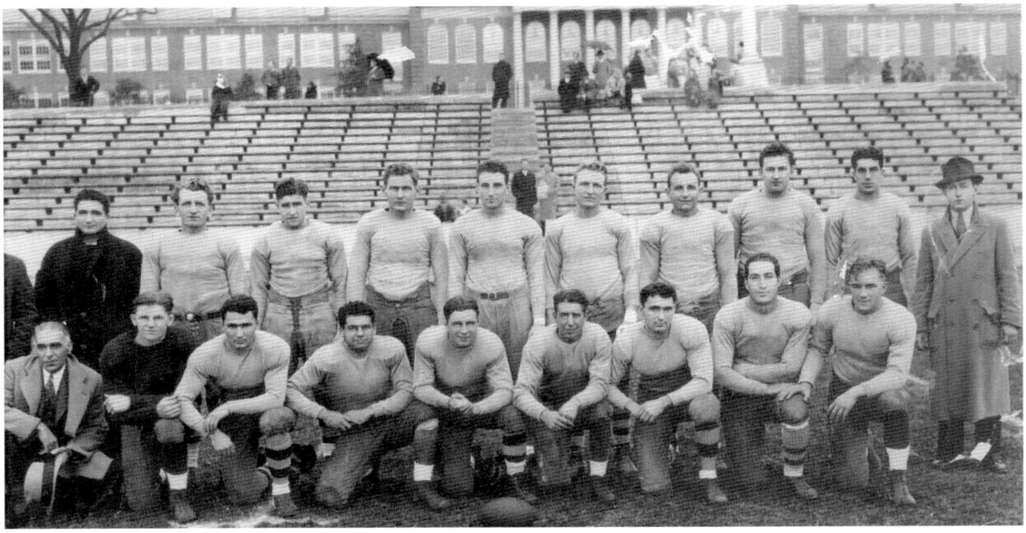

STAMFORD FOOTBALL TEAM, 1935. Stamford's first semiprofessional football team, originally named the Stamford Pros, was managed by Felix LiVolsi.

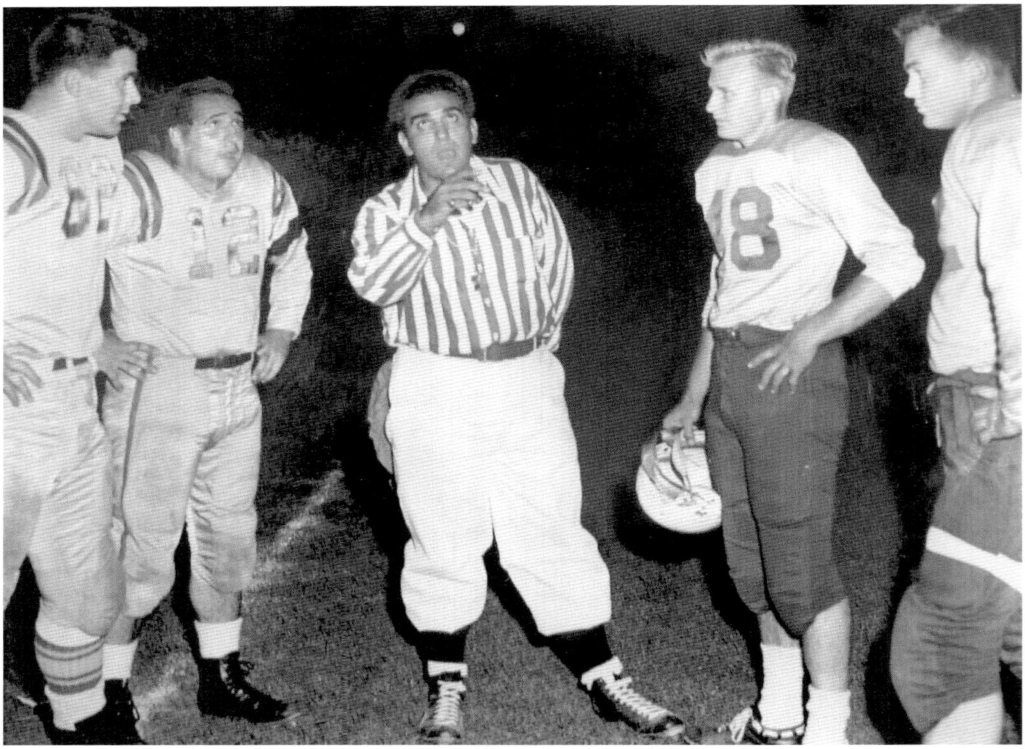

GOLDEN BEARS COIN TOSS, 1957. Stamford had a succession of professional and semiprofessional football teams. The original Stamford Pros evolved into the Golden Bears, seen above at the coin toss of their first game, in 1957. Many of Stamford High's football stars found a new home on the professional team. (Courtesy of Dennis Behunik.)

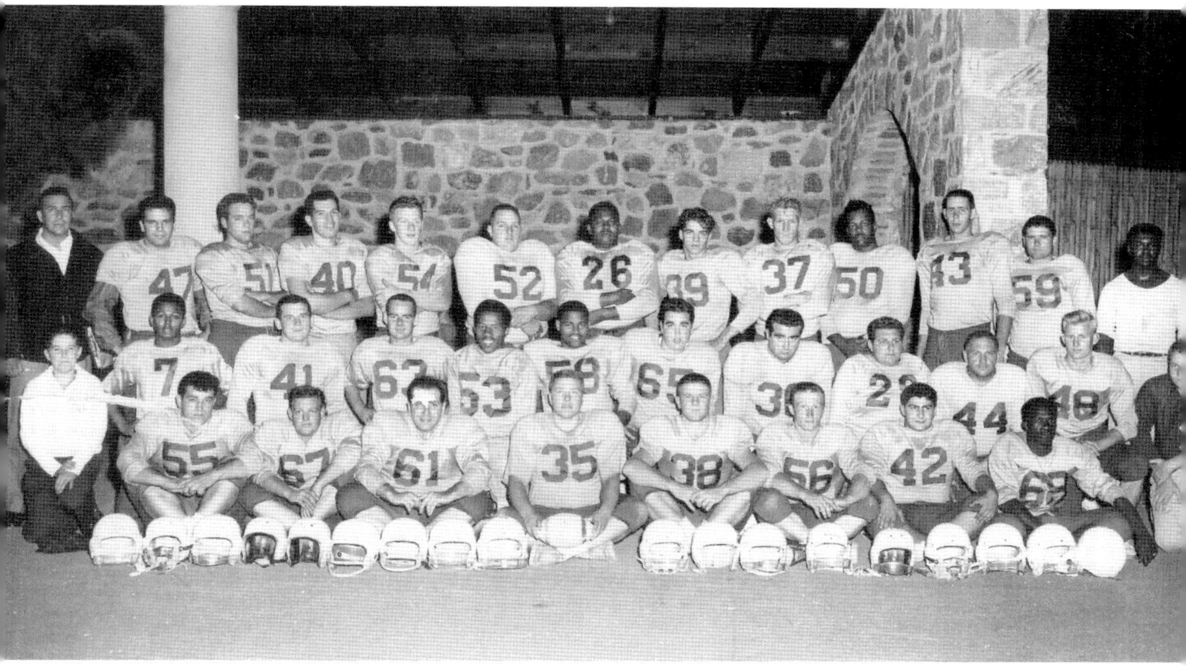

GOLDEN BEARS, 1957. This photograph was taken the year that owners Dennis Behunick and Mike Potenza started the Golden Bears. They played in the New York State Semi-Pro Football League in 1957 and later played in the Eastern Football Conference. (Courtesy of Dennis Behunik.)

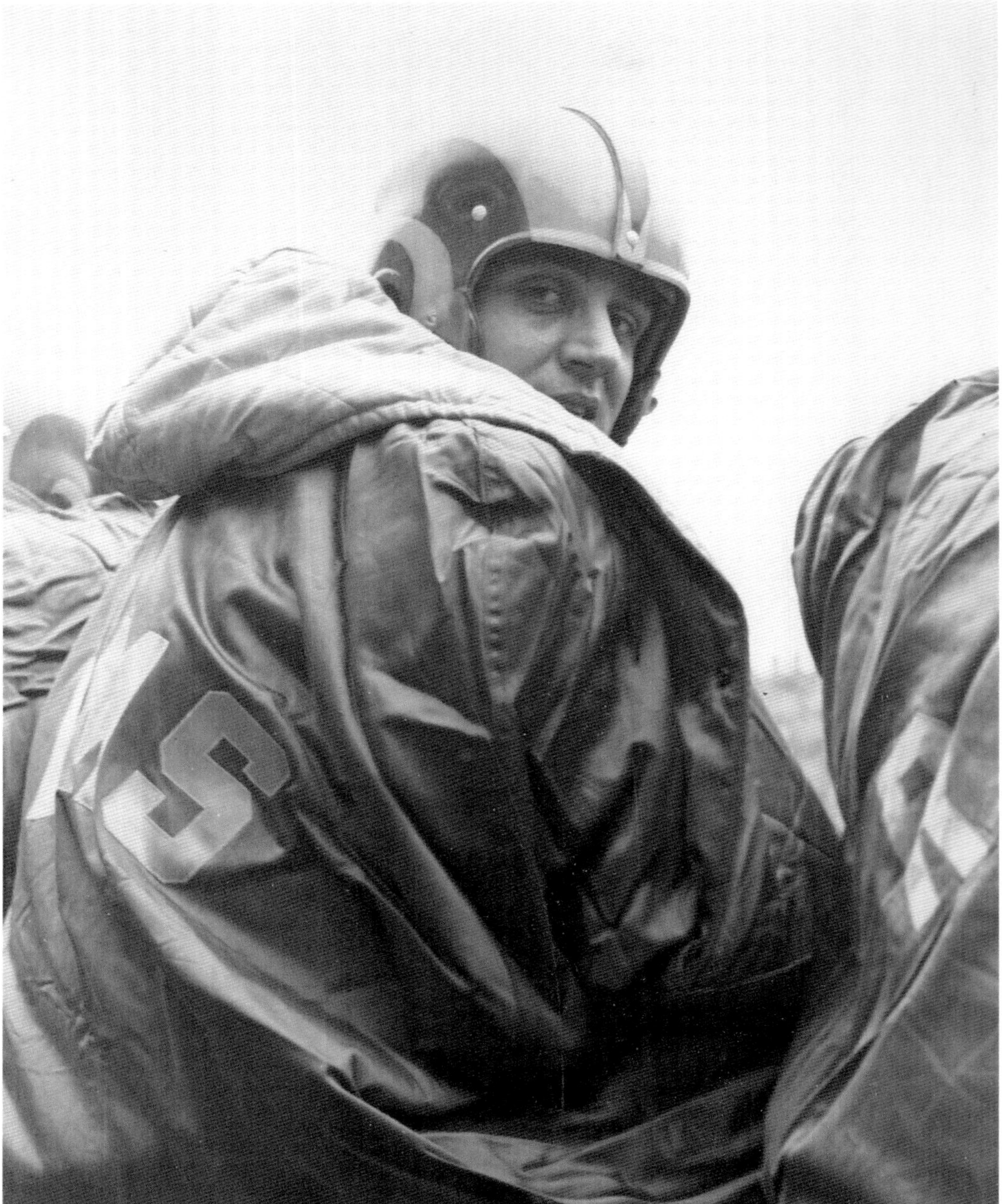

ANDY ROBUSTELLI. Nick Scutti, a well-known Stamford photographer, snapped this shot of Stamford native Andy Robustelli when he played for the Los Angeles Rams. Robustelli was drafted in 1951 and went on to become a Hall of Fame player in the National Football League, playing defensive end for the Rams and the New York Giants. (Courtesy of Nick Scutti.)

6

Gyms, Tracks, and Other Fields of Glory

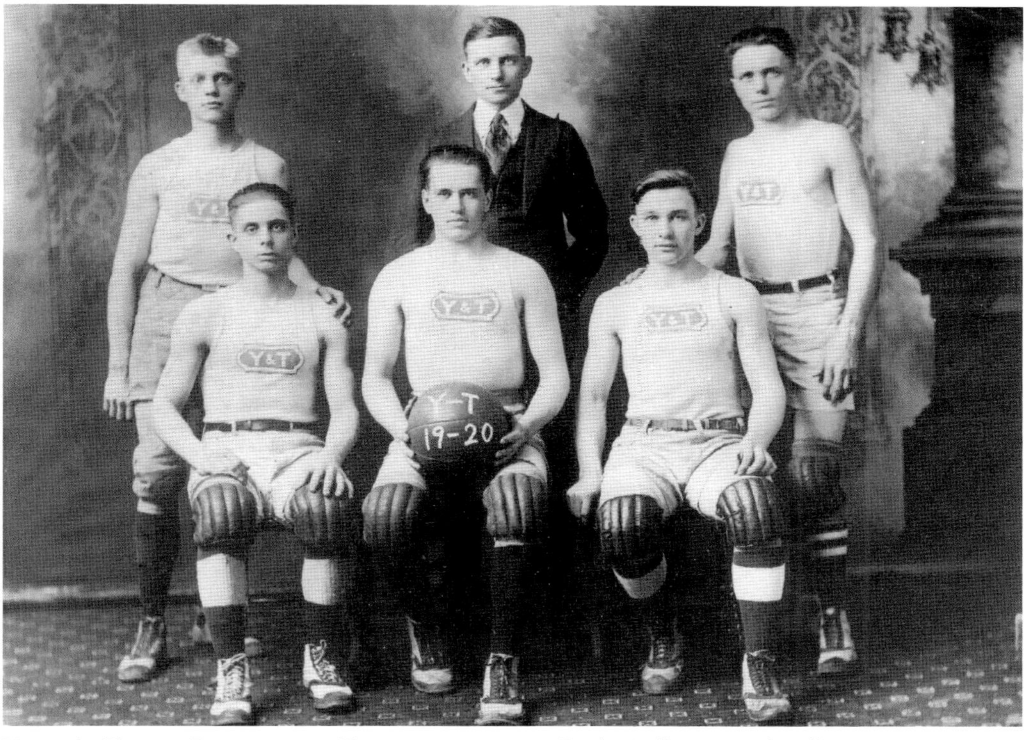

Yale & Towne Basketball Team, 1919–1920. Basketball was, and still is to some extent, the sport athletes play in between the fall and spring to stay active and in shape. Many Stamford legends of the baseball diamond and the gridiron also played basketball. Yale & Towne had its own gymnasium, where athletes could play and work out during the cold winter months. Note the protective knee gear in this photograph, which was not a common sight then or now for basketball players. Stamford picked up the sport shortly after its creation by James Naismith in 1891, who invented the game as a way for his YMCA youths to blow off steam during the winter months. Women began playing a modified version of the game in 1892 at Smith College and in high schools in 1896. Women were playing at Stamford High School at least as early as 1902. The range of sports offered to the youth of Stamford grew over the course of the 1900s, first including sports such as field hockey, volleyball, track, and soccer, and then expanding further to include swimming, gymnastics, lacrosse, ice hockey, and wrestling.

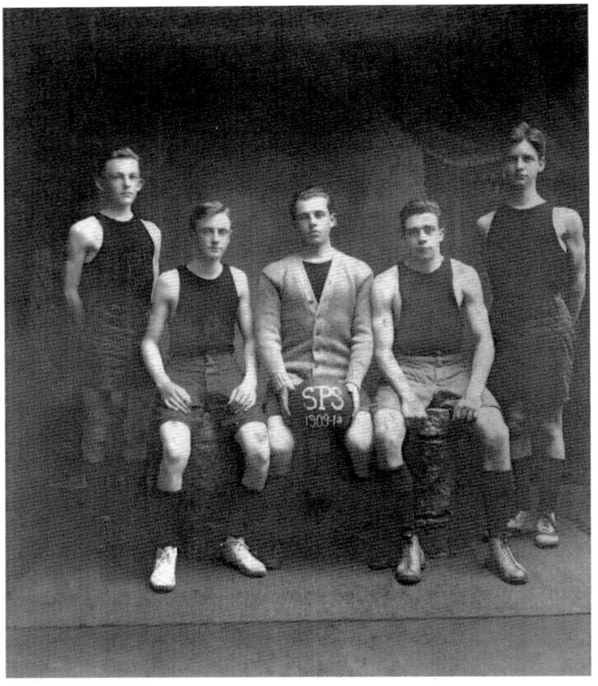

Stamford Preparatory School Basketball Team, 1909–1910. The King School changed its name to Stamford Preparatory School for a few years in the 1910s. It changed its name back to the King School when the Stamford Trade School opened and the two were often confused. Seen here, from left to right, are Leslie Martin, right forward; Malcolm Pitt Jr., right guard; Karl Hoffman Hodge, center; Sereno Sperry, left guard; and Ralsey Scofield, left forward.

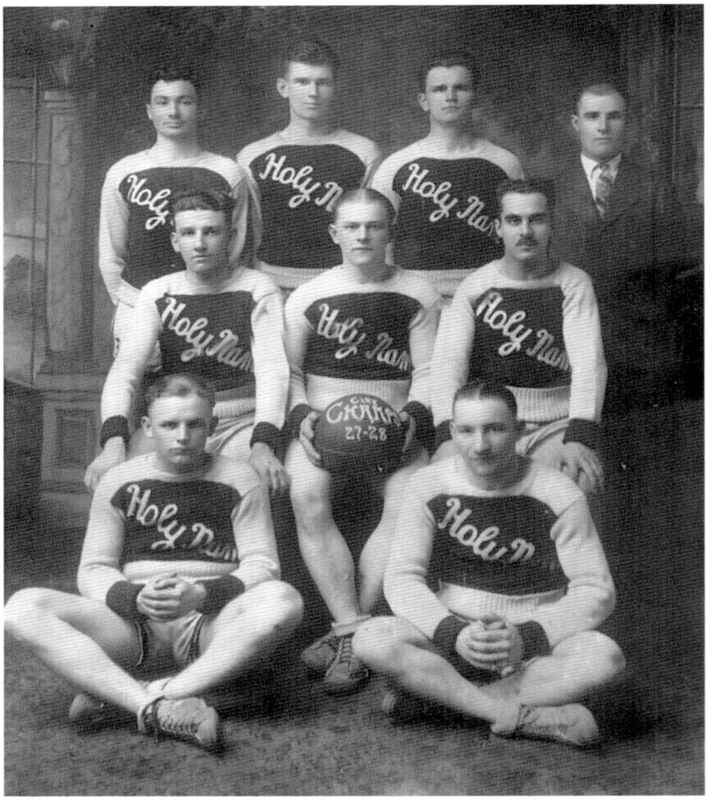

Holy Name Athletic Club Basketball Team, 1928. Already a dominant force in Stamford baseball, this Polish Catholic club showed it could play outstanding basketball as well, winning the 1928 city championship.

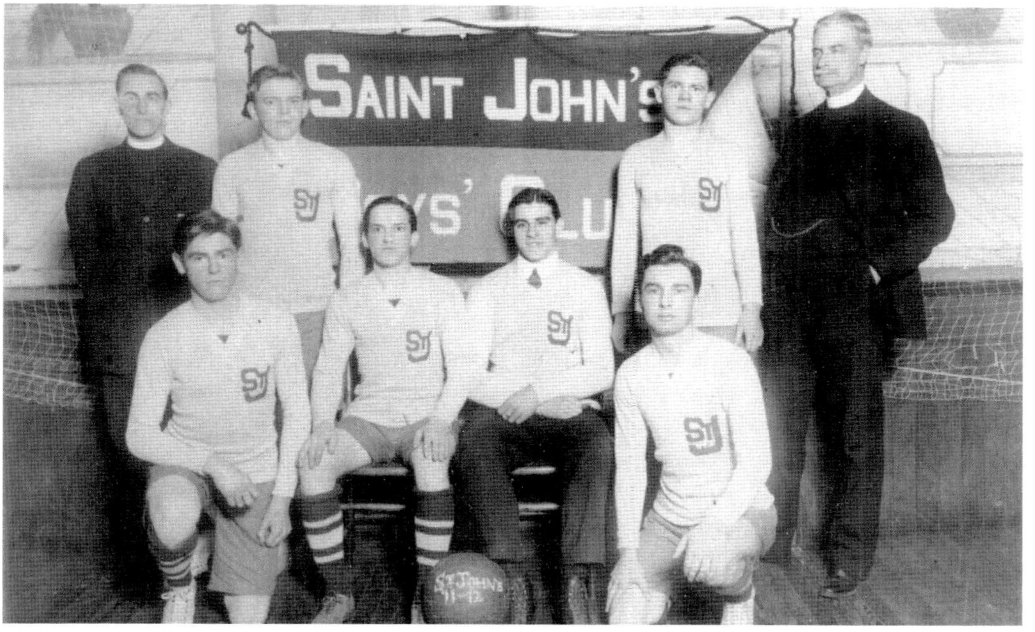

St. John's Boys' Club Basketball Team, 1911–1912. Basketball became a popular choice for smaller schools and organizations that did not have the field space or the large talent pool required for football and baseball.

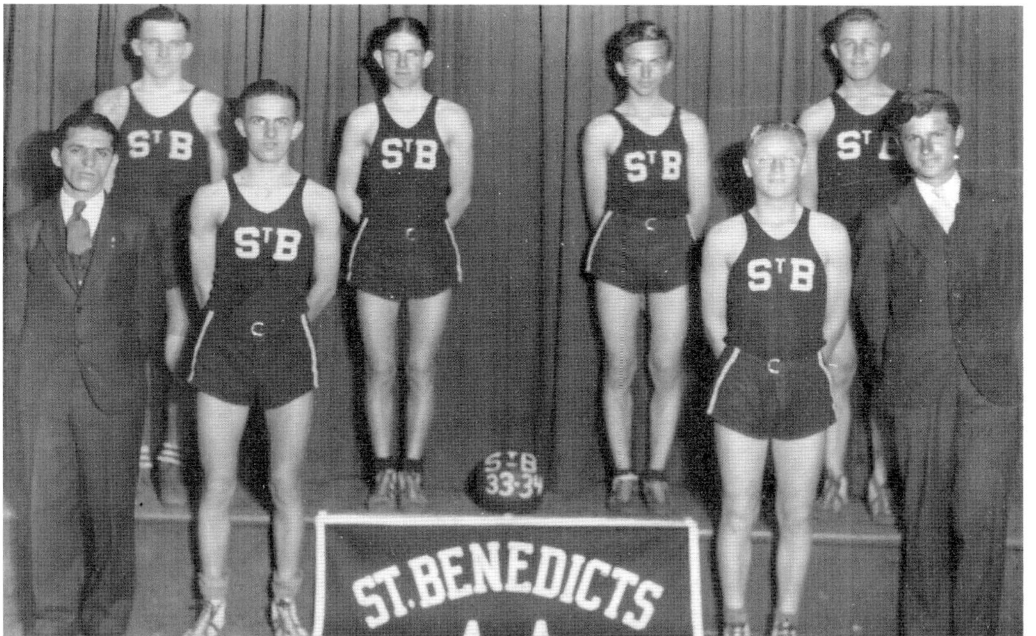

St. Benedicts Athletic Association Basketball Team, 1933–1934. St. Benedicts was formed by Stamford's Slovak community in the Cove section of the city.

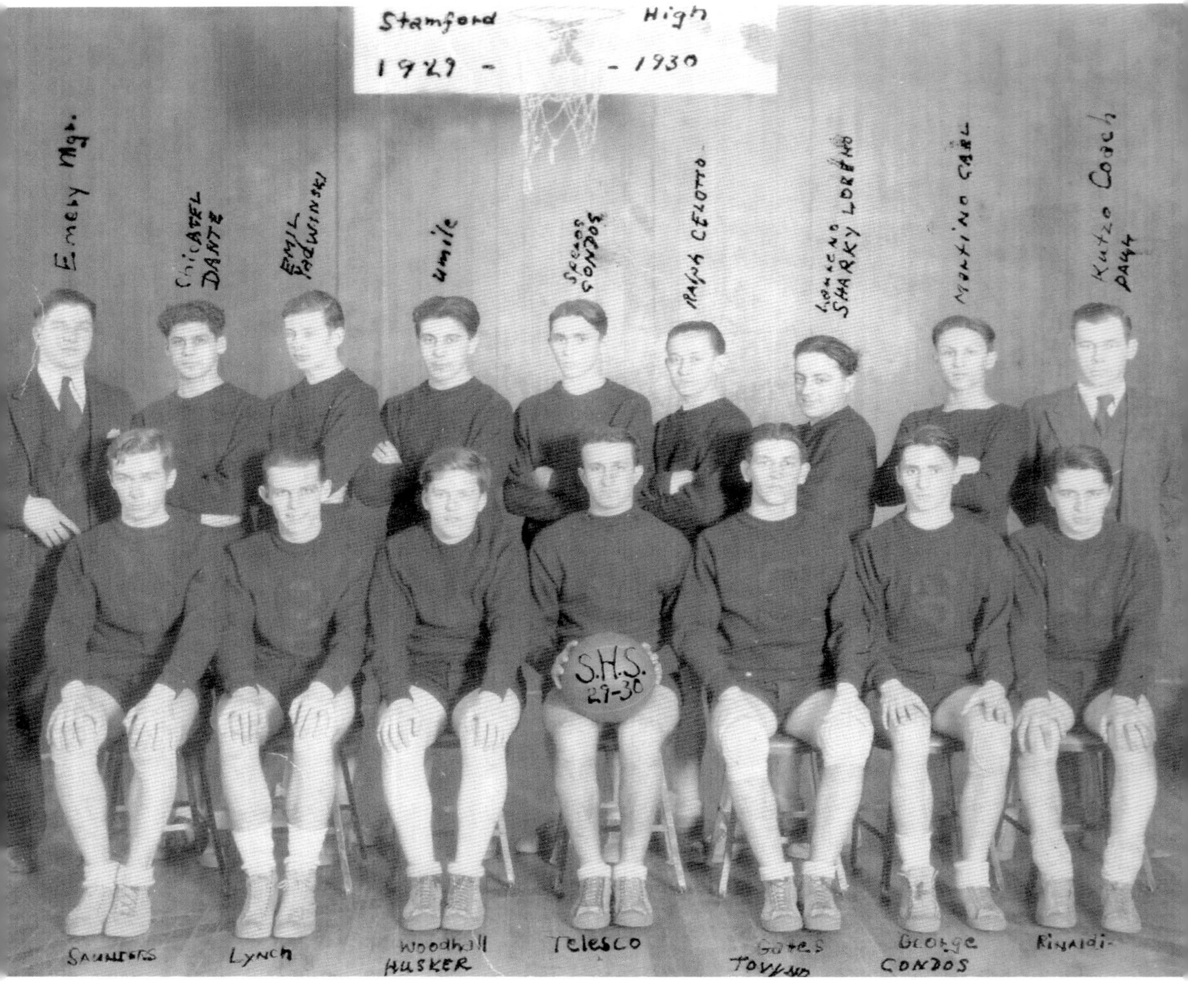

STAMFORD HIGH SCHOOL BASKETBALL TEAM, 1929–1930. This was one of coach Paul Kuczo's first teams at Stamford High. The players are identified, from left to right, as (first row) Saunders, Lynch, Woodhall, Telesco, Gates, Condos, and Rinaldi; (second row) Emery, Chicatell, Yadinski, Umile, Condos, Celotto, Loreho, Martino, and coach Paul Kuczo.

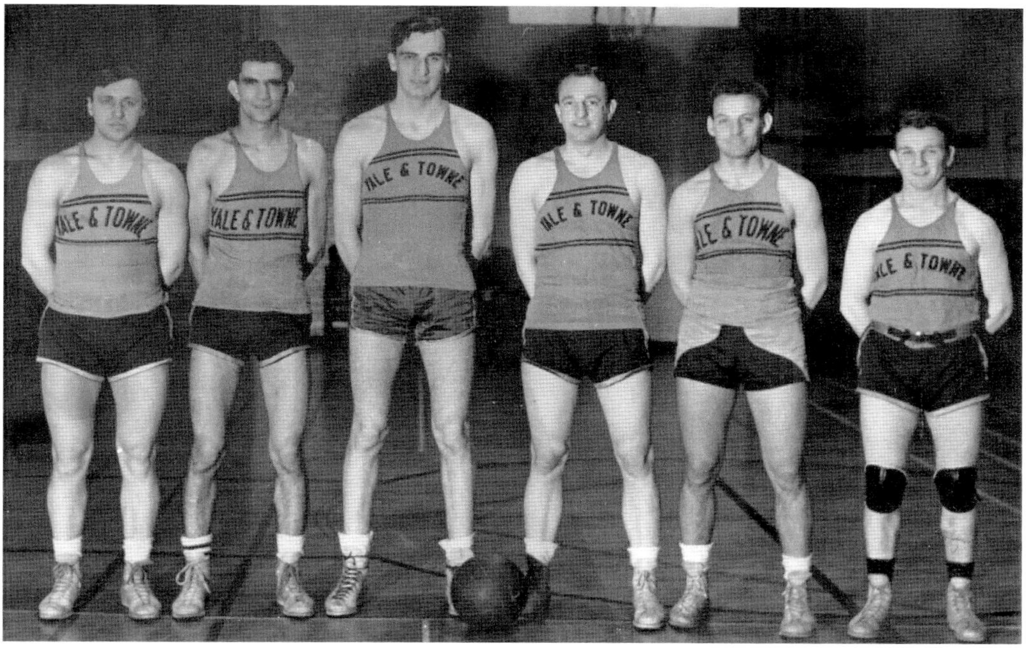

YALE & TOWNE BASKETBALL TEAM, 1937–1938. This team included, from left to right, Pete Merenski, Nick Koules, Truman Smith, Skeets Fitzpatrick, Bucky Celotto, and Steve Richart. Celotto went on to play for Villanova, where he played until the outbreak of World War II.

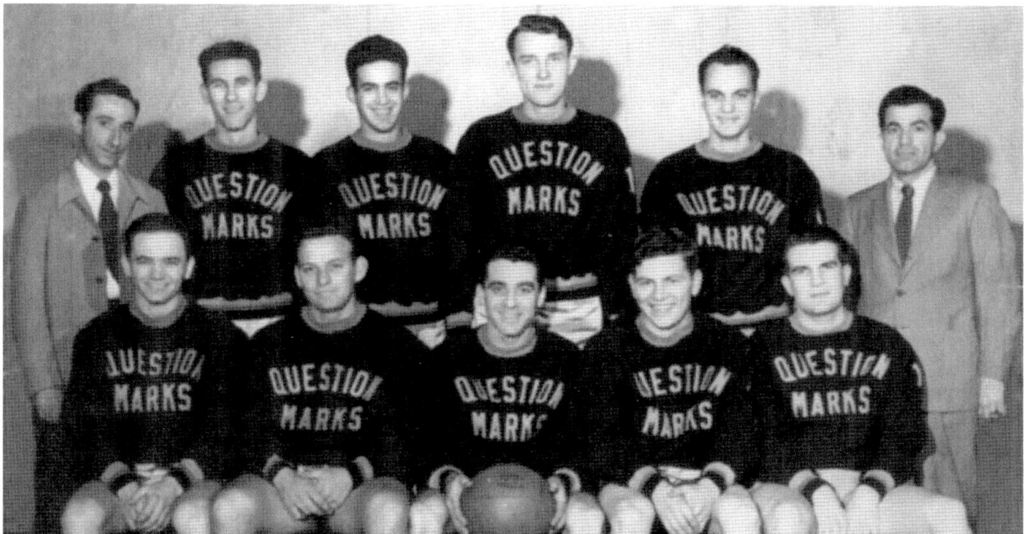

THE QUESTION MARKS. The Question Marks may be the exception to the rule that Stamford crowds only came out for football and baseball games. This league team from the YMCA drew capacity crowds to its games and faced off in interleague play against other big teams from the greater New York City area. In 1953, Andy Robustelli, already playing for the Los Angeles Rams, played with the Question Marks in a March of Dimes fundraising game.

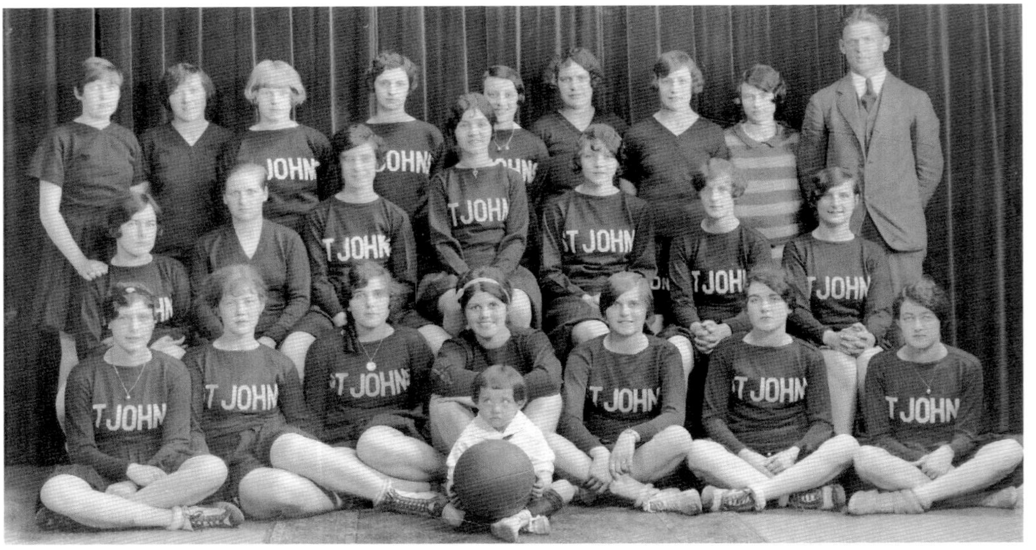

ST. JOHN'S GIRLS' BASKETBALL TEAM, C. 1925. The St. John's Catholic Youth Organization (CYO) sponsored a number of sports, including football, boxing, and basketball. The little girl holding the ball in the front center is Katherine Celotto, who was probably coerced into the photograph by her sister Florence, who is in the third row, fifth from the left.

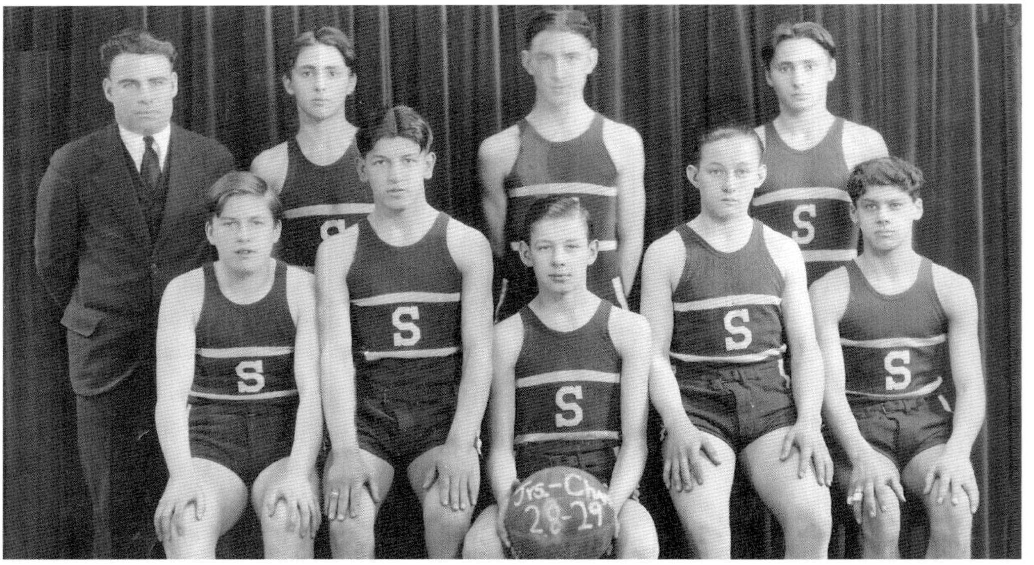

STAMFORD HIGH JUNIORS BASKETBALL TEAM, 1929. In the 1920s, five Stamford boys, George Condos, Spiros Condos, Paul Viola, Dante Chicatell, and Ralph Celotto, became members of the Sterling Boys Club. Many years later, a writer from the *Stamford Advocate* referred to them as a "League of Nations team." The boys played basketball, baseball, and football together through high school and remained close friends for life. From left to right are (first row) Walt Woodhall, Gates Tovino, Emil Yadwinski, Ralph Celotto, and Dante Chicatell; (second row) coach Edward Hunt, Spiros Condos, Paul Viola, and George Condos.

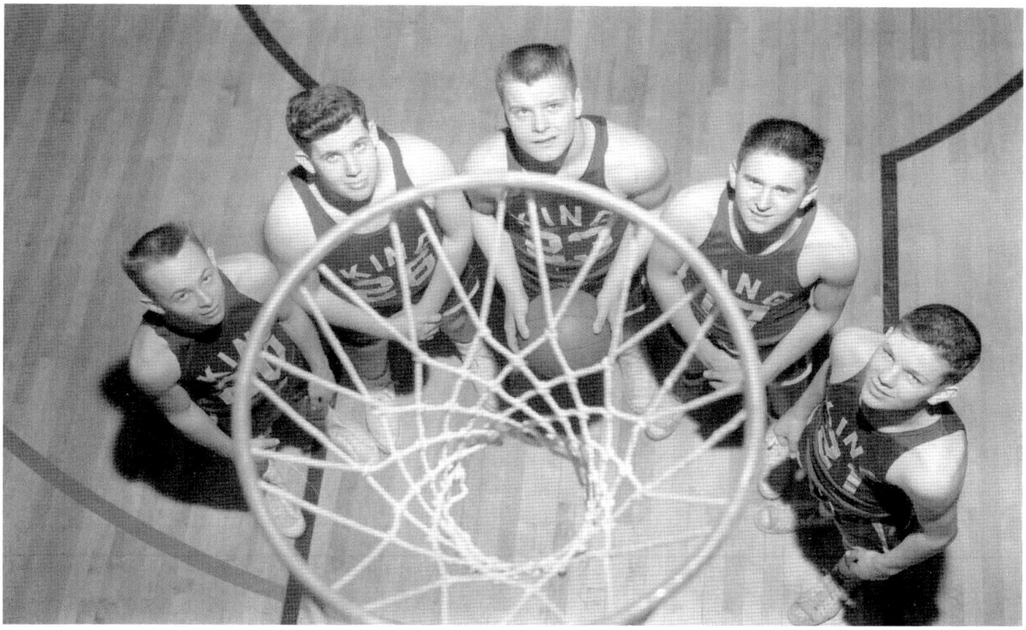

King School Basketball Team, 1956. The Kingsman had a mediocre year in 1956, with a record of six wins and eight losses. This was attributed to their inability to gain scoring momentum early in the game. The starting lineup, seen above from left to right, included Clark Varnum, Abbot Schwebel, Ron Sebra, Fred Willis, and Jack Chesney. Willis went on to write a sports column for the *Stamford Advocate* and later became the head of the sports department at the newspaper.

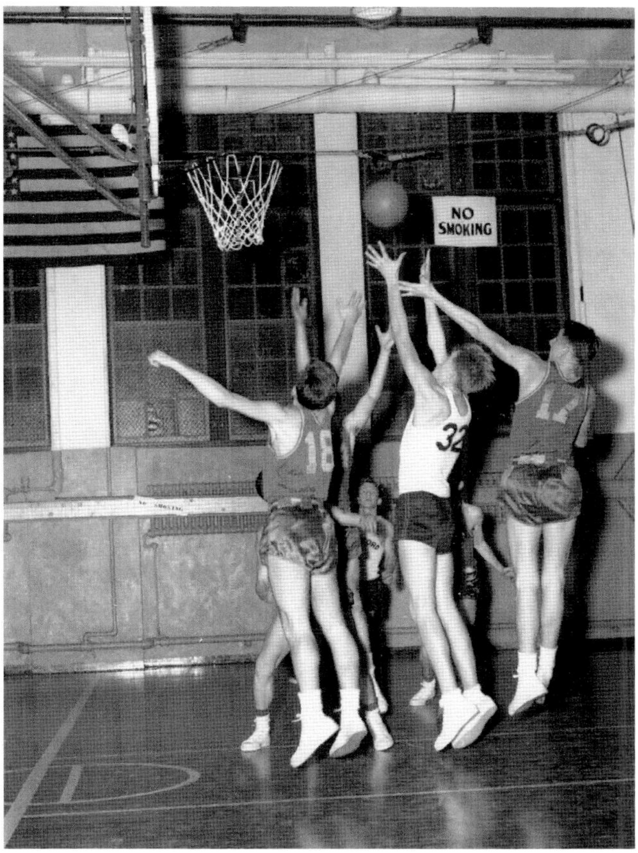

Stamford High School Basketball Game, 1948. A Stamford High player (in white jersey) fights for a rebound during a 1948 contest.

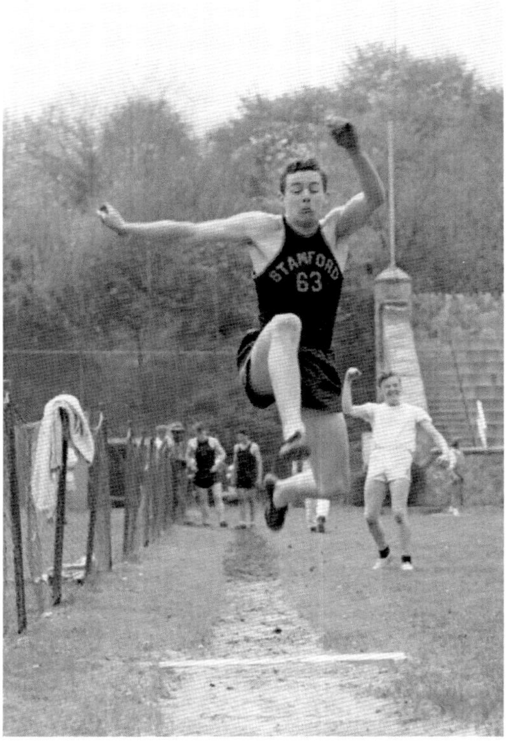

LONG JUMPER, STAMFORD HIGH SCHOOL TRACK MEET, 1948. Although not championship caliber, the 1948 track team was competitive, placing fourth in the Fairfield County meet. Track was just getting restarted at Stamford High in the late 1940s after many interscholastic sports were suspended during World War II due to tight school budgets.

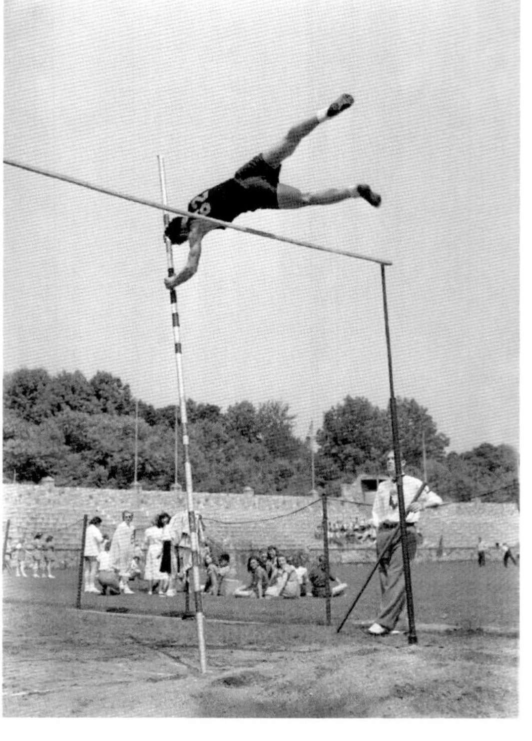

POLE-VAULTER, STAMFORD HIGH SCHOOL TRACK MEET, 1948. Although it is difficult to nail down for certain based on the yearbook, the pole-vaulter seen here is probably William Raymond.

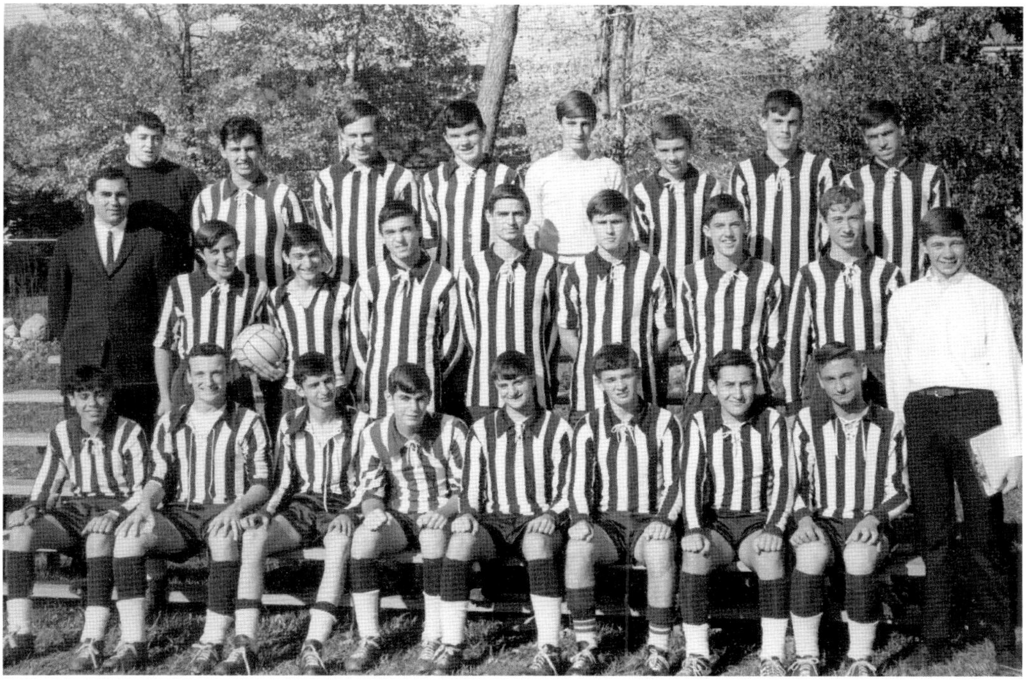

RIPPOWAM HIGH SCHOOL SOCCER TEAM, 1966. Soccer began getting real traction in the late 1960s, and both Stamford and Rippowam High Schools had large and successful teams. The members of the 1966 Rippowam squad (above) are identified as, from left to right, (first row) Sette, Tempone, Castigilio, Lucia, Wirth, Ginn, Mallozzi, Elkies, and Healy; (second row) Webski, Gaurino, Sabia, Nelson, Maruzak, Beszczak, Palmer, and Moffat; (third row) Tozzoi, Sibilia, Caminiti, Chrimbes, Calandrelli, Quigley, Stephenson, and Giamba.

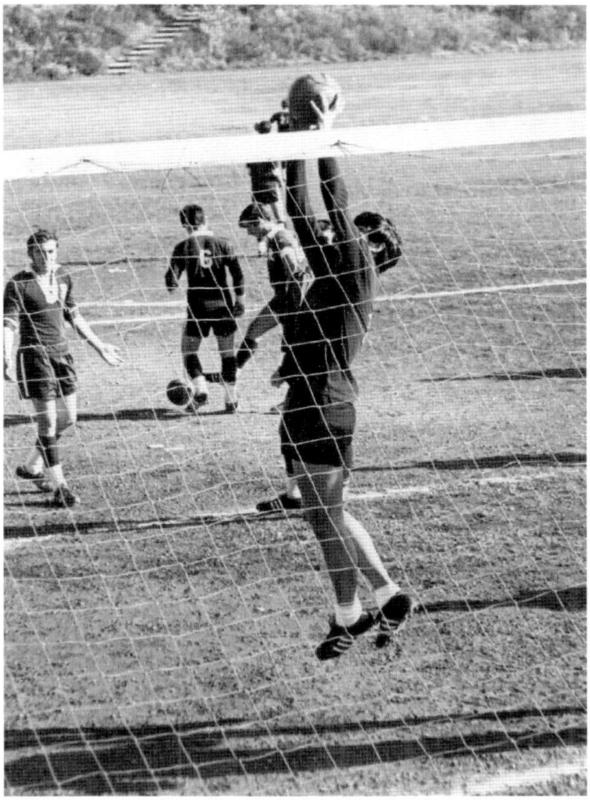

RIPPOWAM HIGH SCHOOL SOCCER GOALIE, 1970. Angelo Mallozzi, seen here snatching the ball to prevent a goal, was the goalkeeper for the 1970 team, which went 6-4-1 and was ranked 16th in the state.

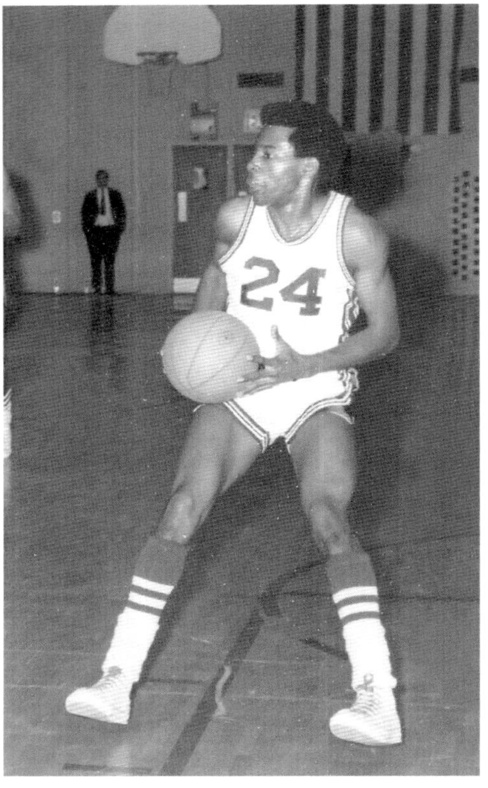

Rippowam High School Basketball Game, 1969. Nick Wright handles the ball during a game against Brien McMahon High School of Norwalk. Wright was the most valuable player of the Fairfield County Interscholastic Athletic Conference (FCIAC). In this game, the Warriors went down to the Senators in a close 49-46 loss.

Rippowam High School Boys' Gymnastics Team, 1969. The late 1960s and early 1970s saw a great expansion of the types of sports available to high school students. Along with wrestling, Rippowam offered football, basketball, wrestling, gymnastics (below), cross-country, soccer, tennis, volleyball, weightlifting, golf, softball, track, field hockey, swimming, and baseball.

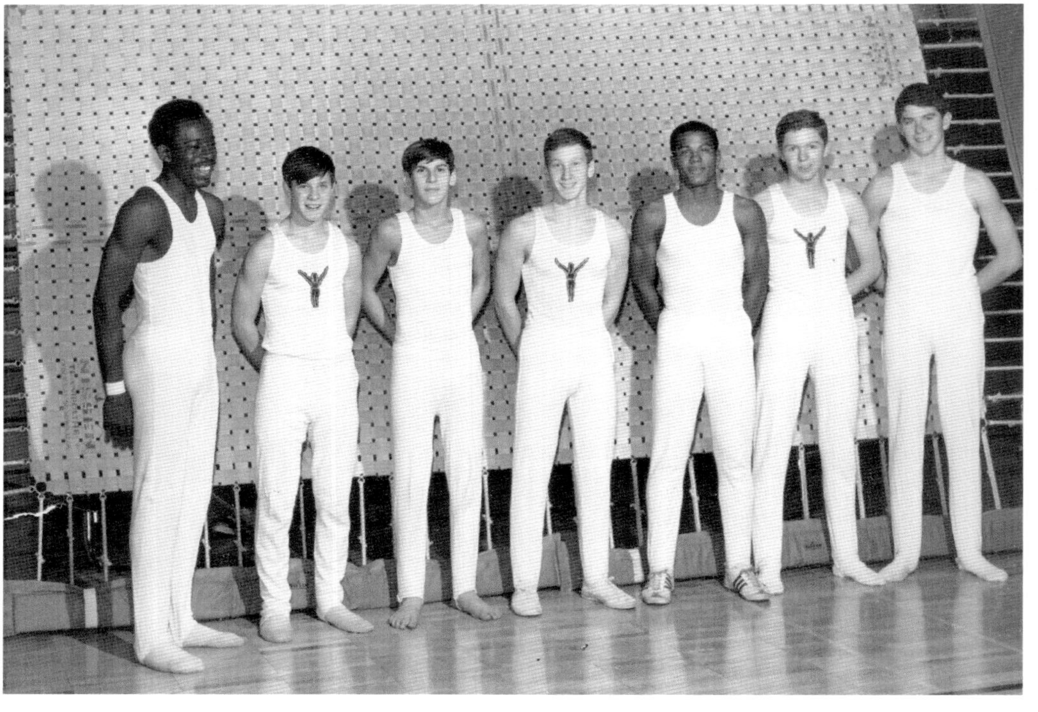

7

WOMEN PLAY BALL

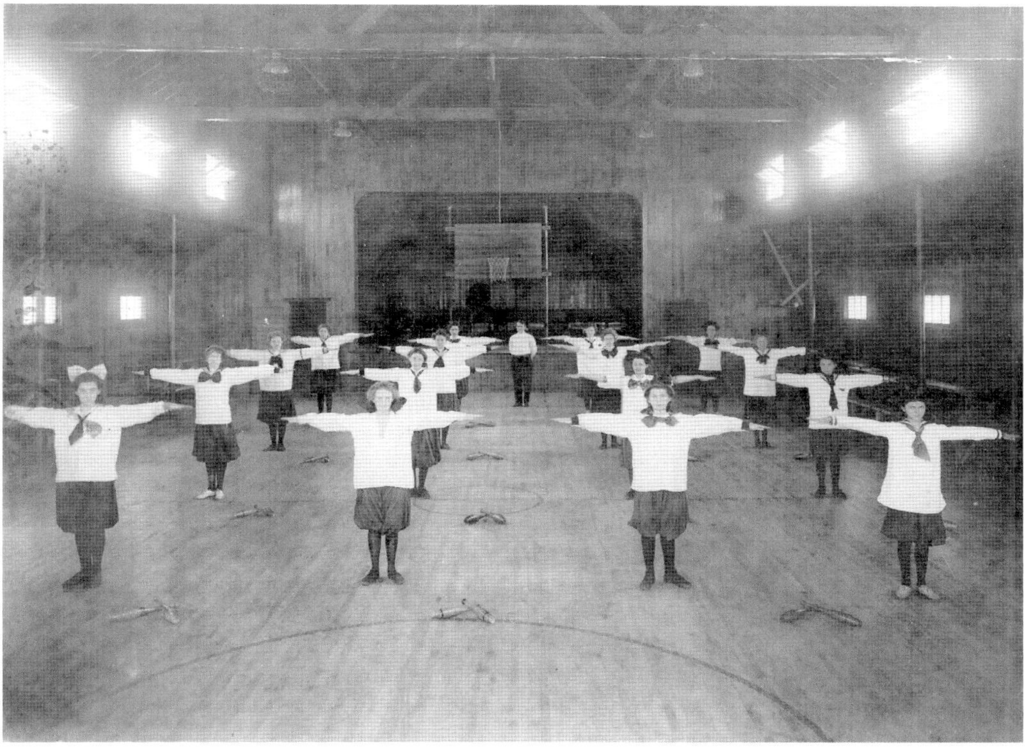

GLENBROOK SCHOOL GIRLS' GYM CLASS. In the late 1800s, when our photographic journey began, scientists and educators were divided about the role of athletics in the lives and education of girls and women. The predominant thinking was that strenuous physical activity could cause permanent harm in women, depleting them of their limited energy reserves and impairing their ability to bear and raise children. Their opponents were primarily educators at women's colleges such as Smith and Vassar, who held that moderate physical activity contributed to the health and beauty of women. In 1885, the Association of Collegiate Alumnae refuted the prevailing notion with a study concluding that "female [college] graduates . . . do not seem to show . . . any marked difference in general health for the average health . . . of women engaged in other kinds of work, or in fact, of women generally." Around 1900, a physical education program was implemented in most schools, with the requisite clothing being the bloomers, tights, and voluminous blouses seen in this photograph.

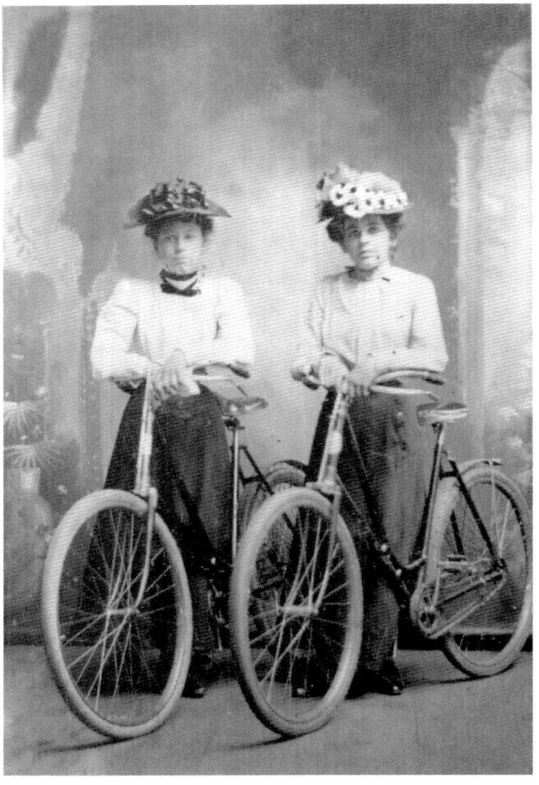

CYCLISTS, UNDATED TINTYPE. In 1896, suffragist Susan B. Anthony said, "Bicycling has done more to emancipate women than anything else in the world. I stand and rejoice every time I see a woman ride on a wheel. It gives women a feeling of freedom and self-reliance." Cycling was a popular pastime in Stamford and one of the few that men and women engaged in together.

WOMEN PLAYING CROQUET, C. 1905. Croquet was considered a genteel game and one that women could play without taxing their energy reserves or compromising their femininity. The women below are identified, in no particular order, as Elsie Mc Nil, Mamie Rivers, Grace (Lester) Bliss, and Nettie (Denike) Walker. The women lived in the Long Ridge area of Stamford.

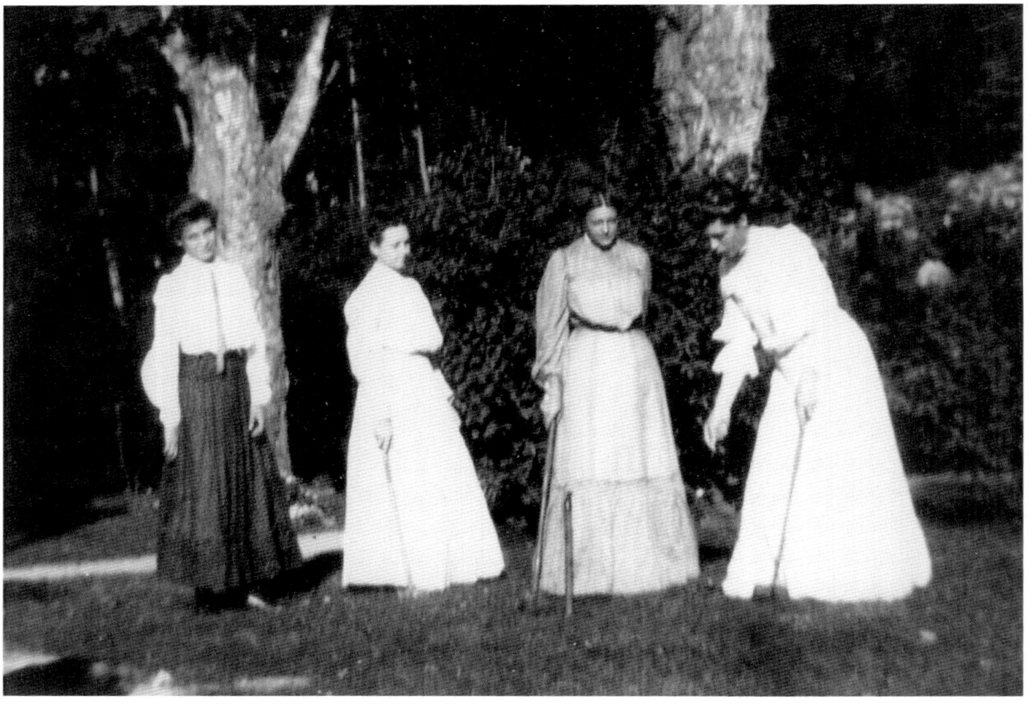

READY FOR THE TOURNAMENT

The Athletic Girl Goes to the Tennis Court Dressed Smartly Yet Inexpensively.

The athletic girl is just now divided between tennis and golf in the way of amusements; and between plain and trimmed costumes on the lines of fashion. The latter subject will worry her for some time to come, for there is a wide difference of opinion.

However natty the untrimmed designs may be, it is certain that the trimmed tennis costumes have an effect that is

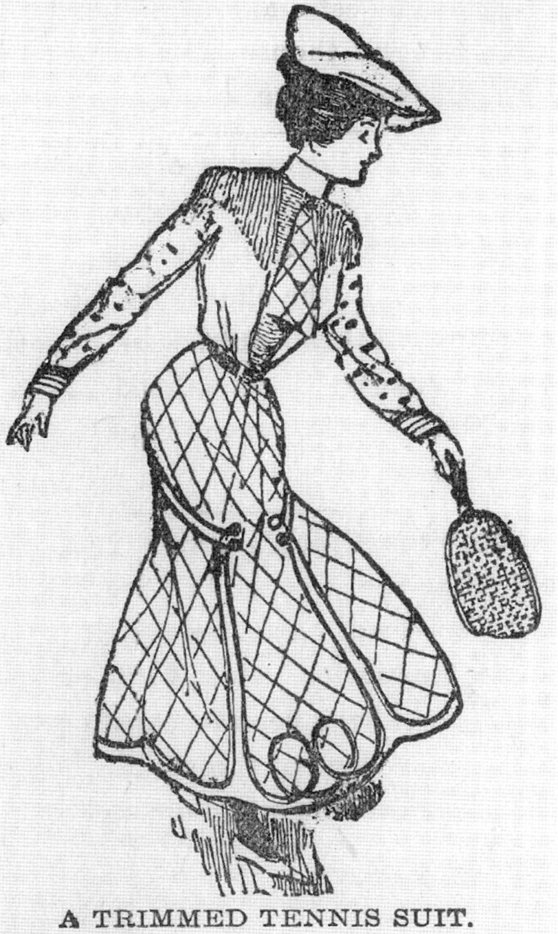

A TRIMMED TENNIS SUIT.

TENNIS FASHION ADVERTISEMENT, 1899. This advertisement from the *Stamford Telegram* puts the emphasis on the outfits and fashion elements of tennis, as opposed to the sport itself. The design in fact restricts movement and breathing to a degree that would make it exceedingly difficult to have an "athletic" match of tennis wearing it. Note that in addition to cycling, croquet, and tennis, golf was considered a game suitable for women at the time.

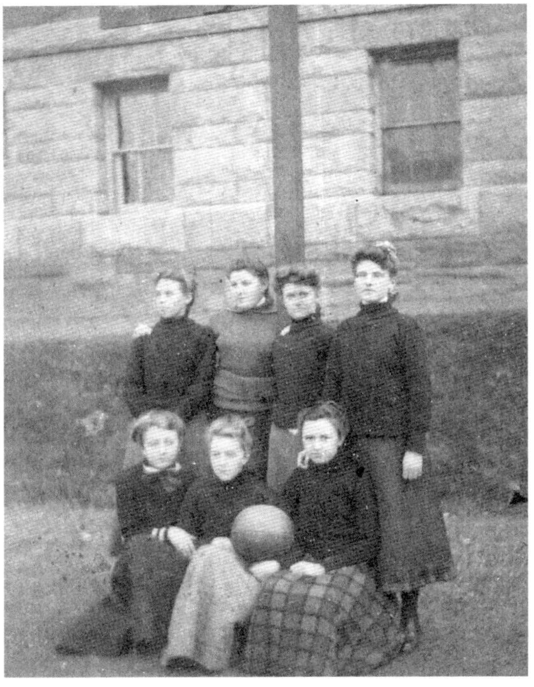

STAMFORD HIGH SCHOOL GIRLS' BASKETBALL TEAM, 1902. Stamford High School's first graduating class in 1881 was comprised of four young women. It fielded its first girls' basketball team in 1902, only three years behind the fielding of its first boys' athletic teams. From left to right are (first row) Edith White, Helen McDonald, and Lydia Mollet; (second row) Ethel Warner, Margaret Darlina, Jennie Boyd, and Josephine Hickey.

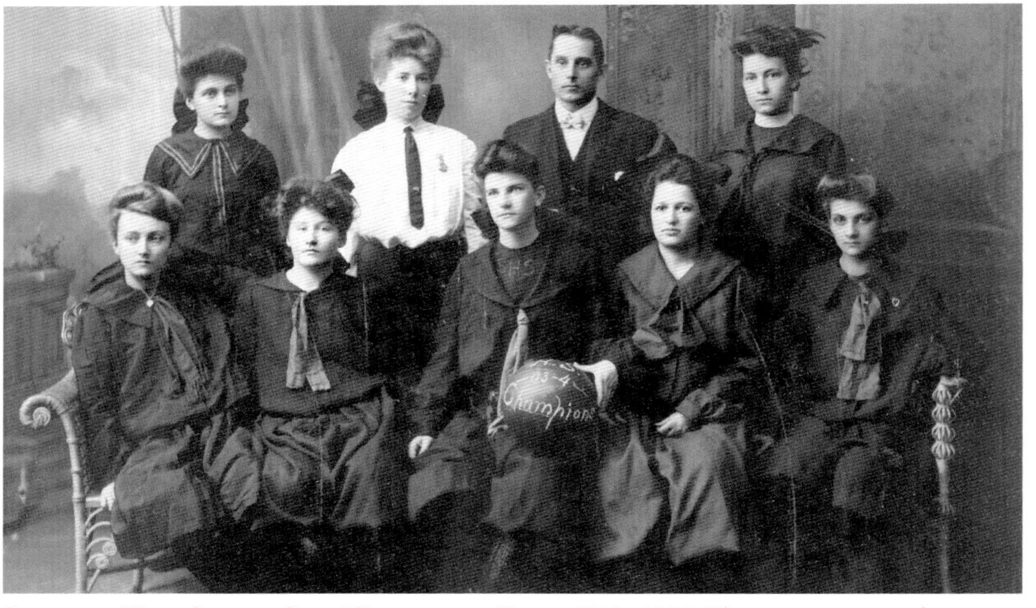

STAMFORD HIGH SCHOOL GIRLS' BASKETBALL TEAM, 1903–1904. This team was state champions in one of the few years before 1946 that Stamford High fielded a girls' varsity basketball team. The girls in the first row were the starters, while the girls on each end of the second row are labeled "reg." The team included, from left to right, (first row) Edith White, forward; Rose McGowan, guard; Cyd Hart, center; Helen Tobin, guard; and Emma "Babe" Banisch, forward; (second row) unidentified, Ida Stark, E. Peckham, and Harriet Church.

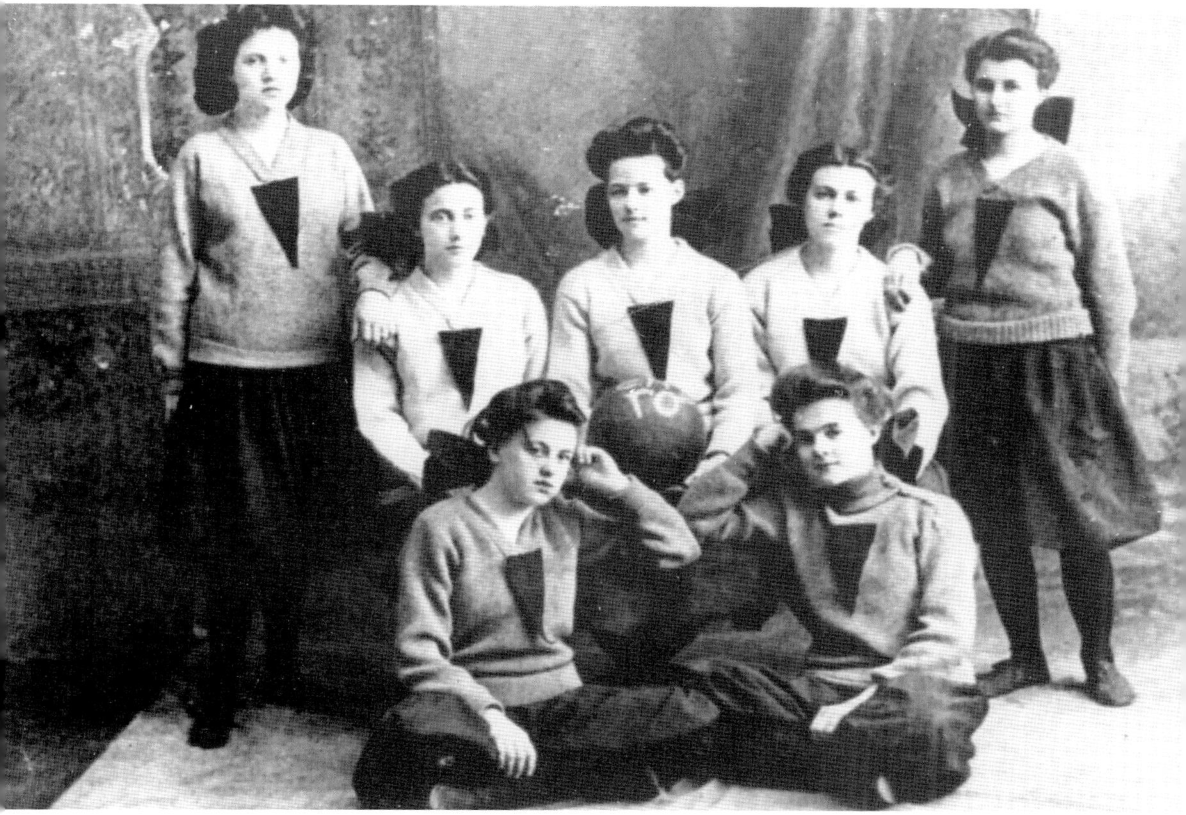

STAMFORD HIGH SCHOOL GIRLS' BASKETBALL TEAM, 1906–1907. Girls' basketball was a very on again/off again phenomenon at Stamford High from its first team in 1902 through the 1940s. While the 1903, 1904, 1905, and 1907 teams played full schedules, the 1906 team played only one other team, the Alphas. After that, there is no record of a girls' team between 1908 and 1915. Play resumed in 1915, but again play was spotty: some seasons included only three or four games, while other years there were 10 to 12. In 1925, the school announced the end of varsity girls' basketball, but it was reinstated in 1928. In 1929, there was a varsity team, but it was only allowed to play on its home court. In 1930, the varsity team was again suspended, and varsity play did not resume until 1947. In contrast, at least two of the private girls' schools in Stamford, the Paxton School and Low-Heywood, consistently sponsored girls' teams for interscholastic play.

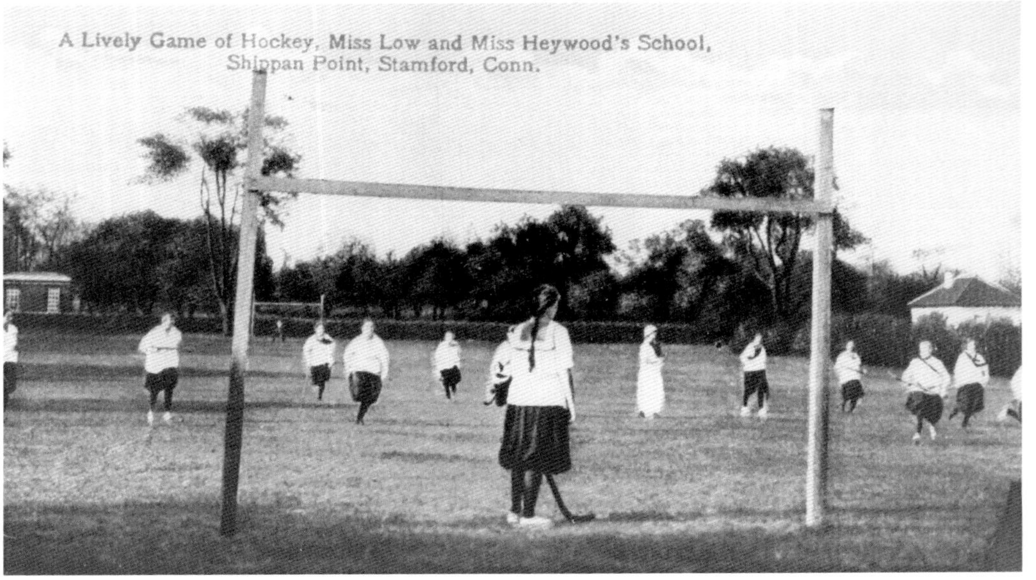

LOW-HEYWOOD SCHOOL HOCKEY GAME, C. 1915. Field hockey was introduced to America by English physical educator Constance M.K. Applebee at a 1901 seminar at Harvard. It was soon adopted as an acceptable sport for girls and women across the United States. In Stamford, the sport was quickly adopted by a number of girls' schools, including Low-Heywood, Willard, and Paxton. The Low-Heywood School showed a particular avidity for sports: throughout the 1920s, their yearbooks included not only season records but a blow-by-blow description of their basketball games. These were included as part of a "Diary of a Low-Heywood Girl." Here is a sample: "Some startling talent was discovered when Ruth Mallory changed from guard to forward, making many spectacular baskets in her new position."

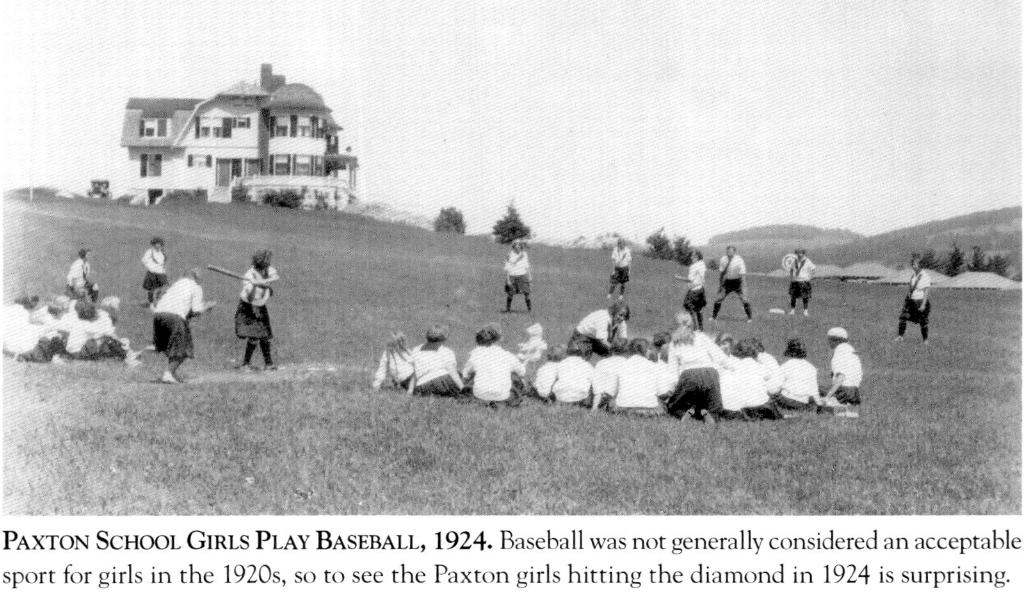

PAXTON SCHOOL GIRLS PLAY BASEBALL, 1924. Baseball was not generally considered an acceptable sport for girls in the 1920s, so to see the Paxton girls hitting the diamond in 1924 is surprising.

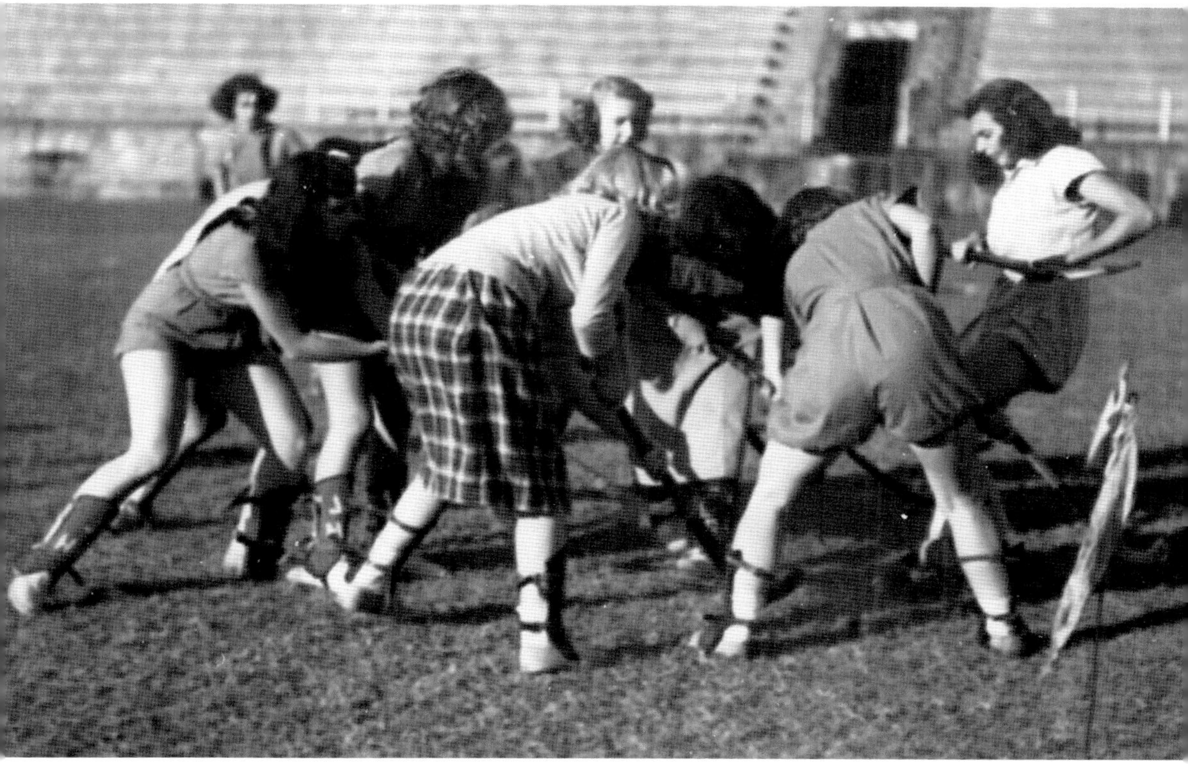

STAMFORD HIGH FIELD HOCKEY, 1948. Players scramble for the ball during a 1948 field hockey game. From the mid-1930s through the mid-1940s, there were no varsity sports for girls at Stamford High School. Intramural sports were offered, but were restricted to indoor games such badminton, volleyball, basketball, shuffleboard, and duckpin bowling. While all sports for boys and girls were curtailed during World War II for budgetary reasons, the war also sparked increased interest in girls' participation in sports as women entered the workforce in large numbers. Varsity teams for girls were finally reestablished in 1947 for basketball and field hockey, which were soon followed by volleyball, softball, and in some years, badminton.

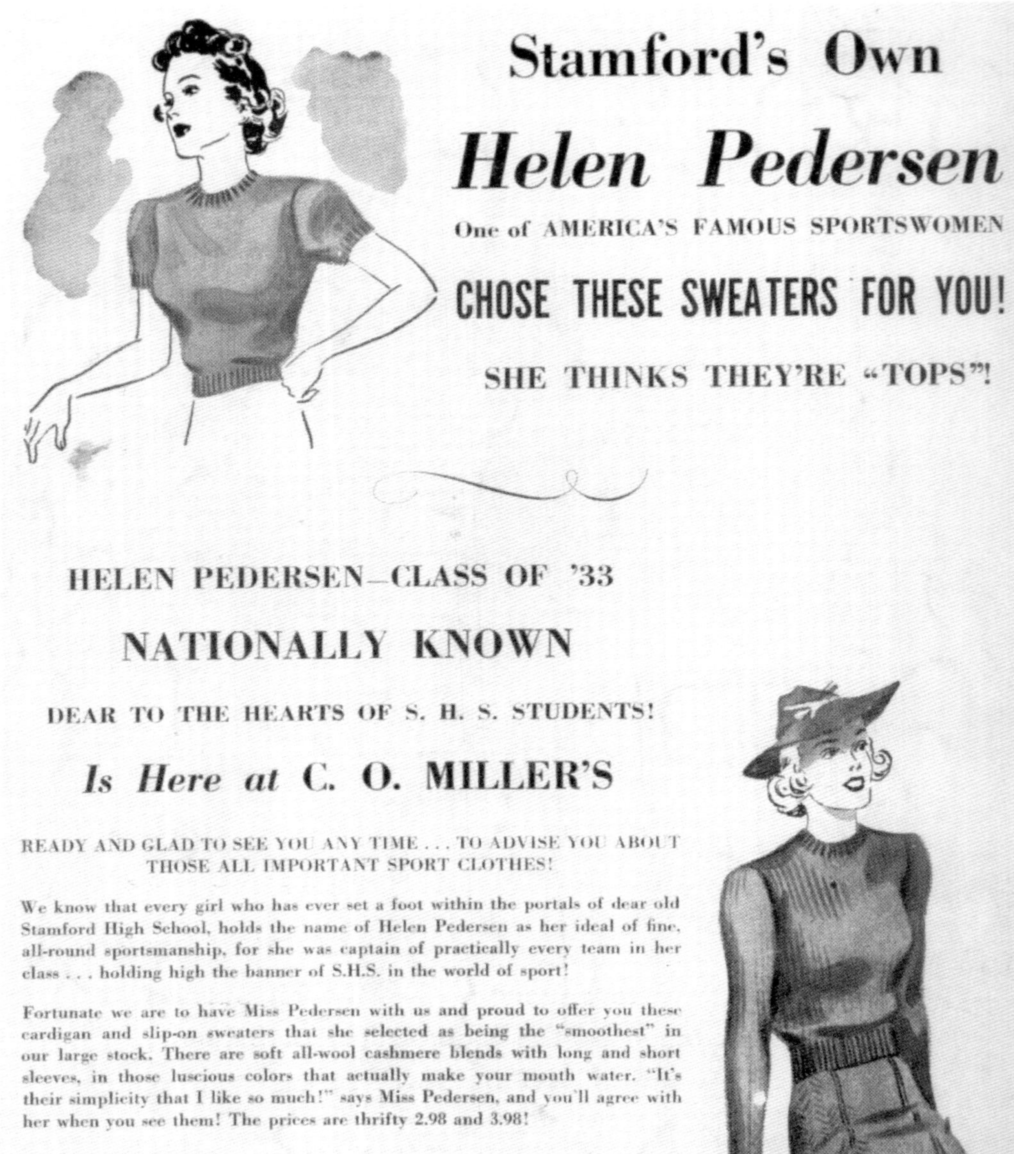

HELEN PEDERSEN IN C.O. MILLER CO. ADVERTISEMENT, 1938. Helen Pedersen was an international tennis champion who played at Wimbledon, the French Open, and the US Open. The advertisement above for C.O. Miller Co., a local department store, mentions her as a standout high school athlete but omits mention of her current professional status. The advertisement is from the back cover of the 1938 Stamford High School vs. Central High School football game program.

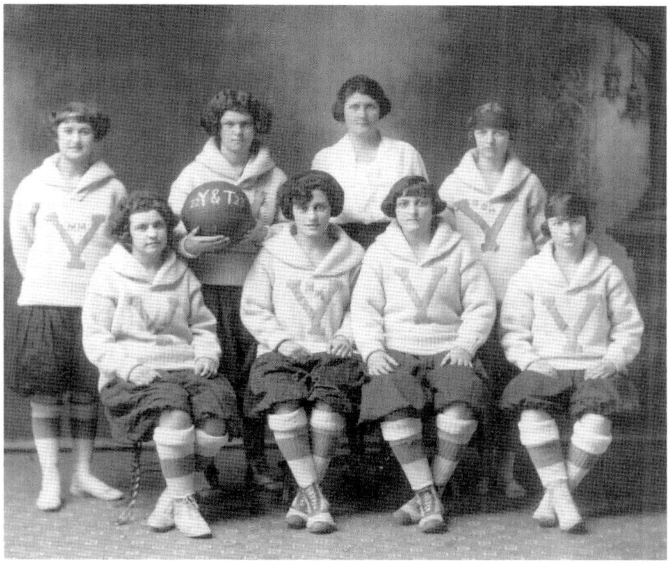

YALE & TOWNE WOMEN'S BASKETBALL TEAM, 1922–1923. Yale & Towne sponsored several women's sports teams throughout the 1900s, including bowling, volleyball, and basketball. According to a 1940 article in the company's newsletter, the *Yale Panel*, the women had to lobby for gym time, which they were granted on Friday nights. The article included suggestions for recreation "well suited to women," such as badminton and volleyball.

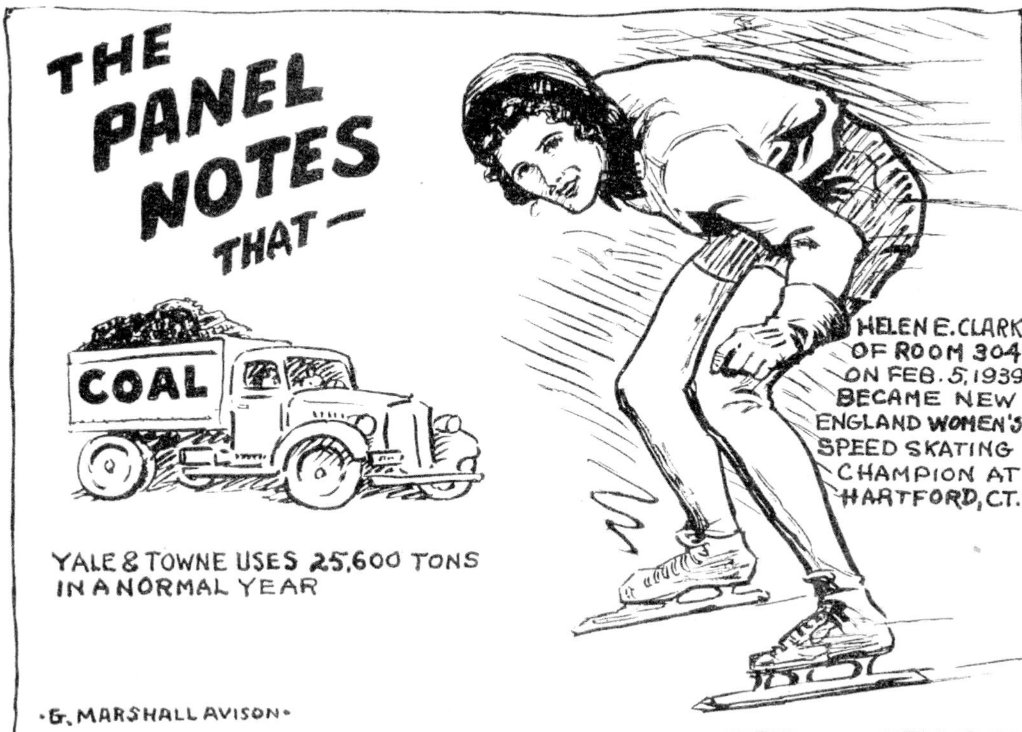

YALE *PANEL* SKETCH OF HELEN E. CLARK, 1938. Yale & Towne had a positive influence on women's participation in sports in many ways. Many women worked alongside men at Yale & Towne, and the company sponsored a number of women's sports teams in addition to its many men's teams. The *Yale Panel*, the company newsletter, often included a feature highlighting one of its employees; here, it features Helen E. Clark, a New England champion speed skater.

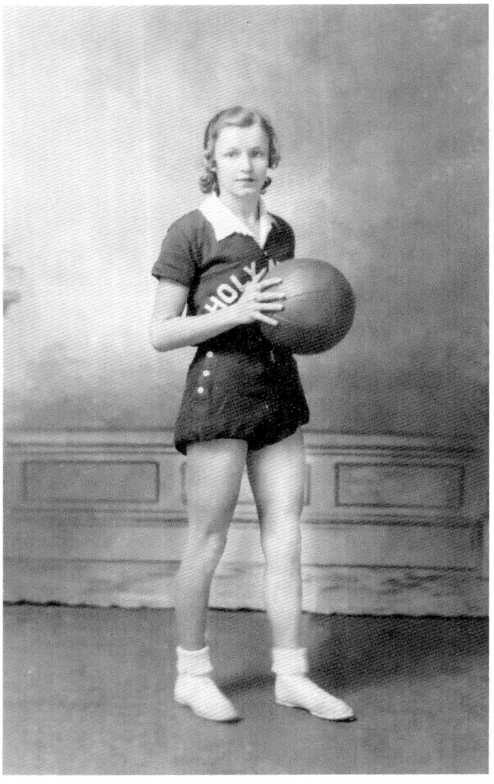

Holy Name Girls' Basketball Player, c. 1945. By the 1940s, women's athletic dress had changed dramatically. The gym outfit, or "middy," evolved from long, baggy shorts or bloomers and voluminous tops to one- or two-piece shorts and a top, with an elastic drawstring around the middle. Also gone are the dark wool tights and long sleeves that ensured no skin was visible. The middy remained the standard gym uniform well into the 1970s, when it was replaced by the standard shorts and tee shirt. Today, women's athletic outfits are designed primarily for performance, and major shifts in uniform design are typically not gender specific.

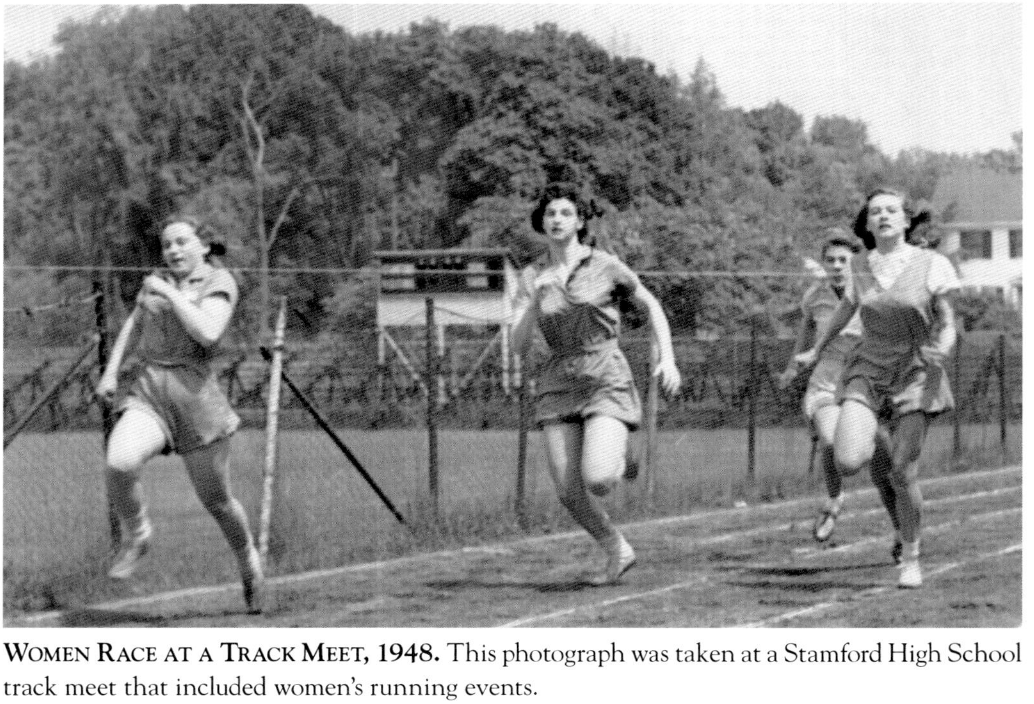

Women Race at a Track Meet, 1948. This photograph was taken at a Stamford High School track meet that included women's running events.

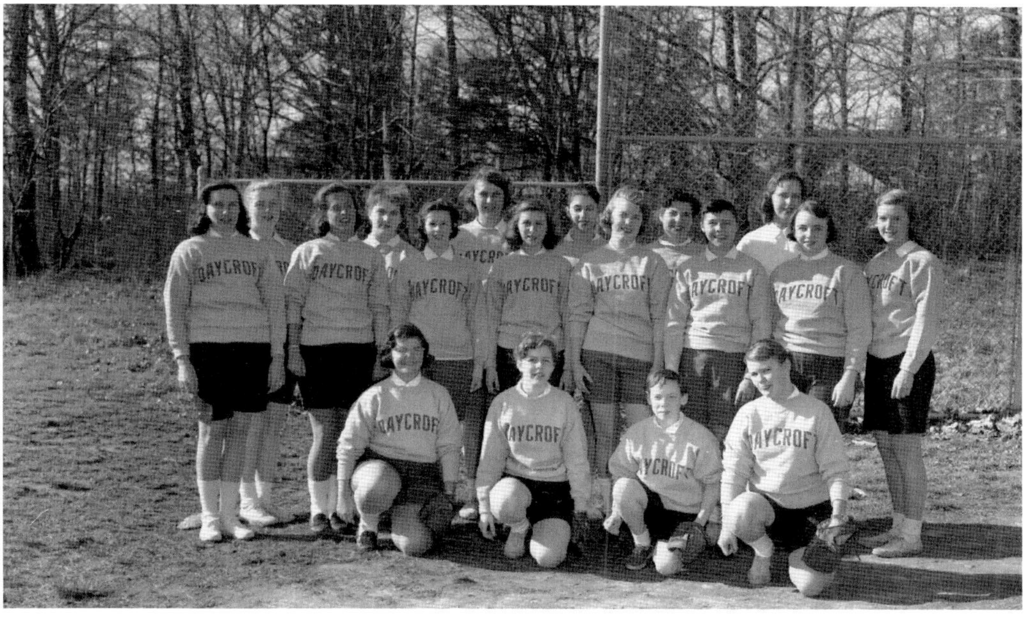

DAYCROFT TENNIS TEAM (ABOVE), C. 1955. By the mid-1900s, sports for girls typically included basketball, softball, and field hockey. Some schools also offered volleyball, tennis, or track. However, competitiveness in women's sports was still frowned upon at both the high school and college levels.

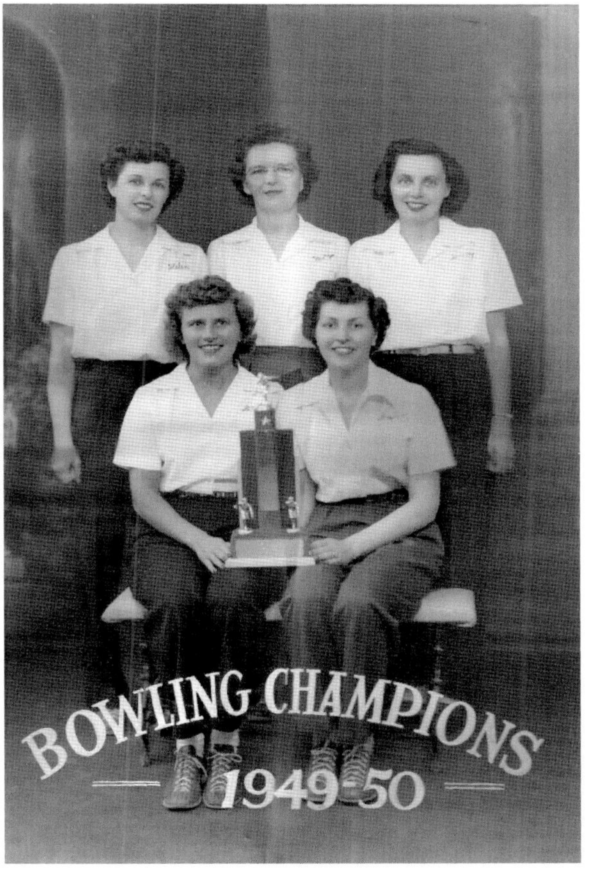

1949–1950 BOWLING CHAMPIONS. Although the name of this bowling team is not provided, the members are identified in no particular order as Helen Glica, Mary Cackowski, Ginny ?, Gladys Rotkiewicz, and Sophie Powajba.

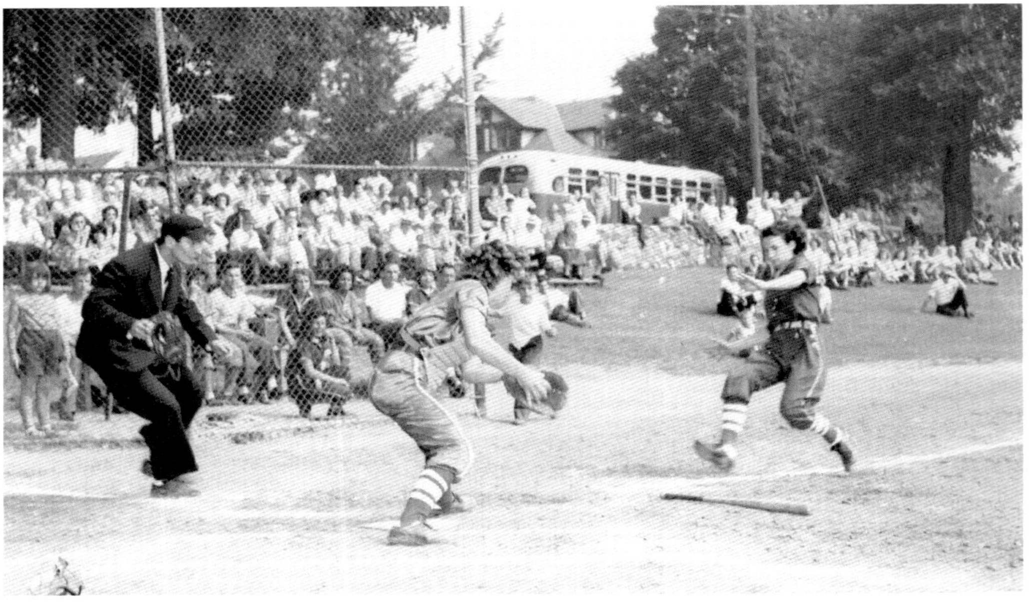

A CLOSE PLAY AT HOME, 1948. The Stamford Nutmegs were a women's professional softball team that played throughout the 1940s and 1950s against teams from Massachusetts, Connecticut, and New York. In this photograph and in many of the shots that follow, note the large crowd turnout for their games. The team, begun in 1939, was especially popular with Stamford crowds in the 1940s.

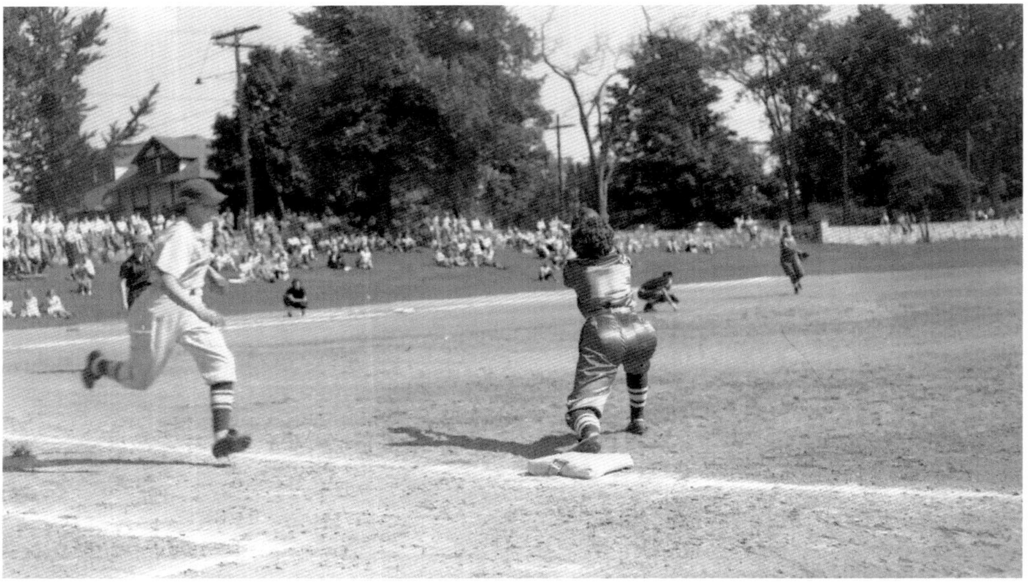

NUTMEGS GAME AT BELLTOWN FIELD, 1948. The Nutmegs continued to play into the early 1950s. When the team closed up shop, some of the players, including Dena Kuczo, Beverly Bowler, and Mary Jane Hagan, went to the Raybestos Brakettes in Stratford, Connecticut. The Brakettes were one of the top softball teams in the country, playing both nationally and internationally.

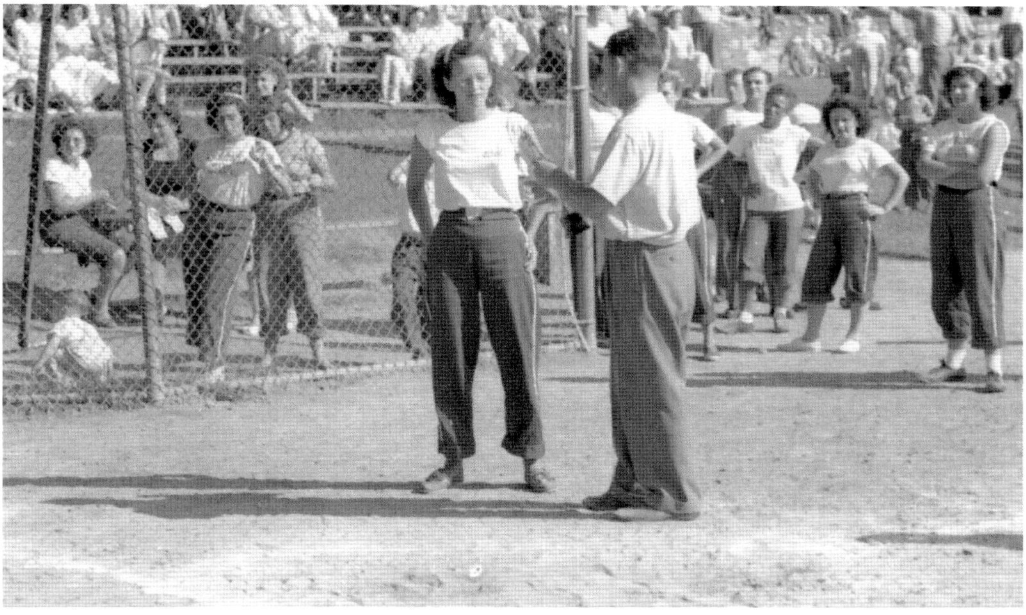

ANSONIA TEAM DISCUSSION, 1948. An Ansonia team member has a plate discussion with a coach while her team members look on. Ansonia was a working-class town that was home to many of Connecticut's iron foundries. The differences in backgrounds between the Ansonia team and the more upscale Nutmegs are evident in both the uniforms and the attitudes—check the players' poses in the background.

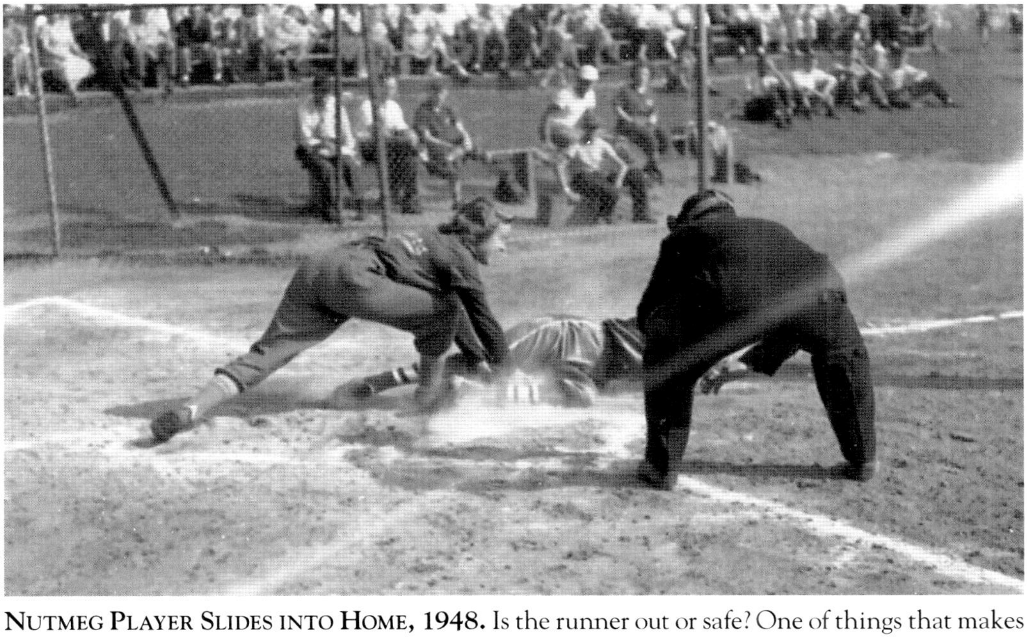

NUTMEG PLAYER SLIDES INTO HOME, 1948. Is the runner out or safe? One of things that makes this a great photograph is that it is not clear—the ball is unseen, the umpire has not signaled, and it is unclear whether the runner is touching the plate.

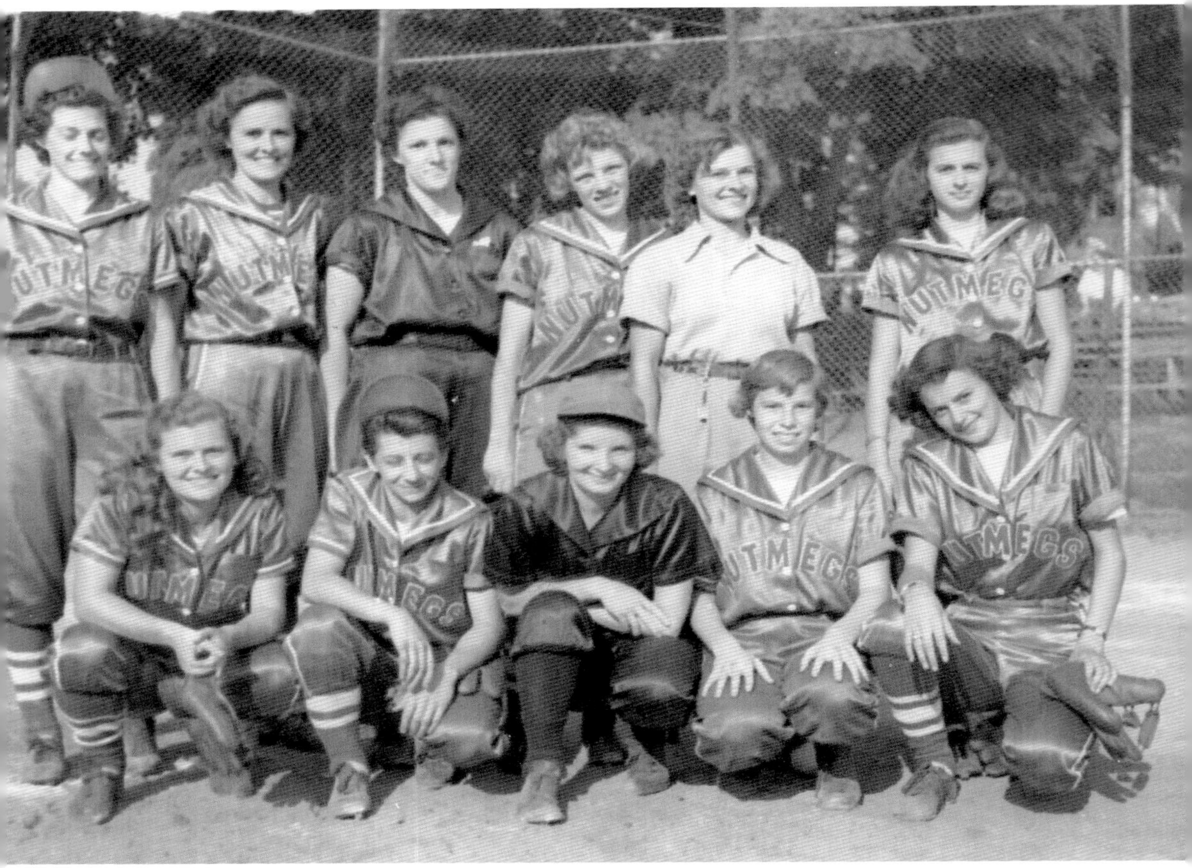

STAMFORD NUTMEGS GROUP PHOTOGRAPH, 1948. The Nutmegs were first known as the Connecticut Nutmegs and later as the Stamford Nutmegs. They won several championships, including three consecutive state and New England championships, in 1941, 1942, and 1943. The women's team drew heavily on the Italian, Polish, and Irish communities of Stamford. In the early 1950s, the Raybestos Brakettes replaced the Nutmegs as the top Fairfield County women's softball team. Martha Rudenfeldt was the Nutmegs' star pitcher and was later inducted into the Softball Hall of Fame. Seen here from left to right are (first row) Toni Uzar, Babe Lasocki (third base), Martha Rudenfeldt (pitcher), Dena Kucszo, and Carol Green; (second row) Irene Romano, Mary Nolan (first base), Doris O'Connell, Ruth Bouton (second base), Stephanie Uzar, and Marie Ottaviano.

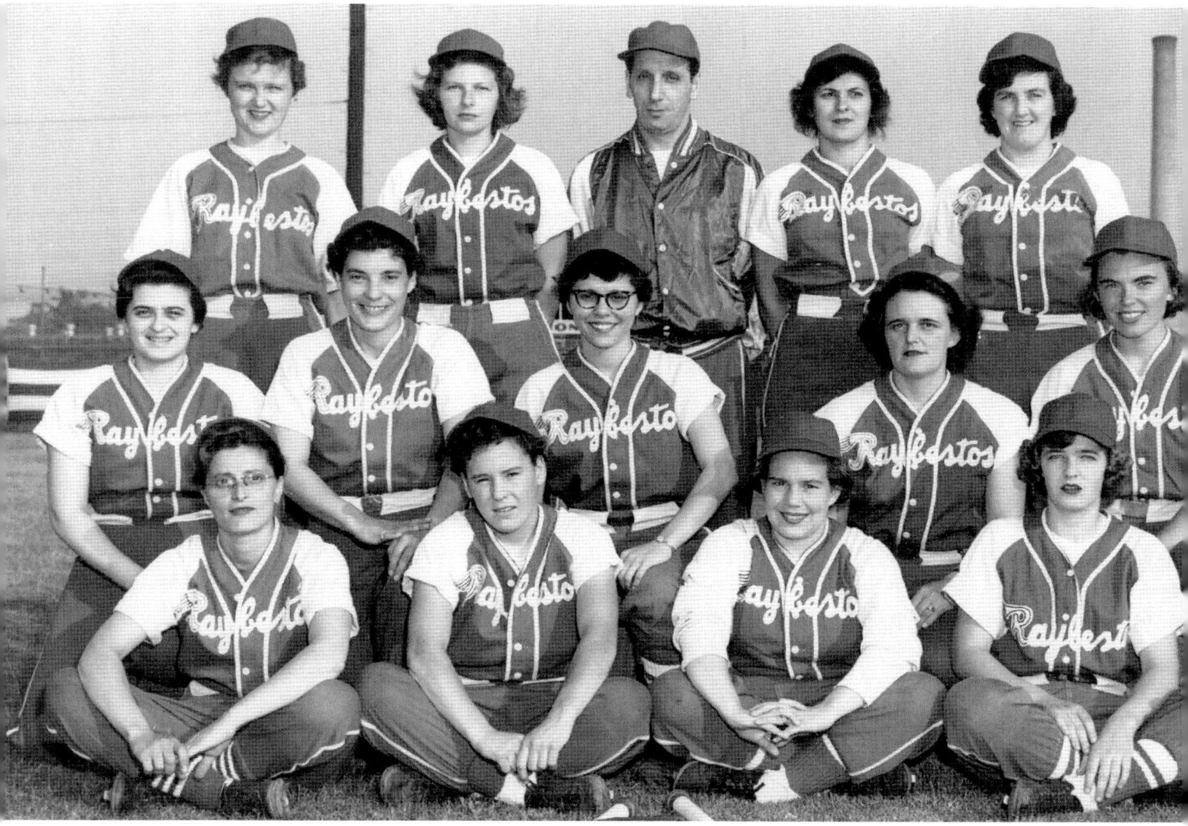

RAYBESTOS BRAKETTES, 1953. When the Nutmegs closed up shop, a number of their top players signed on with the Raybestos Brakettes. The Brakettes were one of the top teams in the country and played around the world. This team included ex-Nutmegs Maria Ottaviano, Mary Jane Hagan, and Dena Kuczo. Interestingly, Kuczo seems to have avoided team photographs—she played with the Brakettes from 1951 to 1953 but does not appear in any of their team pictures. Seen here from left to right are (first row) Tessie Marinelli, Jane Gumkowski, Edna Fraser, and Bev Mulonet; (second row) Marie "Jo-Jo" Ottaviano, Shirley Dubee, Dolores Ruffo, Ann "Punxsy" Edmondson, and Mary Jane Hagan; (third row) Barbara "Rusty" Abernethy, Olive Anderson, manager Bernie Kaplan, Millie Elias, and Lorraine "Chic" Meehan. (Courtesy of the Brakettes Photograph Archive.)

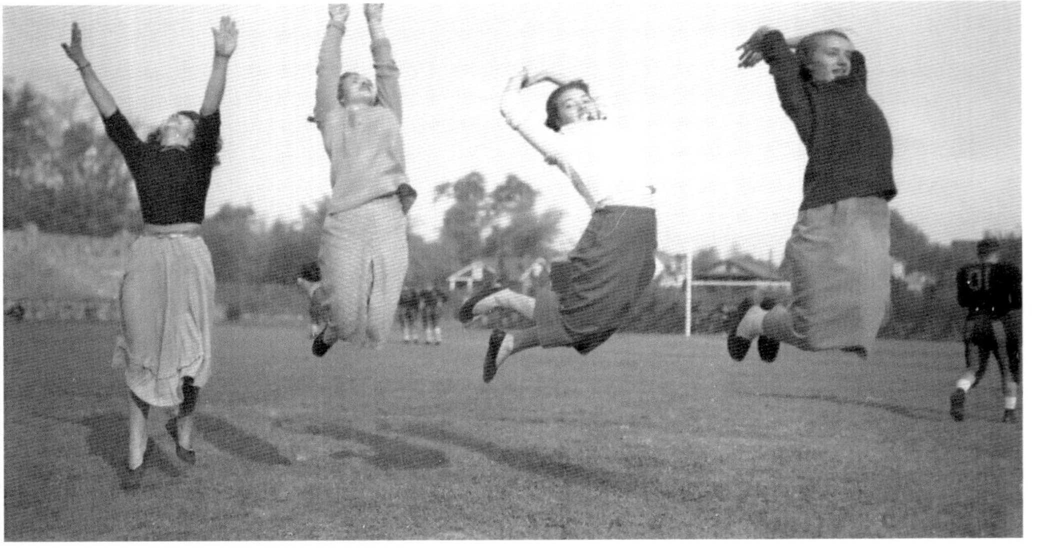

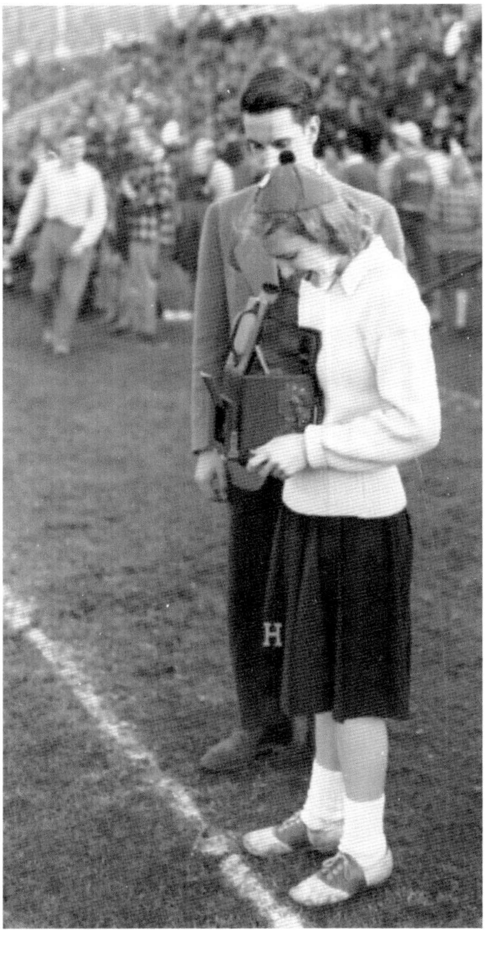

STAMFORD HIGH SCHOOL CHEERLEADERS, 1948. The passage of Title IX was a landmark in the advancement of girls' and women's ability to play the sports they loved. The law requires, in high school and college sports, that the number of women's athletic teams matches the number of men's teams. Cheerleading remains perhaps the most divisive issue in Title IX discussions and litigation. A recent case brought by Quinnipiac College ruled that "competive cheering teams" could not count toward a school's Title IX enforcement numbers. Two factors make this a particularly contentious issue in 2012: first, women now outnumber men at the college level, about 55 percent to 45 percent, and second, as budget cuts hit hard, schools are looking for ways to reduce athletic expenses without violating Title IX statutes. Competitive cheering organizations continue to establish the sport's legitamacy by developing, according to the USA Cheer website, "a new format that would allow a form of competition cheerleading to be recognized as an intercollegiate sport." Above, cheerleaders demonstrate their athleticism and enthusiasm. At left, a cheerleader photographs a game.

8

STAMFORD SPORTS FIGURES

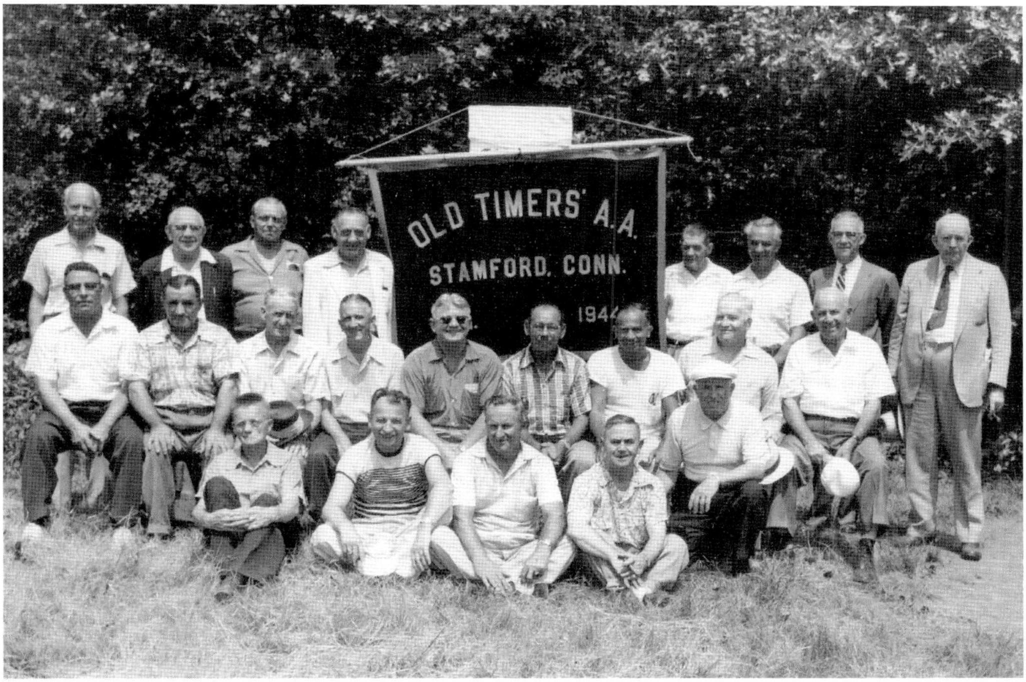

OLD TIMERS' ATHLETIC ASSOCIATION, 1944. While we could not possibly honor every athlete, coach, and sports figure who has impacted sports in the city of Stamford, we can safely say that they are honored and remembered through the Old Timers' Athletic Association. The Old Timers continue to hold an annual dinner honoring Stamford's own, and the programs from these dinners remain a permanent record of all those from Stamford who have performed outstanding feats on and off the athletic field. Many of Stamford's greats, especially the earliest and the most recent, are not part of our photographic record, but we could in no way diminish their accomplishment.

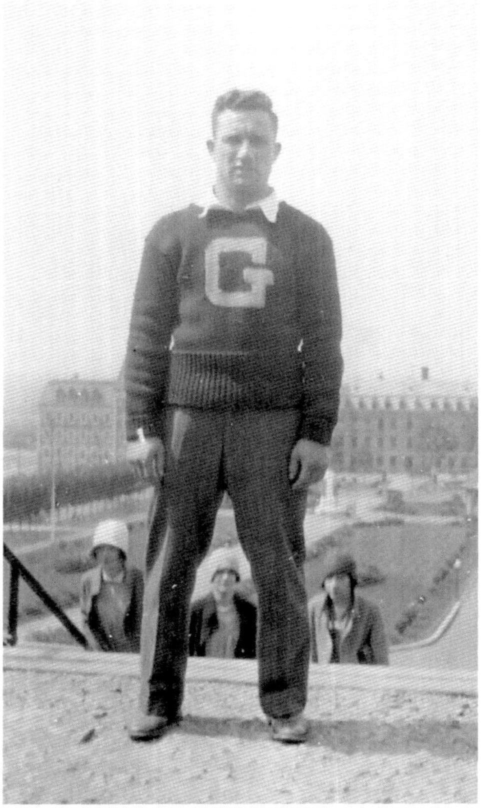

JOHN SCALZI, GEORGETOWN UNIVERSITY. Scalzi played all sports in school but was best known as a baseball player. In college, he played for Georgetown University. After college, he was signed to the Boston Braves and played until 1933. He also played for the Brooklyn Dodgers in the National Football League in 1931 and 1932. Returning to Stamford when he retired from professional sports due to injuries, Scalzi promoted semiprofessional football at Mitchell Field and served as the president of both the Colonial and Twilight baseball leagues.

PIONEER BASEBALL CLUB MEMBERS, 1941. Posing below at Mitchell Field are, from left to right, John Connolly, Ted Mitchell, and John Scalzi.

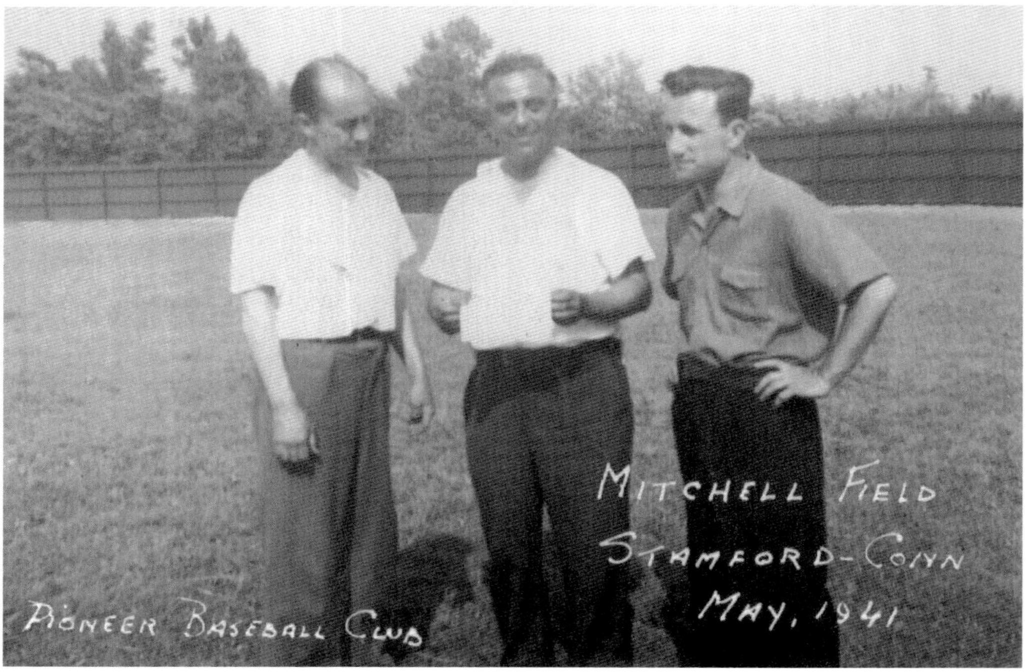

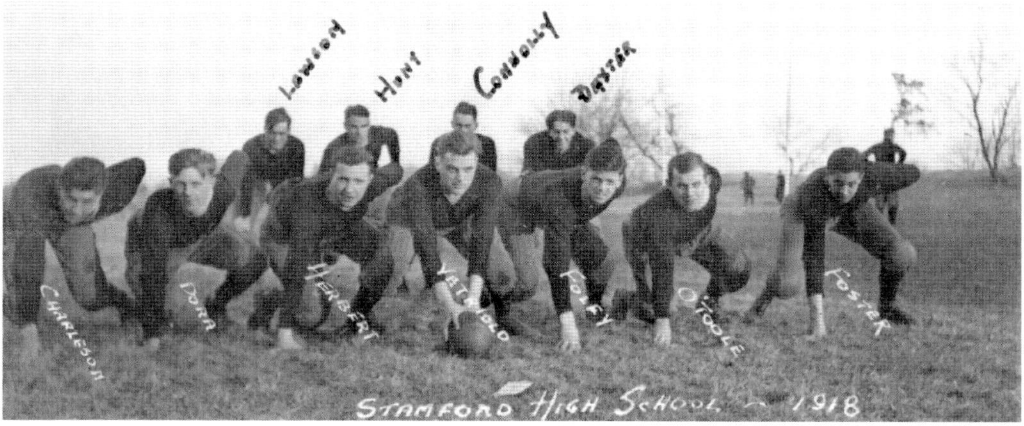

ED HUNT. Born on April 7, 1901, Edward "Ed" Hunt played ball for Stamford High School and Georgetown University. He is seen above (second row, second from left) at Georgetown and below (center) on the 1918 Stamford High School squad. He was an all-state halfback for Stamford High School and an infielder on the school's baseball team. He played semiprofessional football with the All-Stamfords and the Norwalk Pros. He also played semiprofessional baseball with the All-Stamfords, St. Mary's, Yale & Towne, and Stamford Rolling Mills. He later coached the Connecticut Nutmegs (later Stamford Nutmegs) women's softball team to nine New England championships. He served in a number of leadership roles, including director of the board of recreation and commissioner of Stamford Little League, Connecticut Babe Ruth League, and New England Babe Ruth League.

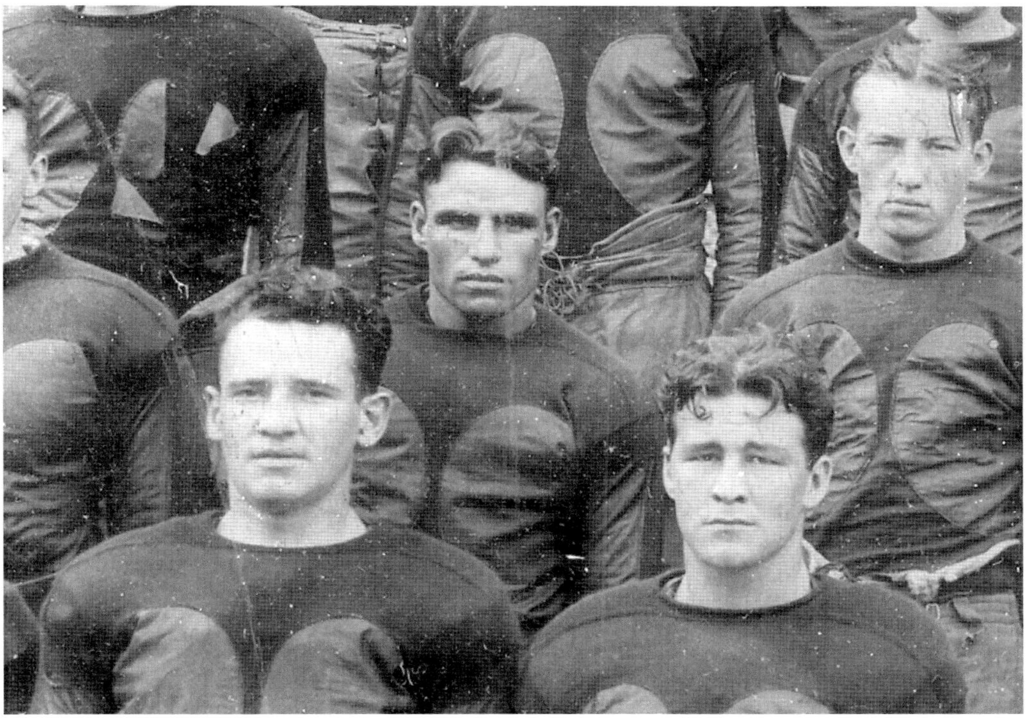

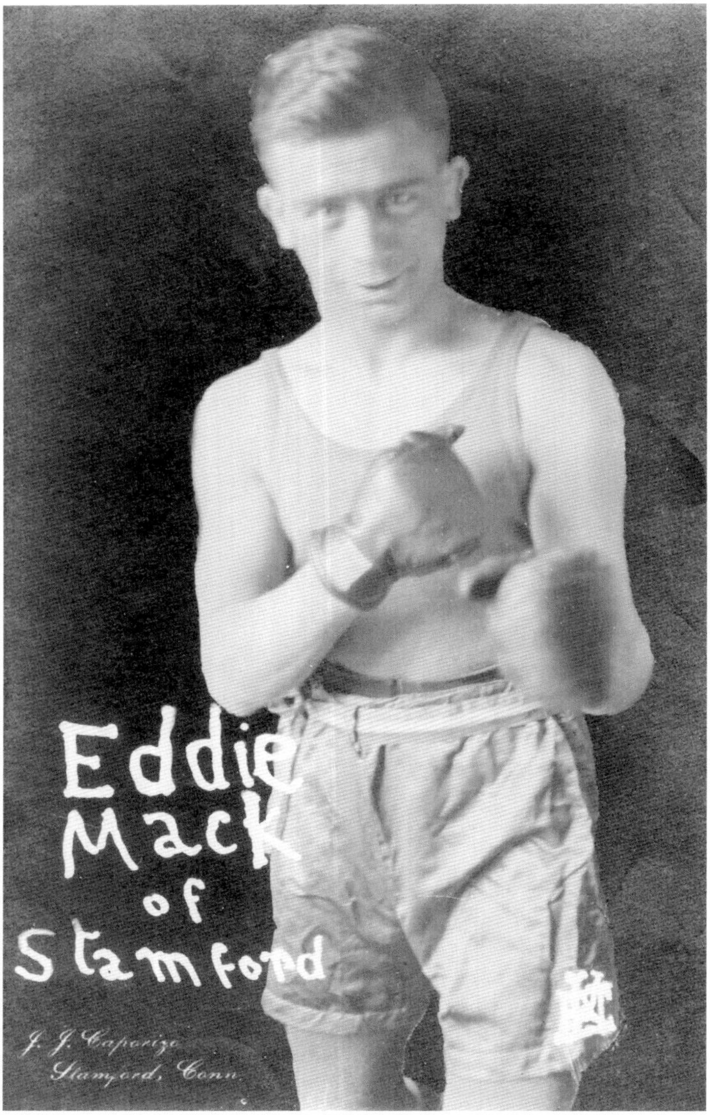

EDDIE MACK. Eddie Mack (born Angelo Morrucco) was one of eight children born to his Italian immigrant parents in Stamford's West End. He boxed professionally from 1920 to 1925 under the alias Young Mack. He racked up 19 wins, 4 losses, and 10 draws and was the New England bantamweight champion. His brother Dave also became a figure of note around Stamford, writing a column for the *Advocate* on local doings that included self-drawn caricatures of people around town. Below, Mack promotes his retirement business in a 1938 advertisement.

LEARN THE ART OF SELF DEFENSE

Weekly instructions in Boxing and Wrestling. NEW BOXING CLASSES Being Organized. Conducted by **"EDDIE" MACK,** former New England Bantamweight Champion. For particulars call 3-2418.

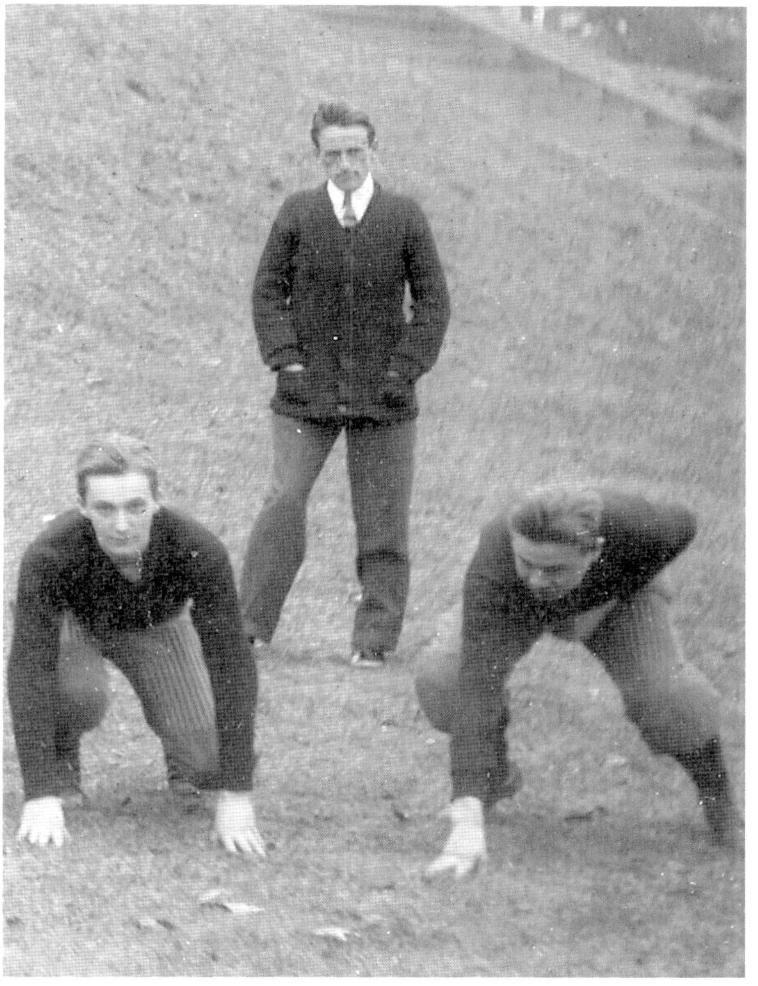

MIKE BOYLE WITH STAMFORD HIGH SCHOOL FOOTBALL TEAM, C. 1920. In 1907, Stamford High School hired Michael A. Boyle to coach its athletic teams, and for 35 years the school was not disappointed. Boyle created a football program that dominated the sport for 31 years, boasting an 81-percent win record and never recording a losing season. He coached multiple sports, including football, baseball, basketball, and women's basketball, and led all of his squads to championship seasons.

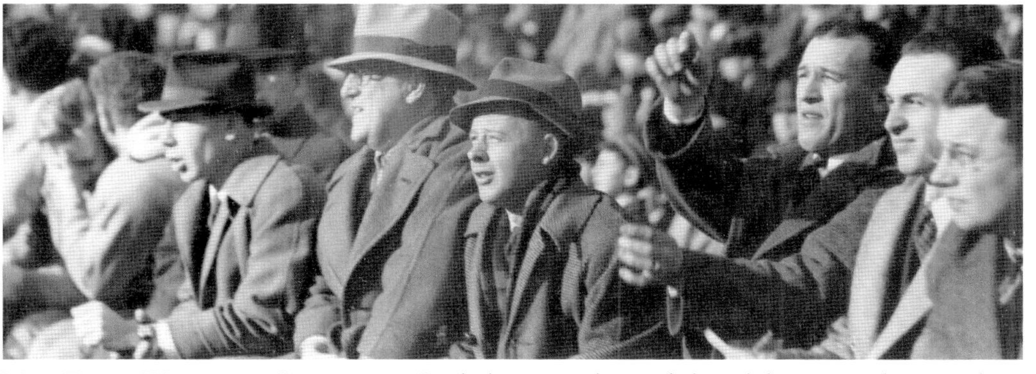

MIKE BOYLE WATCHES A GAME, 1941. Boyle (center, in hat and glasses) focuses on the game from the stands in this photograph, taken shortly before he passed away in March 1942. In November of that year, Michael A. Boyle Stadium was formally dedicated to the memory of the greatest coach Stamford High School ever knew.

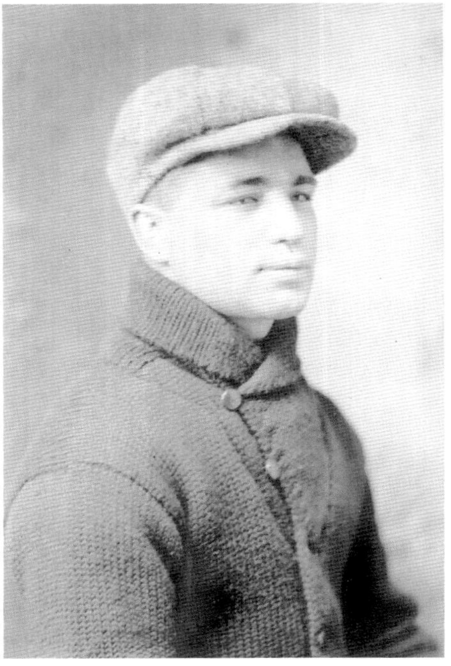

ANGELO PACE, 1922. Angelo Pace, a young Italian fighter in the early 1920s, boxed all over Connecticut as "Young Angelo" and was the Connecticut lightweight champion, with a professional record of 24 wins, 7 losses, and 4 draws. Pace fought in an exhibition match in Halloween Park as part of a Welcome Home program for soldiers and sailors of World War I.

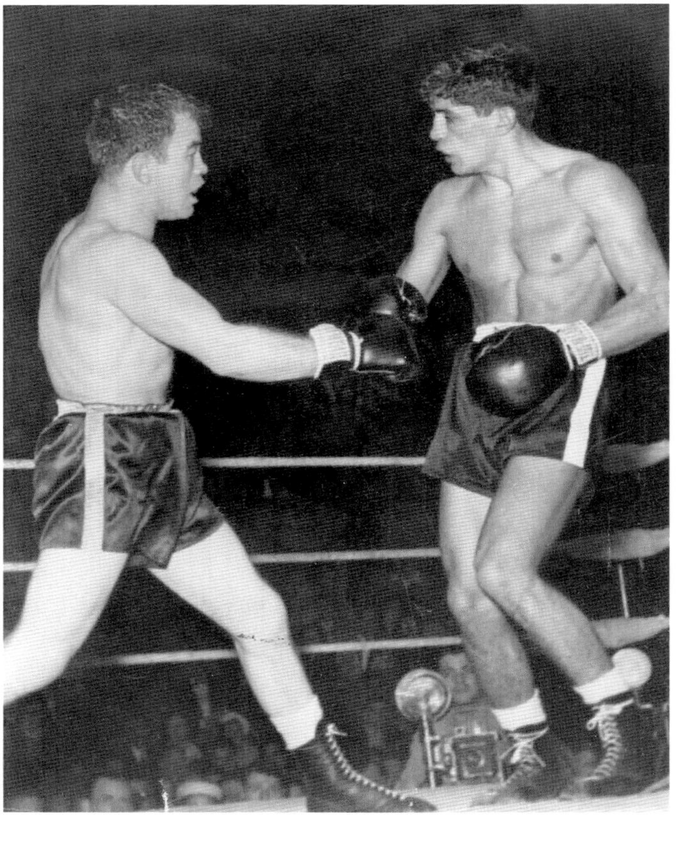

CHICO VEJAR. Born Francis Vejar on September 5, 1951, Chico (right), known as "Stamford's Socking Schoolboy," boxed professionally for 11 years and finished with a record of 93 wins, 20 losses, and 4 draws. As the fifth-ranked middleweight in the nation, Vejar fought often at Madison Square Garden and was a staple on the weekly televised Friday night fights.

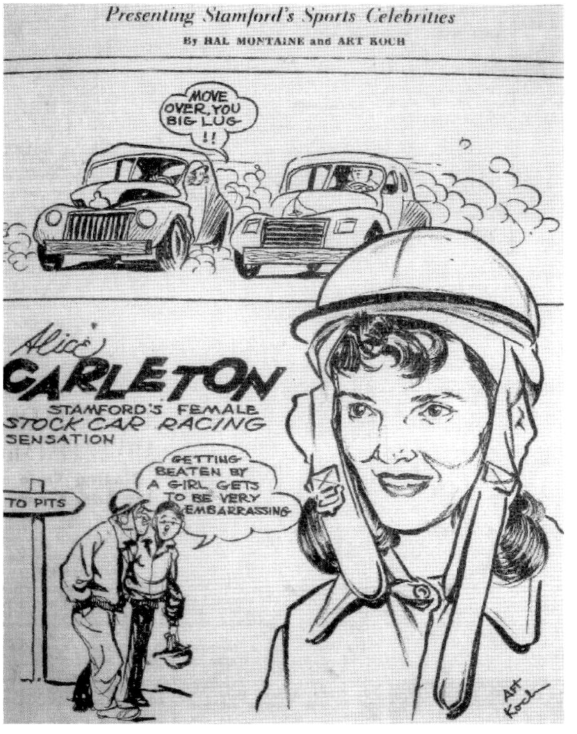

ALICE CARLETON CARTOON, 1949. In the late 1940s, Hal Montaine and Art Koch ran a weekly feature in the *Stamford Advocate* featuring "Stamford's Sports Celebrities." Although the majority of these cartoons featured men, there were a number featuring Stamford's female sports figures, including Dena Kuczo (softball), Pat Kelly (swimming), and Louise DeVivo (golf). Alice Carleton, seen here, competed on the local stock car circuit in the "gal's race" on Friday nights.

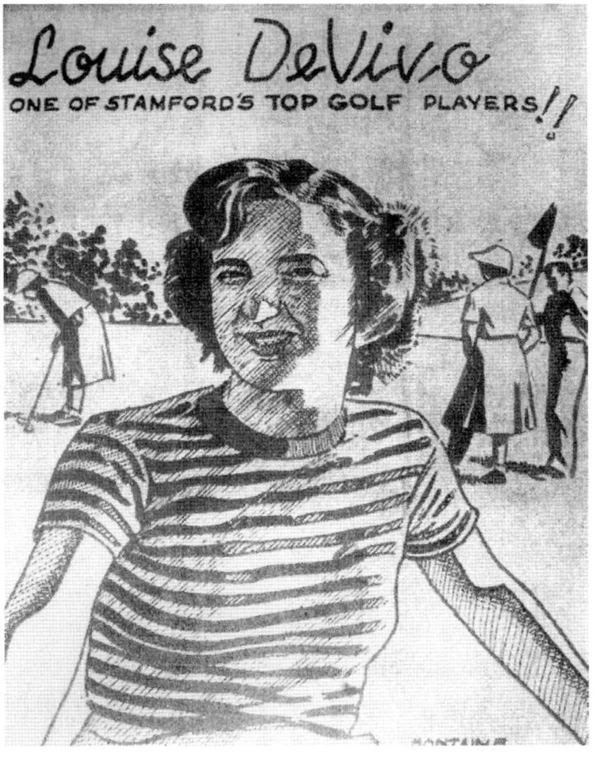

LOUISE DEVIVO CARTOON, 1949. Although she is usually associated with her adopted town of Greenwich, Louise DeVivo began golfing near her home in Stamford at a nine-hole course at Cummings Park. As an adult, she competed in championships across the country and the world, winning more than 50 titles.

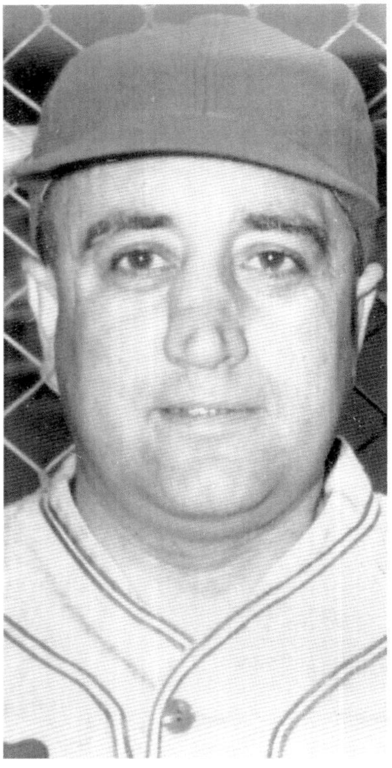

MICKEY LIONE. Michael "Mickey" Lione was a standout athlete at Stamford High School, captaining the 1929 football team to a state championship and playing outstanding baseball as a shortstop and .400 batter. He went on to Georgetown University, returning to Stamford to work as a police officer and to play ball. After playing for Stamford Gas and Electric for several years, Mickey went on to manage teams in the Twilight League. In 1950, with the formation of Little League, Lione coached the Stamford Police team. He co-coached the Stamford All-Stars of Little League with Paul Klinkowski, bringing home the 1951 Little League World Championship. Stamford's Little League was named for Lione as was its Little League baseball field. The photograph at left was taken around 1950, when Lione was first launching and promoting Little League. Below, Mickey strikes a pose during his adult playing days in 1929. (Courtesy of Gerry Lione.)

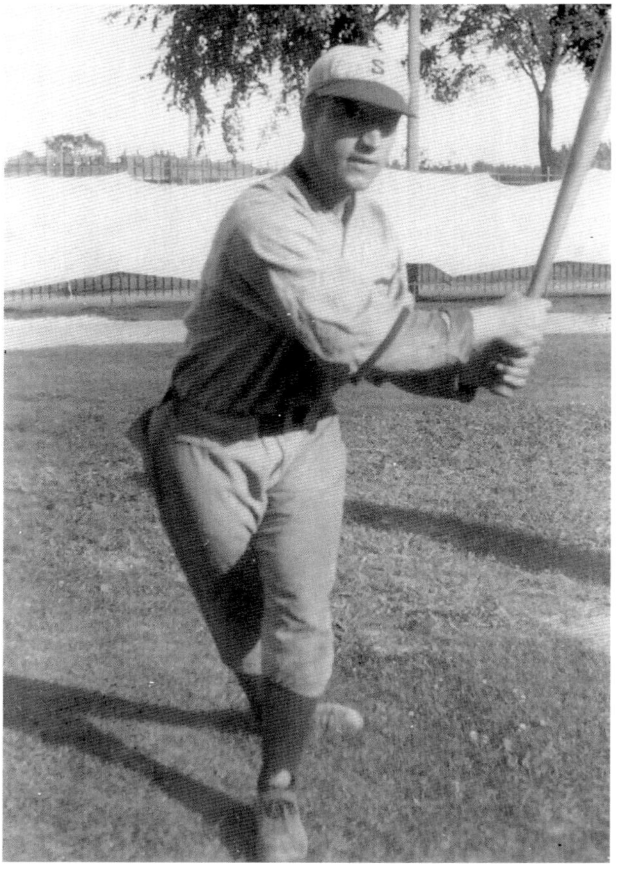

PAUL KUCZO, STAMFORD HIGH SCHOOL. Born on February 2, 1903, in Stamford, Paul Kuczo played baseball, football, and basketball for Stamford High School under legendary coach Mike Boyle. He attended and played ball for Villanova from 1924 to 1927, then returned to Stamford in 1928 as a math teacher and coach, leading the football team to 190 wins and three state championships. His baseball teams won 428 games and his basketball teams won 263. He also played on, managed, and coached a number of league teams in baseball, including the 1938 Twilight League champion Sacred Hearts. In his 30 years of coaching, Kuczo never had a losing season (Courtesy of John Kuczo.)

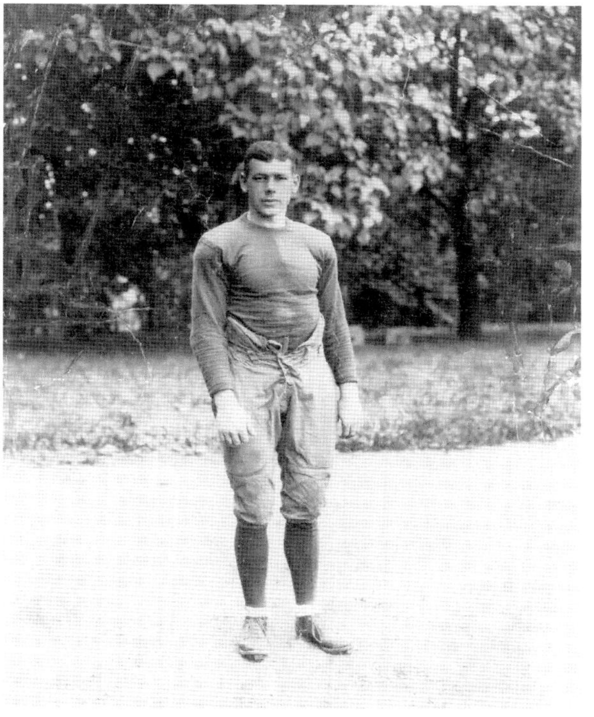

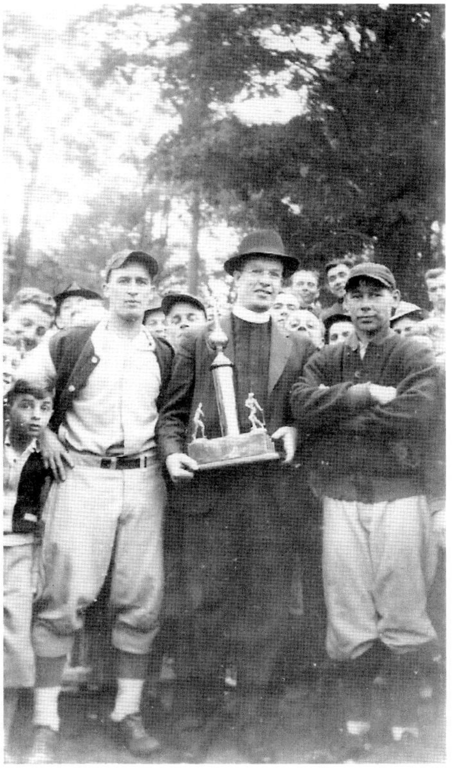

TWILIGHT LEAGUE CHAMPION SACRED HEARTS, 1938. Paul Kuczo (right) celebrates the Twilight League championship with his Sacred Hearts team. (Courtesy of John Kuczo.)

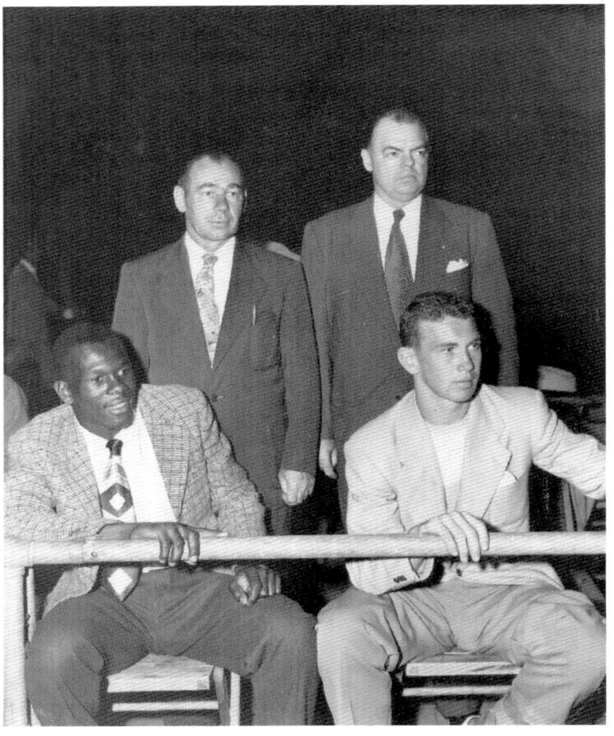

PAUL KUCZO ATTENDS A GIANTS GAME WITH HIS CO-CAPTAINS, 1950. At left, Paul Kuczo (standing, left) attends a charity football match between the New York Giants and the Los Angeles Rams with his football co-captains Russell Going (sitting, left) and Fred Dugan (sitting, right) as guests of Milo MCammon (standing, right), the general manager of the Stamford division of Yale & Towne. In the 1954 photograph below, Kuczo (left) poses with superintendent of schools Reginald Neuwien and Neuwien's son Skip. (Both, courtesy of John Kuczo.)

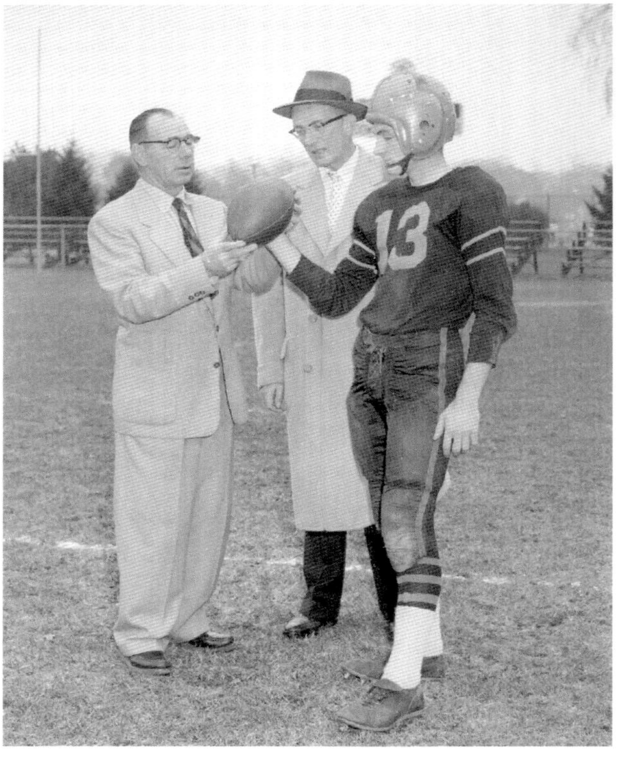

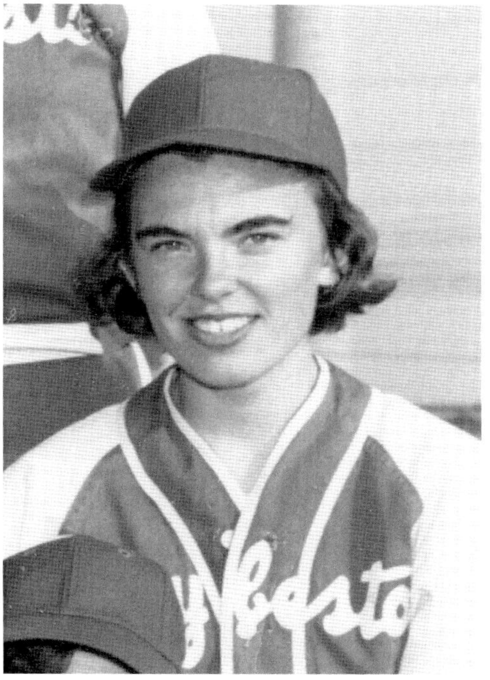

Mary Jane Hagan, 1953. Born on June 12, 1936, Mary Jane Hagan attended Stamford High and earned varsity letters in field hockey, softball, and basketball. After attending Boston University, she returned to Stamford to teach physical education and coach field hockey, basketball, and softball. In the 1950s, Hagan also pitched for the Raybestos Brakettes and was a member of their championship 1956 team. In 1973, she became the coordinator of physical education, health, and safety for Stamford's public schools. She also served as president of the Women's Fairfield County Athletic Conference and worked as a major advocate for the Special Olympics. Hagan was inducted into the Connecticut Basketball Hall of Fame, the Connecticut Amateur Softball Association's Fast Pitch Hall of Fame, and the Stamford High School Hall of Fame. (Courtesy of the Brakettes Softball Archive.)

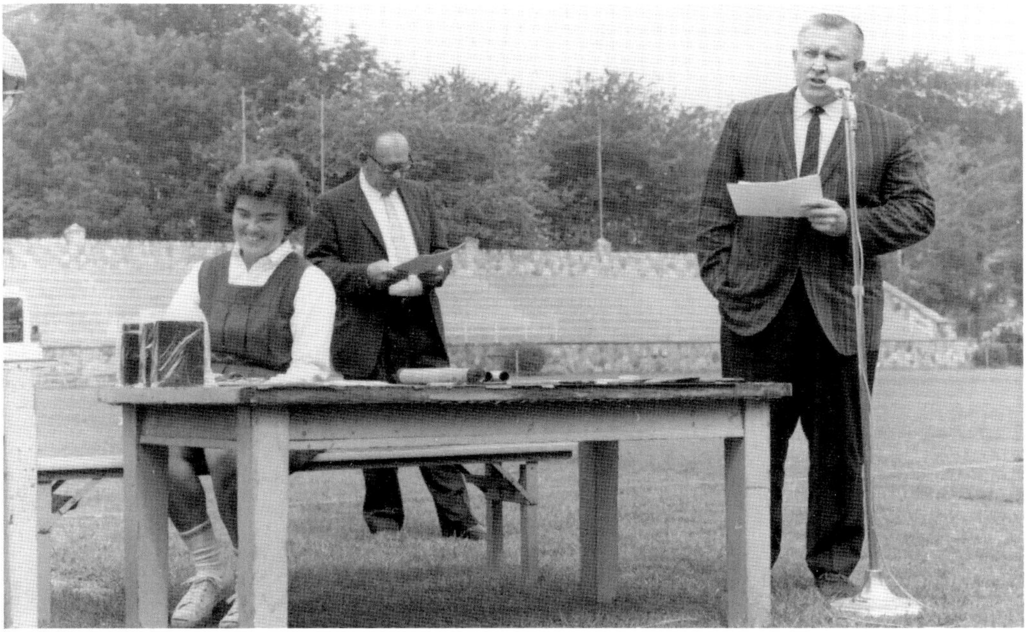

Mary Jane Hagan at Stamford High School Awards Ceremony. Mary Jane Hagan promoted girls' athletics in Stamford well ahead of Title IX. In a 1976 interview, Hagan was asked how Title IX had affected the Stamford school system. "Not very much," she replied. "We instituted a full slate of girls sports several years ago. In fact, in 1970 we sat down and discussed a possible league within FCIAC for girls and this became a reality in 1972." (Courtesy of John Kucszo.)

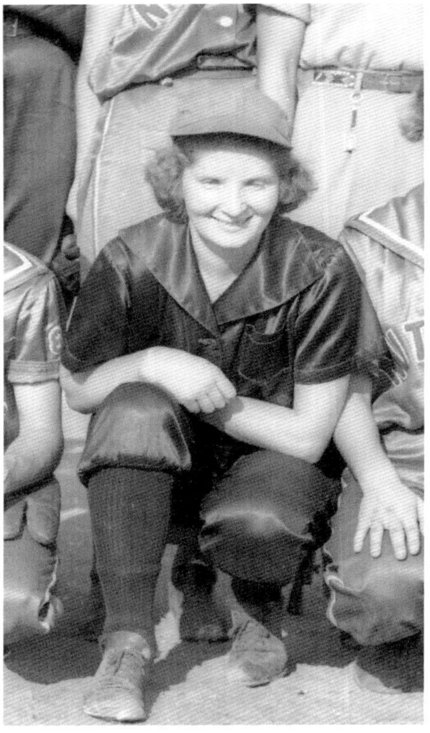

MARTHA RUDENFELDT. Nicknamed Iron Horse by her coach, Martha Rudenfeldt was known for having an indefatigable arm that could pitch both ends of a Sunday doubleheader. She pitched the team to their back-to-back-to-back New England championships from 1941 to 1943. After retiring from softball, Rudenfeldt worked for Stamford recreation under her former coach, Ed Hunt. She served as interim superintendent in 1973 and worked for many years as the director of women's and girls' activities and the assistant to the superintendent. In 1975, she was inducted into the Connecticut Amateur Softball Association Hall of Fame.

ALLYSON RIOUX. Allyson Rioux was born in Stamford and attended Westhill High School in north Stamford from 1976 to 1979. She played basketball, softball, and field hockey and won all-city, all-county, and all-state honors. She continued to play in college, first at the University of Rhode Island and then at the University of Massachusetts. Rioux was with the Raybestos Brakettes for 10 years, playing in 10 national championships and two World Games. She received a number on awards, including Most Valuable Player of the American Softball Association (ASA) National Championship in 1985. In 1987, she was diagnosed with cancer. She passed away on February 9, 1989, at the age of 27. She was elected posthumously to the ASA National Hall of Fame. Her family, friends, and teammates established the Allyson Rioux Memorial Foundation, and Westhill High School renamed their softball field Allyson Rioux Memorial Field in her honor.

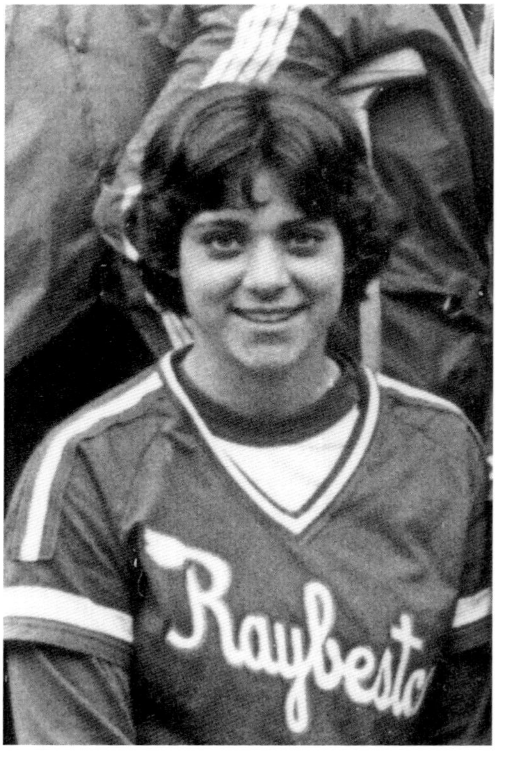

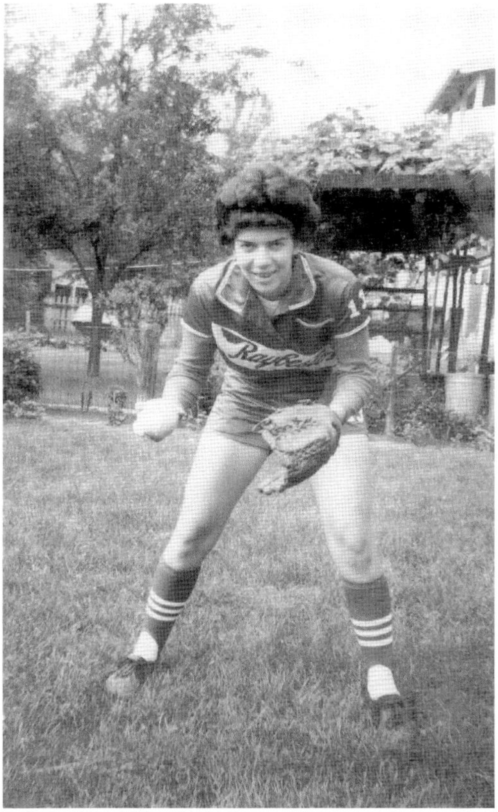

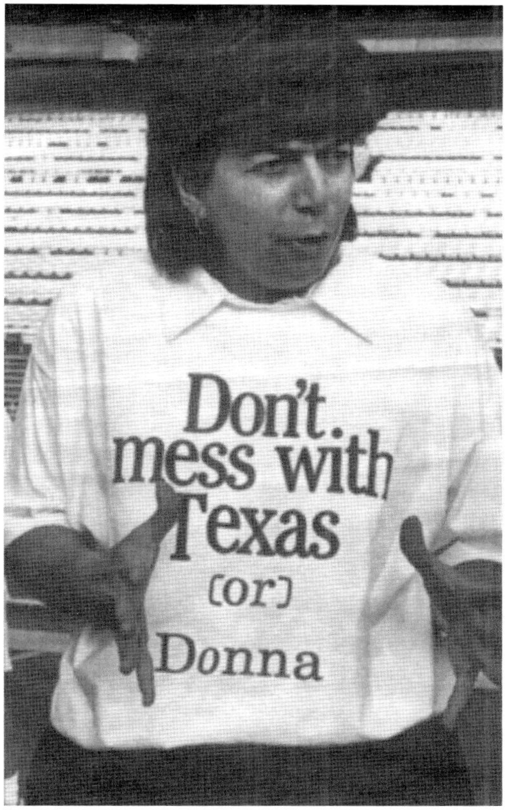

DR. DONNA LOPIANO. Born in 1946 in Stamford's West End, Donna Lopiano has been described by coaches and sportswriters as one of the most influential people in sports. At age 11, she tried out for Stamford's Mickey Lione Little League and was the number-one pick for pitcher. Waiting in line for her uniform, she was told by a parent brandishing a rulebook that "girls are not allowed." Lopiano went on to become an outstanding athlete and a driving force behind equal opportunity and excellence in athletics. She played multiple positions, including pitcher, for the Raybestos Brakettes beginning at age 16, and continued through her college years. She earned her doctorate from the University of Southern California in 1972, the same year she helped lead the Brakettes to a national title. In 1975, she became the director of intercollegiate athletics for women at the University of Texas, where she greatly expanded and improved the women's athletics program. Within a month of her starting the position, she was asked to testify before the Senate Education Committee during hearings on Title IX. In 1992, Lopiano became the CEO of the Women's Sports Foundation, an advocacy group for female athletics. Dr. Lopiano's approach to any issue is to come armed with data, argue reasonably, and not bring in the personal. In an interview for the Oral History Archive at the Connecticut Women's Hall of Fame, Lopiano said, "The personal becomes idiosyncratic. People will say, you got where you are because you're lucky, or oh, it's Ellen, or it's Billy Jean. That's not the point. It's that every human being has the right to be their own person." The photograph on the right was was taken during Dr. Lopiano's tenure as director of women's athletics at the University of Texas, where she rightfully earned the motto on her shirt. (Both, courtesy of Donna Lopiano.)

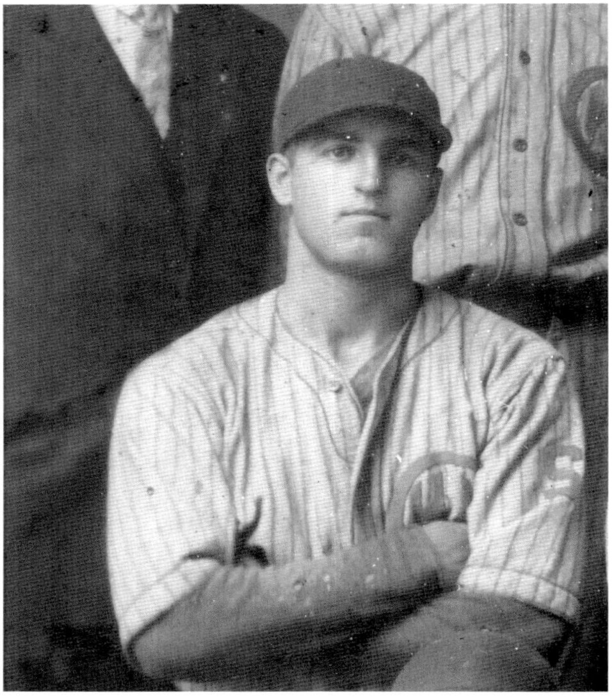

ALEXANDER KOPROSKI SR. Born on October 25, 1904, Alexander "Al" Koproski grew up in Stamford's heavily Polish South End. He began his baseball career playing for the Harbor Giants in 1919. With other members of the Polish community, Koproski founded and organized the Holy Name Athletic Club, which became one of the strongest baseball clubs in the area. The "Namers" joined the Twilight League in 1934 and clinched the title that year over rival Stamford Gas and Electric. Koproski was appointed to the Stamford Police Department on December 5, 1938, and served as a police officer for 31 years.

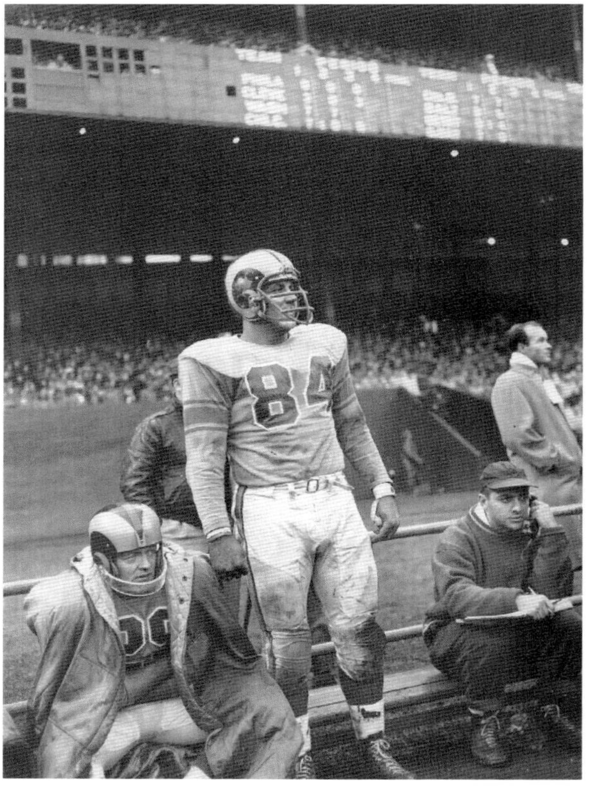

ANDY ROBUSTELLI. Born on December 6, 1925, in Stamford, Andy Robustelli played football and baseball for Stamford High School before serving in the Navy aboard the destroyer USS *Cole* during World War II. After college, he was drafted into the National Football League by the Los Angeles Rams, playing there until he was traded to the New York Giants in 1955. He was selected to the all-pro team nine times and played in nine championship games. In 1971, Robustelli was inducted into the National Football Hall of Fame in Canton, Ohio. This photograph was taken by his close friend, Nick Scutti, shortly after Robustelli (84) was drafted by the Los Angeles Rams. Jack Dwyer (29) is to the left. (Courtesy of Nick Scutti.)

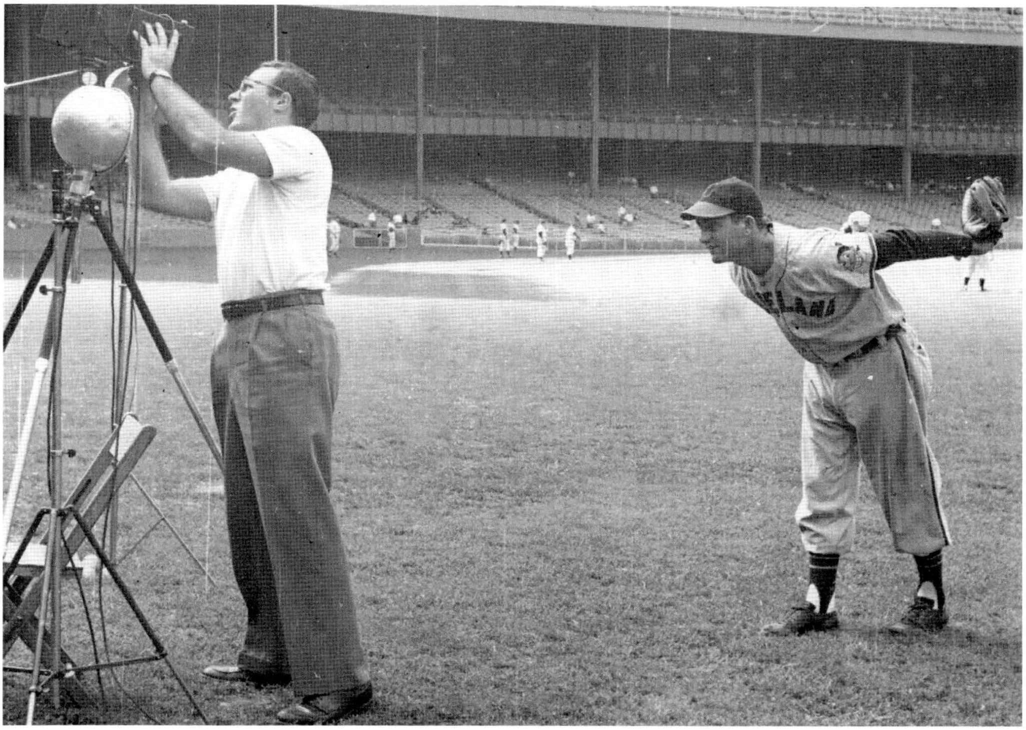

OZZIE SWEET PREPARES A SHOT. Above, Stamford-born photographer Oscar "Ozzie" Sweet worked with another Stamford native, Nick Scutti, on posed photographs of athletes. Sweet specialized in posing athletes realistically for "action" shots. (Courtesy of Nick Scutti.)

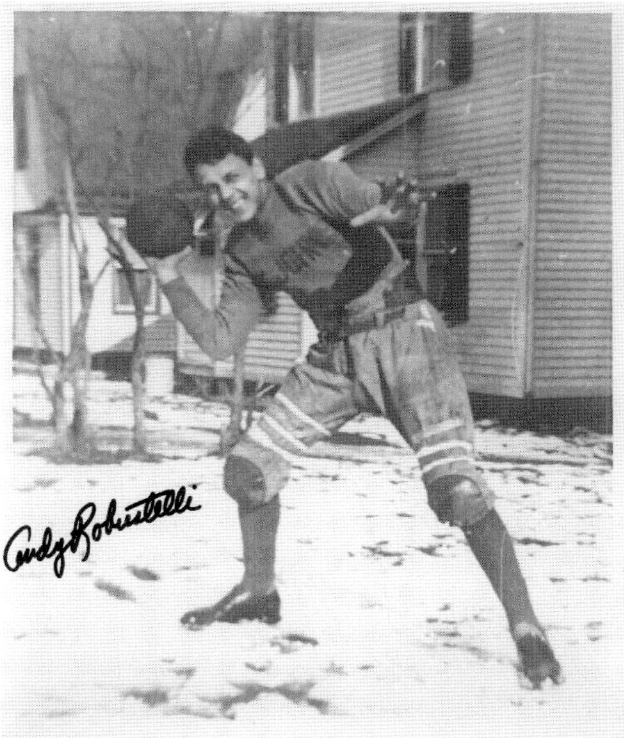

ANDY ROBUSTELLI, 1939. Nick Scutti snapped this picture of his close friend, 14-year-old Andrew "Andy" Robustelli, in 1939. Notice that the precocious Robustelli signed it. (Courtesy of Nick Scutti.)

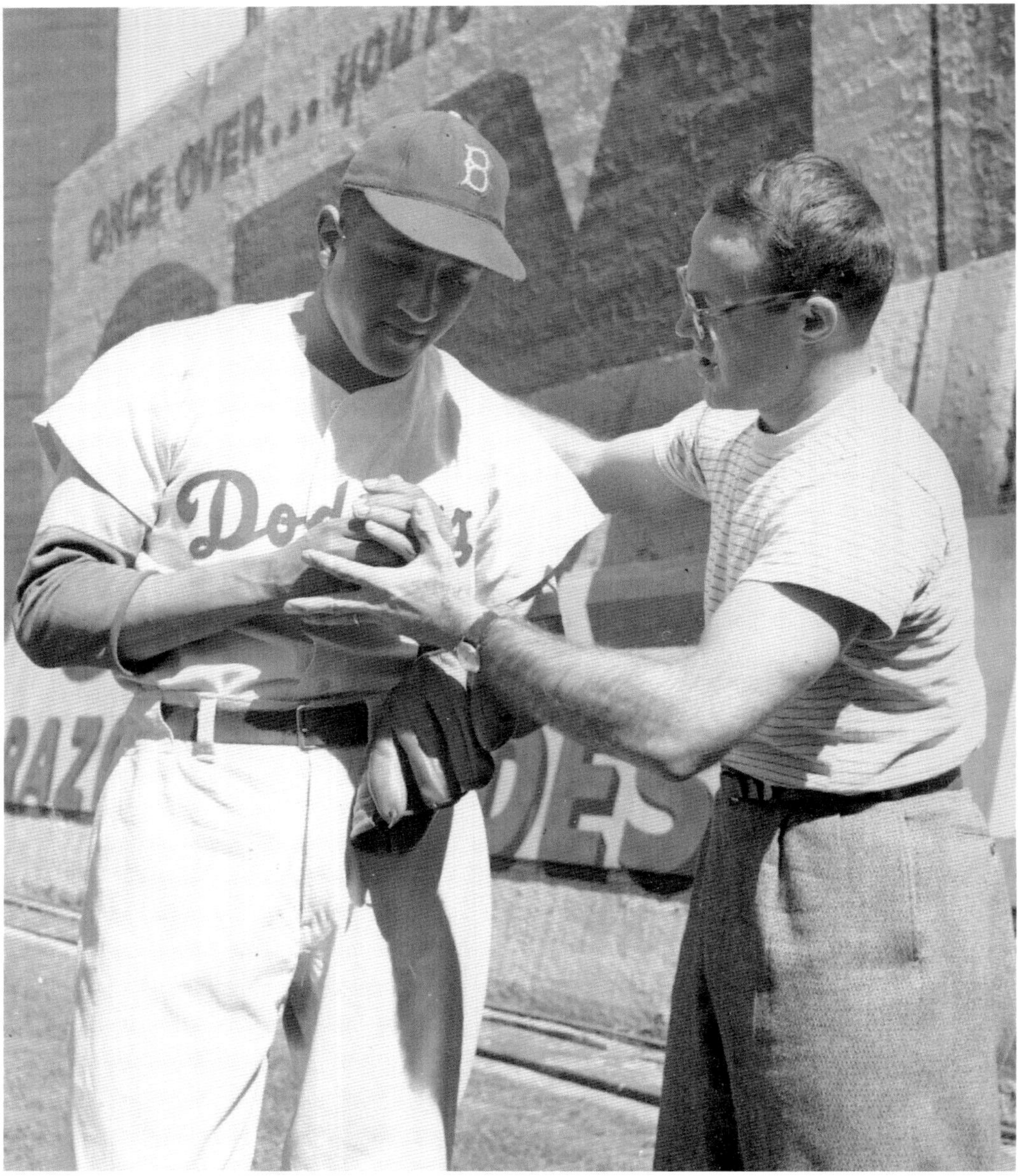

Ozzie Sweet Poses Jackie Robinson. In another photograph taken by Nick Scutti, Sweet prepares Jackie Robinson for a posed shot. Robinson moved to Stamford, where he lived for 20 years. (Courtesy of Nick Scutti.)

BIBLIOGRAPHY

Burke, Deborah. *Getting in the Game: Title IX and the Women's Sports Revolution*. New York City: NYU Press, 2010.

Burns, Rosemary H. *Springdale Remembered, 1640–1949*. Stamford, CT: The Stamford Historical Society, 1982.

Epler, Stephen E. *Six-man Football, the Streamlined Game; Principles of Six-man Football for Players, Coaches and Spectators*. New York City: Harper & Brothers, 1938.

Feinstein, Estelle F. and Joyce S. Pendery. *Stamford: An Illustrated History*. Woodland Hills, CT: Windsor Publications, 1984.

Gillespie, Edward T.W. *Picturesque Stamford: A Souvenir of the Two Hundred and Fiftieth Anniversary of the Settlement of the Town of Stamford, Containing an Historical Sketch, Covering Salient Points of Stamford's History from 1641 to 1892*. Stamford, CT: Gillespie Bros., 1892.

Grundy, Pamela. *Shattering the Glass: The Remarkable History of Women's Basketball*. New York City: New Press, 2005.

Krom, L.J. "The Development of a Rolling Mill." *Metal Industry*, Vol. 15, No. 12. 1917: 244–251.

Lopiano, Dr. Donna. Interview by Tracey Felcher. Oral History Archive at Connecticut Women's Hall of Fame. November 19, 2003.

National Collegiate Athletic Association. *2004–2010 NCAA Gender-Equity Report*. Indianapolis: National Collegiate Athletic Association, 2012.

ABOUT THE STAMFORD HISTORICAL SOCIETY

The Stamford Historical Society, Inc., the municipal historian of Stamford, is an educational and research institution whose primary functions are to collect, preserve, conserve, interpret, and exhibit materials relating to Stamford and our region in order to engage citizens in the telling of their stories. Established in 1901 and incorporated in 1909, the society is dedicated to preserving local history and providing opportunities for the community to understand and experience the past through the presentation of exhibits and displays, lectures, demonstrations, special events, and participatory programs. In particular, we preserve and offer tours of the unique Hoyt Barnum House, built in 1699. As Stamford's history center, we have a responsibility to all the citizens of our community to preserve the varied experiences that reflect our cultural heritage.

For more information about the Stamford Historical Society, please visit our website at www.stamfordhistory.org or visit us in person at 1508 High Ridge Road in Stamford.

Consistent with our mission to preserve history on a local level, this book was printed in South Carolina on American-made paper and manufactured entirely in the United States. Products carrying the accredited Forest Stewardship Council (FSC) label are printed on 100 percent FSC-certified paper.

MADE IN THE USA